THE RED QUEEN

LAMENTS OF ANGELS & DARK CHEMISTRY, #3

Meg Xuemei X

First edition
Silver Wheel Publishing

ISBN: 978-0997996302

Printed in the United States of America
Cover design by Laura Gorden

ACKNOWLEDGEMENTS

"...not by might nor by power, but by my Spirit," saith the Lord of Hosts.

Many thanks to Alexis Razevich, Richard Casey, Randal K Jackson, and Dan McNeil for their friendship and help in shaping The Laments of Angels & Dark Chemistry. To John Briggings and Lucinda Leavens for editing The Red Queen and Mehgan Tea for proofreading it.

I heartily thank all the readers for keeping reading *Laments of Angels & Dark Chemistry* series.

TABLE OF CONTENTS

PART I...7
Chapter 1. RED RAGE.....................................9
Chapter 2. BEATEN......................................24
Chapter 3. DUEL...47
Chapter 4. CONFESSION OF LOVE...............70
Chapter 5. PARTING....................................79
Chapter 6. MAD DANCE...............................87

PART II...93
Chapter 7. CAPTURE....................................95
Chapter 8. COLD BATH...............................104
Chapter 9. BERLIN.....................................118
Chapter 10. BAYROSE..................................127
Chapter 11. DESERT WRAITH......................134
Chapter 12. THE SHADOW...........................138
Chapter 13. ATHENS...................................150
Chapter 14. SNIPERS IN PLAKA...................152
Chapter 15. ASHBURN.................................165
Chapter 16. RITUAL....................................171
Chapter 17. THE SHIELD.............................176
Chapter 18. SERAPHEN'S HEAD....................183
Chapter 19. JEKATERINA.............................201
Chapter 20. THE THIRD SCROLL...................221
Chapter 21. POISON OF LOVE.......................234
Chapter 22. BEACH AND BOYS......................248
Chapter 23. SISTER IN LOVE........................252
Chapter 24. HERITAGE................................267
Chapter 25. THE EYE OF TIME......................274
Chapter 26. GIRL SCORNED..........................280
Chapter 27. SLEEPLESS NIGHT.....................297
Chapter 28. A PIE.......................................301
Chapter 29. THE TALK.................................304
Chapter 30. RIVER OF FIRE..........................309

Chapter 31. ONE NATION...323

PART III...331
Chapter 32. CODE...333
Chapter 33. DEVOURER...336
Chapter 34. DOUBLE BETRAYAL.......................................343
Chapter 35. PHOENIX IN ASHES.......................................346

Sneak Preview of *The Empress of Mysth*...............................359
Also by Author...369
About the Author..370

Part One

Chapter One

RED RAGE

Where am I?

A sea of red. Was it fire or blood? Lucienne Lam couldn't tell. Fog filled her mind, clouding her judgment. She twirled around in difficulty and found herself trapped underwater.

She felt heat. It was fire. It licked the surface of the ocean. She'd drown if she didn't go up, but who would take a chance with the endless fire? Her burning, bursting lungs answered the question. Kicking her legs, Lucienne swam up, looking for gaps in the inferno.

Every stroke was an ordeal. Something was wrong with her body—she was combusting inside.

Forbidden Glory, she summoned.

The power from her Siren's mark responded like a trail of static.

The venom. Blood Tear had infected aether, one of the five elements of Forbidden Glory. That was what had brought the sense of wrongness. She was on her own, forced to keep moving up. The sound of water pounded harshly in her eardrums, and yet, amid the rushing water, she heard voices. Distant voices, but distinct nonetheless.

"Are we just going to sit around, watching her like this?" She made out Kian's voice, and it was laced with fear, despair, and anger.

Her people were around her somewhere. Relief washed over her. But where were they?

"We thinned her blood," said Dr. Wren, her family doctor. "We've tried everything possible, but everything we've done has only worsened her condition."

"We need to figure out the hidden code in her genome." That

sounded like Dr. Christophersen, the Norwegian geneticist.

"Your team will work around the clock until you find the cure," Kian said. "From now on, the lab is where you eat, poop, and sleep."

Lucienne wanted to tell Kian that that was an unreasonable demand, but first she had to reach him. "Kian," she called, "put out the fire!"

He was still barking orders at the doctors and scientists. For a split second she was upset that he ignored her, but then she realized he couldn't hear her. She was this distant, floating body that couldn't talk underwater. With one strenuous stroke, she approached the surface, but immediately fell back as the flames bore down on her.

A wall of fire sealed every inch of the sea. The temperature was too high for her to break through. She had one choice—drown or be torched.

She bit her lip. No, this couldn't be her end. She'd survived Blood Tear's poison. She'd passed the trial of fire at the age of eight when she became Siren. Fire was part of her. It was her lifeline.

She would live through this.

Quenching her fear, she summoned Forbidden Glory again. *Fire is your element. Take me through this fire.*

Her power whimpered.

If I die, she said, *you'll be trapped in ash and bone.*

This time, Forbidden Glory responded like a raindrop.

At least that's an improvement. She could only hope her power still had a spark left—a spark that would shield her flesh from the earthly fire.

She went up again. Despite the unbearable heat, she pushed on, at least until she touched the flame. Only the fear of drowning kept her from screaming in agony.

Her hair singed. Her skin peeled from her face.

Lucienne plummeted. Drowning would be easier.

Water poured into her lungs. They burned too.

"What is happening to her? She's choking!" Kian shouted in raw fear. "Lucia, wake up! Wake up, kid! Please."

So this was a dream? A nightmare? That could be good news. All she needed to do was wake up, and the flood and fire would leave her alone. She blinked hard, once, twice, three times. She still couldn't breathe. She pinched herself. She bit down on her tongue and tasted blood. Nothing worked. No, this wasn't a dream. She couldn't wake herself. The burning was real.

"Bring her back!" Kian yelled in fury.

Just put out the fire and I'll get through! she shouted at her audience, but it was as if they were on the other side of a soundproof door unaware of her cries.

What kind of hell was she in this time?

Drowning and burning.

"She isn't waking!" Dr. Wren's panicked voice passed by her ear in the rushing water. "Her heartbeat is weakening."

"Should we use the defibrillator?" Christophersen asked.

"This isn't a guessing game!" Kian grated. "A wrong move will kill her. You kill her, and I'll skin you."

Cold metal hit Lucienne's chest. The doctors tried to jumpstart her heart. Forceful electricity shocked through her. *You're electrocuting me!* she roared to no effect.

Lucienne went limp and plummeted, face up.

Someone charged into the room and cussed profusely. Was it Ash? He never swore, yet the harsh voice was his.

Where was Vladimir? Why didn't she hear him? Had Kian and the men taken him out while she was incapacitated and unable to protect him? Fear pumped vigor into her. She surged up again toward the surface fire and instantly dropped back with another shriek.

"You never should have sedated her!" Ash said.

"She had an episode," Wren said with a pang of regret. "She turned violent. We couldn't let her hurt herself or the others."

"I don't care if she hurts a hundred of them. You never, ever put her under again," Ashburn said in a stormy voice. "She's struggling to come back but can't make it. The drug neutralized her power. Next time, just get me!"

"Never sedate her again!" Kian yelled through his clenched teeth.

Lucienne could imagine the doctors cringing under Kian's menace. Then she stopped falling toward the abyss of the ocean. An unseen force held her waist.

"Lucia, fight." Ashburn wasn't present, but his voice whispered in her ear, "Take my strength."

The water around her pulsed. She tried to raise her hand, but the electrified water passed through her fingers.

"It's not working!" Christophersen said. "We must try something more scientific than—"

"Come back to me, Lucienne Lam!" Ashburn called. "Do not abandon me again!"

She abandoned him? When?

Warm, soft lips found hers, slating over her open mouth. Ashburn was not just giving her air—he was branding her as his. He was kissing her from the other side. Normally she'd fight back; resist any man's attempt to brand her, but in this world, trapped underwater, forever drowning, Lucienne hadn't much choice. She blinked under the water, then kissed him back. She was surprised that she had the strength to reciprocate.

Something shimmered in the water. The Lure. It whisked around her with a song. The ancient siren's song. She felt her heartbeat at the connection.

You found me, Ash, she whispered.

I'll always find you, love. His kiss deepened, and air streamed into her lungs.

Forbidden Glory switched on. Its angel's fire erupted from Lucienne and swept away the earthly fire that dominated the surface of the ocean.

Lucienne gasped, and her eyes flashed open.

She was in bed in her room in Sphinxes.

A hand, masculine and beautiful, lay on her chest, its heel against her cleavage. While scorching pain cleaving to her, pleasure sprouted from the touch point and spread outward, downward. The Lure had followed her back from the other side.

The Lure originated from TimeDust, an ancient power inside Ashburn. It forced a supernatural attraction between her and Ash. Whenever they resisted its pull, it was like being hit by a runaway train.

"Ash, thank you," Lucienne whispered. Her mind had cleared of the fog, though her head still throbbed.

Ashburn pulled her into an embrace, his face buried against her shoulder blade. "Lucia." He was trembling. "I thought I'd lost you again."

She stroked his silver hair to comfort him and show her gratitude, but then her hand halted. Where was Vladimir? A quick scan of the room showed he wasn't here. Over Ashburn's shoulder stood Kian and Dr. Wren; behind them were Christophersen and her tearful nanny, Aida. All hovered over her as worried as Ashburn that she'd been lost forever.

The guards blocked the door, their expressions grim. Oliver had red scratches across his boyish face. The young guard joined Sphinxes' team a year ago. His uncle, Orlando Sutherland, had been one of Lucienne's most trusted guards. The man sacrificed himself to save her from the fatal blow of Seraphen, an unidentified species, a year ago. Had she hurt Orlando's only family? Dr. Wren had said she had become violent. Her face paled. No, it couldn't be. She would never hurt her own people, but guilt fell in her stomach like iron, followed by shame and anxiety. She turned to lock her gaze on Kian, in desperate need of assurance and consolation, but all she saw in his sapphire eyes was a churning sea of uncertainty and agony.

Kian collected himself and warmth returned to his eyes, easing his edge. "How are you feeling, kid?"

"My head hurts like a bad hangover," she groaned, still sagging against Ashburn.

"I'm glad you haven't reached the legal age for drinking," said

Kian.

She might never reach that age. When she was named Siren, her family had attempted to make sure she'd never reach adulthood. Ten years later, her ancient enemy, the Sealers, had finally succeeded in poisoning her with Blood Tear.

"We have aspirin," Christophersen offered.

"I said all drugs are banned!" Kian said, unnecessarily harsh on the geneticist. "And Lucia won't be taking any painkillers either."

Lucienne desperately wanted an aspirin to reduce her horrible headache, but painkillers weren't for Sirens. Her race regenerated faster than ordinary humans, but narcotics prolonged their recovery time. The Sirens had to experience pain—part of the curse for her bloodline.

She didn't want to complain anymore how wrecked she felt, so she smiled at Kian, then at the others. "Why do you all look like you're at my funeral?" she said, trying to lighten the mood in the room.

Their faces only paled.

"Look, I'm okay," she groaned.

Then she saw shards of a broken Qing dynasty vase on the floor, one of her favorite antiques. Aida and the guards hadn't had the time or mood to clean up the evidence of her outburst. She shot a glance at Oliver again. He looked back at her. There wasn't the slightest accusation in his eyes—just sadness and regret.

She'd lapsed again, and it was worse this time. She'd hurt one of the guards. In dread, she looked down at her red gown.

Ever since the ancient poison had entered her blood, she started to wear only two colors. When she sank into insanity, she craved red. When she was herself again, she dressed in white, fully repulsed by the mere sight of red.

Aether's color was pure and white before the poison had polluted it. Red symbolized sin and revenge, brought by Blood Tear. And now all she wanted was to tear the crimson gown from her.

"I need a moment alone," Lucienne said.

Everyone except Aida filed out of the room in grave silence. Lucienne shrugged off the red gown and tossed it to the floor. The nanny selected a white, flowery dress from a closet and helped Lucienne put it on, then quickly removed the gown from her sight.

Aida brought Lucienne a glass of white grape juice. Lucienne drained it and put the glass on the desk. "Aida, I've become such a burden to you."

"You're never a burden, my sweet girl." The nanny perched on the edge of the bed and wiped beads of sweat off her charge's forehead. "You're more than a daughter to me."

Lucienne rested her head against Aida's shoulder and let her nanny hold her. "Raising me wasn't an easy task. The only reason I do not become a monster is because of you and Kian." Then she was stuck in a thought. Would the poison turn her into that monster?

"I wish I could take your poison into me," Aida said.

"I forbid you to say that or pray to your gods for that," Lucienne said, then sat upright. As soon as she stood up, she dropped back on the bed as smoothly as she could manage. The throbbing in her head exploded at her sudden movement.

"Where's Vlad?" she asked casually to conceal her anxiety.

She'd kept him near to protect him from her men's wrath.

Vladimir and Ashburn had moved into her mansion, after she'd returned from the war, despite her protests that she didn't need babysitters.

Kian also placed a team of round-the-clock guards in adjoining guestrooms. He checked on her every morning before hurrying off to his chief's duties. Dr. Wren often accompanied him. Nothing Lucienne did could drive these men away. Ashburn hovered around her whenever Vladimir showed up. Kian, who no longer trusted the Czech prince, backed up Ashburn's every move. The two didn't want her and Vladimir to be alone. Not for a second.

Ziyi Wen, a leading force on her tech team, had also tried to move in with her. No matter how much Lucienne loved that girl, she knew Ziyi would be a pest if she let her friend reside in her house.

"Why don't you have everyone move in, and then I move out?"

she had once asked Kian.

He'd ignored her sarcasm.

"Aida, where's Vlad?" Lucienne asked again.

"That scoundrel went to shower," said Aida, "so he can smell like prince charming when he comes back."

"Aida, you've been mean to him. It's not his fault."

"Even that devil didn't deny it, and he usually denies every wrongdoing," Aida snorted. "You're the only one who still defends him. I'd toss him to a pack of wolves, if I could!"

"Aida, please," Lucienne said. "Vlad has given me everything he has."

The nanny murmured something inaudible. Lucienne sighed. Not just Aida, the men all blamed Vladimir for her being poisoned, and he wasn't helping himself. He hadn't acted like a sorry dog with his tail between his legs. On the contrary, he became more provocative, as if he welcomed the men's antagonism. He was only sunshine when he was with her.

A thought hit Lucienne. Vladimir went to great lengths to make everyone hate him because he hated himself even more. She must set him straight and stop his self-destructive behavior.

A knock rapped on the door, and Aida went to open it.

Ashburn stormed in with doctors and the guards in tow. The men looked reassured at her white attire. They'd learned to judge her state of mind by the color of her dress.

"The Sealers wanted a war, and we delivered it to them." Kian's voice carried through the open door. "The UN can object all it wants. I don't give a rat's ass. They have no jurisdiction over Sphinxes." He shut his encrypted Eidolon and spat a curse, "The lot of hypocrites," and strode back into the room.

"I'm fine now." Lucienne waved off her family doctor. "You should get back to your other patients, or go take a nap, Dr. Wren. You've been on edge lately."

Wren and Christophersen looked at Kian, and he nodded. The doctors hurried away. It suddenly occurred to Lucienne that they didn't go to tend to other patients; they were returning to the lab to find a cure because they hadn't yet learned that the ancient poison was out of their league. She sighed inwardly. They wouldn't find the antidote by spending their sleeping time carrying on numerous tests, but no one listened to her while she was in this condition.

"Problem with the United Nations?" she asked Kian, pressing her fingers on her temples.

"Nothing you need to worry about," Kian said. "The sedative is a bad business. It was a lack of judgment on my part."

"No one knew it would mess me up," she said.

"We're at wits' end with this poison," Kian said. "I've sent for the best doctors in the world."

"Send them back," she said. "My condition is beyond anyone's expertise." She darted her gaze toward Ashburn, signaling him to back her up.

Ashburn leaned against a desk, watching her. His eyes were gray with concern. She would never get used to his smoldering gaze. She blushed and cursed under her breath. She'd demonstrated less control over her body's reactions since being poisoned.

Fueled by her hyperawareness of his closeness, the Lure grew more vivid and in turn made Lucienne's pulse speed up. Ashburn stirred.

"Ash," she called to distract him and herself from the Lure. "Kian wants to have a group of new doctors from all around the world come in to poke me. What do you think of that?"

"It will be torture to Lucia, Mr. McQuillen," Ashburn said over Kian's glare. "The best doctors can't help her. I need to observe her for a little longer before I can construct a cure."

"Make it quick then." Kian gave Ashburn a curt nod. "Time is ticking!" As he turned back to Lucienne, his hard sapphire eyes softened and warmed. "See you later, kid." And he left.

Lucienne rose to her feet. Thankfully, her vertigo had passed after some rest and a full glass of grape juice. She emerged at the door but didn't see Oliver among the guards.

"Where is Oliver?" she asked Adam, the captain of the guards. Marloes, her former captain, had perished to save her in southern Russia.

"Ashburn sent him home," Adam said.

Oliver was assigned as Ashburn's assistant and guard, but most of the time he couldn't even tag Ash. Ashburn often took off with his Spike and was gone in the blink of an eye, leaving the poor guard having to find his own way home.

"When he returns, tell him I'm sorry, and that I need to talk to him," Lucienne said and retired to her room, where Ashburn waited.

The Lure was with them.

Lucienne's gaze moved to the bluish circles in the hollows of his eyes. He was spent after lending her his energy to bring her back. He held her gaze.

"Walk with me?" she asked. And he nodded.

The guards trailed after them into the forest of maples that half-enclosed the white mansion. The wind sent scarlet leaves drifting in the air, then abandoned them.

Lucienne walked toward the side of the forest that led to the cliff. The guards tensed up and rushed to her side.

"Cousin, we should get back," Thaddeus urged.

Lucienne didn't know when her cousin had joined them. Adam, Duncan, and Thaddeus decided among themselves to take turns watching her. One of them was with her at all times.

"The weather report says there'll be storm in the afternoon," Adam added. "The storm will hit any time now."

Lucienne turned to her captain, who bore scars for her after battling the Sealers' knights. Whenever she became difficult, Adam always used her cousin to sway her. "Even if the storm comes two hours early, and I doubt it will," she said, "I can manage some wind and rains."

Running out of excuses to make her return to the house, the guards traded anxious looks.

"It's okay," Ashburn told them. "I'm with her. Spike can bring her back in a second."

The guards pulled back. They trusted Ashburn, at least to protect their Siren, though they were still uncomfortable in his presence.

Lucienne stopped at the edge of the cliff and looked to the horizon, far above the waves that rolled against the ancient rocks beneath her. Sphinxes' fleet patrolled at the border of international waters. Pride rose in her. Sphinxes had the best military hardware and the most disciplined, loyal soldiers.

They'd made a home here, knowing they would always need to fight in order to protect it. Their old enemies were far from extinct, and new ones rose fast.

And her fight was far from over.

She hadn't expected such a harsh reality—this wandering between sanity and insanity. She'd already had three lapses in a week, each time worse than the previous. Her team wasn't prepared or equipped for this, and they had to suffer her disasters.

The air rippled; the Lure was impatient, demanding her full attention. It couldn't care less that she was half-mad as it drove her toward Ash. Her old resentment toward it vanished after it had helped bring her back from the influence of the drugs.

The world wasn't made of black and white. Nor was the Lure.

But that didn't mean she wasn't wary of it.

It was now taking advantage of her vulnerability. She'd just narrowly escaped being torched or drowned—she could die in the virtual world. A physical comfort would calm her nerves, and Ashburn was right here.

The Lure intensified its appeal. Ash's eyes glowed silver. Lucienne sensed his desperate need to have her in his arms, which mirrored her want, but he stepped a few inches away from her to defuse the Lure.

She could see the pining on his face as his white throat rose and fell, but she'd sworn never to break her oath of faithfulness to Vladimir. At present, it was the hardest thing to do.

She curled her hands into fists and let her fingernails sink into her palms to stop herself from jumping on Ash. Wisely, she also moved a few inches away from him.

The pain—the Lure's punishment—sliced her stomach. Lucienne grimaced and stole a glance at Ashburn. He also winced, then stared ahead, as if only the horizon held his interest. She followed suit.

Instant gratification could lead to deepest regrets. She and Ashburn both understood that. But how long could she maintain this control, battling against her need, heart, and sanity? How long could she fight an ancient force that was hell bent on bringing them together?

"Kian had the guards remove all things sharp from the house," she blurted out, not knowing what else to say when she couldn't go near Ash or stay away from him.

"To—to protect you from yourself," Ashburn said. He was having a hard time concentrating.

"And the others."

"You didn't mean to harm them."

"But I did." Had she used her fingernails to attack Oliver? When she'd first woken up, she'd been so ashamed that she couldn't look in Oliver's eyes.

"You aren't responsible when you weren't yourself."

"You think I can make that excuse?" She shook her head, unable to squash the rising fear in her voice. "What if this is just the beginning?"

Her dread broke Ashburn's self-control. He moved toward her, and she didn't have the will to stay away from him anymore. Every fiber of her being craved him. His strong hand held her chin, and the touch sent a delicious shiver throughout her body.

"It was an accident," he said, gazing into her eyes and slowly tearing his hand from her skin. "You were careful not to hurt anyone, but rage took you. Oliver rushed ahead of other guards to take the vase from you. They knew how much you cherished the antique. They knew you would feel heartache at breaking it when you came back to yourself. As you wrestled with Oliver for control of the vase, you scratched him. He didn't think badly of you. None of them did. They were sorry they didn't preserve the vase, and they were sorrier they didn't stop the doctors from sedating you. I—they almost lost you."

Lucienne swallowed. "What triggered my rage?"

"How much do you remember?"

"I caught a glimpse of my first lapse. The second time I had only a vague recollection. This time, I have no memories."

"Complete blackout," he said. "We don't know what set you off. It might be an epidemic burst of Blood Tear in your system."

The poison had turned aether into the most volatile element in Forbidden Glory, which in turn made her a ticking time bomb.

"We should get back to the house," Ashburn said. "You look exhausted."

"Stay a little longer, please," she pleaded.

They stood quietly for a minute before Ashburn broke the silence. "Nothing has changed for me, Lucia, no matter how you're changing."

She turned to him, her eyes inquisitive.

"What I mean is," he said softly, "you'll always have me."

She'd once promised him that no matter what dark place he was in, he'd never need to feel alone, for she'd always be there for him. But now she no longer had the capacity to be there for him or for anyone. How fragile a promise was made by a mortal. She wouldn't hold Ash onto that.

"It was mostly my fault anyway," he said. "I was supposed to watch over you."

"I'm not your responsibility," she said. "I'm so sick of everyone blaming themselves for my slip."

"I saw it coming, but I didn't stop it," he said. "I knew you would never stand still. It's in your nature to move forward, but you backpedaled for my sake. You couldn't bring yourself to harm me with the Eye of Time, so you tried a new angle and went after Nexus

Tear."

"Is it your fault that aether was the one missing element of my Siren's mark?" she asked. "Is it your fault that I felt restless before it united with the other four fundamental forces? My ancient enemies knew of my coming from the prophecy on the third scroll. They had planned this revenge since ancient time. Should I let you or anyone take the fall for them?"

Lucienne possessed the first two scrolls. One-third of the first scroll remained undecipherable without the last. Only when she had the last one could she crack the full prophecy and decode the mysteries of the new universe.

Her expedition teams had spent years trying to locate the last scroll. At the Temple of Lemuria, her treacherous father had revealed that it was in the keep of the Sealers. Her enemy had succeeded in decoding the partial prophecy on it and used the prediction to lure her into a trap and poison her.

"I had only a glimpse of the last scroll from a memory," Ashburn said. "Ancient inscriptions, runes, and dead languages are scrawled upon it. Even if I had the full view, I couldn't decipher them." After a pause, he continued, "TimeDust is insufficient."

And they both knew why. Without linking to the Eye of Time, TimeDust in him remained incomplete. As long as it stayed that way, as Ashburn insisted, he'd be safe and still be Ashburn. That was why Lucienne had locked the ancient entity inside the Twilight Water to prevent herself from unleashing it on him. The temptation was too great.

"I've tried to reboot TimeDust and have it run a full system diagnosis," Ashburn added.

Lucienne's heart skipped a beat. He wouldn't have actively sought to engage TimeDust if not for her. "Any success?" she asked casually while holding her breath.

"We'll see," he said in a measured voice.

"If you can help me locate the last scroll by accessing the Sealers elders' memories—"

"I did, but there's a problem."

"When is there not?" she said, crestfallen. "I should have known the Sealers would keep the scroll in the submarine. Black Lightning Seven blew it to pieces."

"The scroll survived."

Lucienne whipped around toward Ashburn, eyes sparkling with hope. Her hand grabbed his arm, and the Lure immediately spiked. She rasped at the pleasure it provided, reluctantly withdrawing her hand after lingering a little longer. Now, she had to embrace the punishing pain for letting go.

"Your Siren's mark shields you, so I can't read your memories," Ashburn said. "But for some reason, I can't see your mother's either. I believe the Eye of Time erased her from the collective consciousness."

Her face showed the subject of her long-gone mother wasn't something she liked having brought up. "What does Jekaterina have to do with this?"

"The last scroll has fallen into her hands," he said.

She looked at his darkened expression, and her face sank. "And she falls off the grid, doesn't she?"

Chapter Two

BEATEN

Lucienne awoke to a beam of sun dust dancing in front of her face.

Aida made it a routine to open the curtains and let the sunlight in each early morning ever since Lucienne returned from the war.

She's terrified I won't wake up one day if she doesn't do so.

Even Dr. Wren, her family doctor since her birth, wasn't particularly positive that she could last long if they didn't find her a cure in time.

Widely awake now, Lucienne took in her open-style bedroom. The tone of the room stayed rich white—a vanity set, a rug with silver lilies, and flowery curtains. All valuable, breakable things had been evacuated. Kian had also taken great care to have the crew remove the chandelier of crystals from the ceiling, fearing it would fall on her next time she went berserk. He banned mirrors after she smashed one with her bare hand in a rage.

The team replaced her treasured Chinese Shui-mo painting *Nymph of the Luo River*, which told of a doomed romance between a goddess and a mortal prince, with calendar photos of snowy forests.

Her people were protecting her property from her.

With a sigh, Lucienne threw off the quilt and swung her legs out of the bed. A relief settled over her as she found she was in a white sleeping gown.

She headed to the bathroom to take a two-minute shower. A bath had become a luxury. The last thing she wanted was to be caught in a transition from sane to crazy in the nude.

After her quick shower, she put on a white shirt and jeans with wide belt and jogged toward the sun room for breakfast. Duncan and another guard escorted her.

The smell of coffee, bacon, and French toast floated down the hallway. Her mouth watering, Lucienne quickened her pace, but then paused before reaching the glass door to the sun room.

The air crackled with electricity. The Lure had arrived before her. Lucienne took a moment to brace herself. Ash wasn't the only one inside. Vladimir must be waiting for her as well. Neither of them would let the other be alone with her.

She hadn't seen Vladimir since her episode yesterday. He'd gone for a shower and hadn't returned after that. He deserved a break from her.

She evened her breath and approached the door. Recognizing her heat signature, it slid open. Lucienne sauntered in.

A flood of sunshine poured through the spaces between the red maple leaves dangling over the glass roof. Vladimir and Ashburn, positioned as far away from each other as possible, took the two seats facing the door.

Ashburn sensed her coming before Vladimir did. He sat there expectantly, hands on a steamy teacup. "Lucia," he said, his bored, annoyed expression vaporizing at the sight of her. "You can sit beside me."

Vladimir, who was adding spoons of sugar into his mug of coffee on the counter, turned to her at once. "No freaking' way," he said. "She sits with me."

Lucienne stifled a sigh. This never got old, but at least they evolved a little. Vladimir didn't demand Ashburn get lost. He knew she needed Ash, though he stubbornly assumed it was a temporary thing— that she needed Ash to improve her health, and then he'd be gone.

Before Ashburn retorted, Lucienne cut in, "Let's start the day with getting along, shall we?" She chose a middle seat on the opposite side of the boys. "And good morning—" Her bright greeting choked in her throat as she saw what had become of Vladimir's face.

It was bruised and swollen with two cuts on his left cheek. His lower lip was nastily split. That was why he hadn't showed up last night. He must have looked worse.

Vladimir never lost a one-on-one duel. The men had ganged up on him again. Lucienne's eyes hardened. Her Czech boyfriend had become the most hated man in Sphinxes. The first week after they'd returned from the war, he'd constantly engaged himself in a fight whenever he left her residence. When she'd asked how he'd gotten his bruises, he'd always found some excuse.

She was a warrior herself. She understood pride. She couldn't interfere in his struggles with her soldiers. Vlad couldn't take it if the men despised him—and they would if she stepped in. She'd given him and the men time to sort out their differences, but she underestimated the scale of her warriors' fury. So he'd come back damaged. This, she decided, must end. If she continued to tolerate their violence and his pride, one day they would deliver her a body bag with Vladimir inside.

Rage fell into Lucienne's eyes.

Ashburn was at her side in an instant, his hand grabbing her shoulder. "Lucia," he said, "easy. Reel in your anger." And then he pulled her into his arms.

His woody scent filled her world. His warmth and hard chest was the haven she'd been searching for. Pleasure rushed over her. Ash was using the Lure to distract her so she wouldn't let fury take over. Anger was the major cause of her insanity.

Lucienne's temper ebbed away at Ash's touch.

Vladimir was beside her. He was always fast. As he watched his rival embrace her, his jaw tightened, but he didn't attack. In the past, he'd have assaulted Ashburn for that, but her condition brought the two of them to an understanding. Vladimir tapped Ashburn on the shoulder to indicate that he could take over hugging Lucienne.

Ashburn gave Vladimir a sinister glare, but Lucienne extricated herself from him to avoid a further conflict. Vladimir immediately pulled her into his arms, his hands, rough and strong, tight against the small of her back. Lucienne could read his intention to replace Ashburn's scent with his, and she was momentarily confused by the sudden shift. Both scents were intoxicating, but now wasn't the best time to make a comparison.

With clenched fists, Ashburn returned to his seat, his death glare glued on Vladimir. Ashburn was more conservative and considerate. He wouldn't do anything to provoke her; Vladimir, on the other hand, was reckless even in the most hazardous situation.

"Will you let me have my breakfast?" she asked Vladimir and he released her reluctantly. She noticed his limp as he went back to his seat, though he was very careful to hide it. The men had beaten him up terribly.

"Did you get into a fight again?" she asked.

Vladimir shrugged. "Just a quarrel."

"A quarrel?" She stared at him. "They mauled your face."

Ashburn looked alarmed again. Lucienne gave him a nod to tell him that she would get hold of herself.

Vladimir had the nerve to flash a grin at her. "You should see how they look."

Ashburn snorted at Vladimir's bravado. Lucienne could imagine how the men looked and how many men it took to take the prince down. He'd finally admitted it was more than one man. She could guess who the ringleader was—the battle-hardened Finley. He'd hated Vladimir since the Brazil raid.

Vladimir saw the dangerous glint in her eyes and went rigid, his grin gone. "Lucia," he said, not forgetting to give her a frown of disapproval. He'd been pretending she was just like before, and that everything was normal. As if by making believe, things would be fine for the two of them. "It was just a fight," he stressed. "Men are like dogs. Men fight."

Ashburn shook his head in disgust and turned to drink his Irish tea.

Aida stepped through the adjacent inner door with a cart of a full-course breakfast.

"Ah, Aida," Vladimir said cheerfully, shifting his attention to the food, "just in time. I'm starving."

Aida didn't look in his direction. It took more than a touch of willpower for her not to poison his food. Had it not upset Lucienne, she just might have done it. The nanny stopped the cart beside her charge. "My sweet girl," she said, "I made you your favorite omelet." She laid out several dishes in front of Lucienne, then placed a glass of almond milk on the side. As Lucienne eyed Vladimir's coffee, the nanny said firmly, "No coffee, Lucia. Doctor's orders."

Lucienne heaved a sigh and gestured for the guards to join her for breakfast, and they eagerly took seats on either side of her.

"No man can resist Aida's full English course," Duncan said.

"I'm not English," Aida said. "I'm a Mongolian."

"Sorry," Duncan murmured, "I didn't mean English. I meant course."

"I know what you meant!" said Aida.

"Uh, your English is very good," Duncan said. "I can barely hear any trace of an accent."

The other guard nodded an impressive approval.

Aida hissed, "I was raised in Chicago." She pushed the cart away without the slightest intention of serving the guards, and they traded a glance.

As Aida strolled past Vladimir, he called, "Slow down, Aida darling. Can I have an omelet too?"

"I'm not your darling," Aida said coldly. "You want anything, make it yourself."

Vladimir kept his grin, but Lucienne caught fleeting hurt in his hazel eyes.

Aida stopped again beside Ashburn and placed a plate full of pancakes in front of him. She poured syrup on top of the stack. "More syrup, Ash?" she asked fondly.

"Yes, please," Ashburn said. "And thank you, Aida."

The nanny drizzled more syrup on Ash's pancakes, then left the whole bottle on the table directly in front of him. Lucienne watched silently. Aida refused to serve Vladimir, but at least she hadn't spat on his food or mixed sand in his steak and sandwiches as the chefs in Sphinxes' castle did.

Lucienne cut her omelet in half, placed a portion on another plate, and pushed it toward Vladimir. "Share mine," she offered.

"Jsi můj miláček," Vladimir said in Czech, meaning, "You're my sweetheart." He cut a piece of creamy spinach omelet and put it into his mouth. "Good stuff," he said and swallowed it.

Ashburn glared at Vladimir. Standing behind Ashburn, Aida also looked daggers at the Czech prince. Vladimir took in another mouthful of omelet and moaned as if he were in heaven.

"Aida is a softie inside." Lucienne turned to the guards. "She's made plenty of toasts, bacons, and beans for everyone in the kitchen. Help yourself."

"We take turns," Duncan told a young guard. "And I outrank you." With that, he rose and exited into the kitchen.

The guard murmured a complaint.

Lucienne ignored the tension in the room, determined to enjoy her breakfast. She put a forkful of omelet into her mouth and chewed. It didn't have the delicious flavor of fine egg, cheese, and spinach. It tasted like rusty metal. Then the smell of blood permeated the air.

No, Lucienne cried silently, as a heated wave hit her face.

"*No*," she heard Ashburn's whisper as she looked up from her food and locked eyes on him.

The wave dragged her toward a pit as she kicked and screamed, struggling to pull free.

It was gone, leaving her in the center of a sunny room, where everything appeared distorted.

She blinked in confusion, and everything returned to normal.

"Oh, gods, it comes more and more often," an old woman cried. "My sweet girl suffers."

She ignored the woman, who posed no threat, but the men surrounding her were warriors. They were young and virile, and she could sense they were always itching for a fight. Tensing up, she grasped a string of beads on her wrist. She never went anywhere without a weapon, and though the beads didn't seem dangerous, they were lethal in her hands. The enemies who underestimated her had paid dearly.

"Láska?" A hazel-eyed boy called to her.

Why did he call her "love" in Czech? She didn't even know him. Was this some kind of trick to make her lay down her defense? Narrowing her eyes, she plucked three open beads from the string, twirling them between her fingers. Any wrong move from these men, and she'd attack first. She could put down two or three at once.

"Lucia, we're your friends." A silver-haired boy gestured for the others to fall back as he moved toward her like approaching a small carnivore. But she wasn't small. She was tall and deadly and feeling backed into a corner.

The men all looked tense, but they obeyed the silver-haired boy and stepped back, their eyes not moving from her.

The hazel-eyed boy ignored the silver-haired boy's warning and competed to reach her. *A rebel type*, she thought. Should she take him down now?

"Don't be an idiot, Blazek!" the silver-haired boy hissed at him. "You should not provoke her."

The hazel-eyed glared at the silver-haired, but stopped. When he turned back to her, there was tender boldness in his eyes. "I'm not provoking her. I want to show her I'm her boyfriend."

Boyfriend?

She rolled a bead between her fingers as silver-hair growled. He didn't agree, but one of them could be her boyfriend. Which one, though? The two were clearly rivals and much more likely to attack each other than her. Lucienne loosed a tight breath and tilted her head to study them. They were both striking, yet in opposite ways. It was hard to judge which one was more attractive. Her grandfather warned her not to trust a man, especially a pretty one, and she had two in front of her.

They both wanted her. The way they looked at her—they knew her well and pined after her. But why didn't she remember them? She decided it best not to trust either one.

Then, from a distant memory, a song reached her. The lyric was ancient— a language she couldn't place. It entranced her. She was a princess in a blooming garden; a moonbeam of gold dust twirled around her. Winged fairies put a crown of delicate flowers on her head before shooting back into the air. A prince stepped into the picture. It was the silver-haired boy. He gazed at her with love, yet she wasn't sure about her own love for him. Still, her desire for him arose in response to his presence.

"Ash?" she asked, her eyes sparkling with delight at the recognition.

"Lucia." Ashburn blew out a breath.

She liked the way he said her name, as if she was indeed his princess. He was grateful that she identified him. Fondness toward him swelled in her, and she had an urge to touch him. She put her beads back on her wrist and stepped toward him, but then stopped in her tracks. Maybe she shouldn't do that. There were so many people around them, gawking at her.

"Láska," the hazel-eyed boy called again, trying to step in front of Ash and remove him from her sight.

She darted her gaze toward him, amused that he was trying so hard to get her attention. Fine, she could give him a few seconds for his effort. As she fixed on him, her eyes widened, not at the nasty cuts on his face, but at the amount of pain in his eyes. *Did he lose someone dear to him?* Sympathy for him brought back a memory. She realized who he was. He was the real prince, not the other boy.

"What happened to you, Prince Vladimir?" she asked.

"I picked a fight," he said.

"Why would you do that?" she asked.

"My opponents were extremely annoying," he said.

"You can't fight everyone who is annoying," she advised. "Soon you'll be fighting the whole world."

"Then I'll fight the whole world," he said.

He's a wild card.

A light illuminated another slice of memory. Why did she keep having fragmented flashbacks? "Vladimir Blazek," she said. His name associated with so many things.

He quirked an eyebrow to flaunt his carefree charm, but Lucienne had caught a flash of disquiet in his eyes. Did he often brace for the worst? She wouldn't doubt that by looking at his swollen face.

"If I'm not mistaken," she said matter-of-factly, "'being extremely annoying' is what everyone usually says about you."

Vladimir blinked. Then there was a spark in his eyes. She used to talk to him like that when they'd met at Desert Cymbidium, her family's military school.

"That's slander," he said. "Now you see why I had to teach them a lesson and show them the consequences of infuriating me."

She cocked her head to the side, regarding his slit bottom lip. "It seems you got the consequences."

Ashburn snorted in delight at her mockery of the other boy, as did the men in the room. Lucienne swept her gaze to Ashburn. His hostility toward the Czech prince was like an open furnace. Obviously, he wasn't thrilled that Vladimir grabbed her attention. Was Ash the one who gave the prince bruises? No, Ash didn't seem like a fighter. He had an air of cold calculation and tight self-control.

Vladimir followed her gaze and glared at Ashburn, who returned it at full measure. Both desired to give the other a death sentence. Did it have anything to do with her?

"You two are like a pair of buffaloes," she said, "ready to charge each other."

The boys at once relaxed their poses, evidently not wanting to be regarded as buffaloes, but the muscles in their jaws still twitched in tension. Lucienne giggled at their display, yet they didn't find it funny. They looked alarmed, which made her giggle more.

The room was quiet, except for her laughter. The older woman stopped crying and came to pat Lucienne's back as if afraid of her choking. This compassionate move, as if for a baby after feeding, promoted another of Lucienne's memories. This woman was her nanny. Feeling a twinge of embarrassment, then irritation, she shrugged off Aida. "I'm a big girl."

She then paid no mind to her nanny. Her interests lay with the hot boys. Why did they look so grim? Maybe it was—

She looked down and saw her white shirt and jeans. The cold, empty white wardrobe enveloped her like a stone coffin. White conjured impending doom. She must expel it with fire. Bright red fire.

"Where is my red gown?" she asked with a snarl, tearing at her white shirt.

"I'll bring it." The nanny scrambled out of the sun room and returned soon with a red robe in her hand. She covered Lucienne. "Now calm. Here's your pretty red gown."

Lucienne caressed the red velvet, her confidence returning, which put her in a much better mood. She even let Prince Vladimir wrap her in his possessive arms.

She laid the side of her face on his broad shoulder. From this angle, she glanced up at Ashburn through thick eyelashes. He looked so stunning, and he watched her with a pained, stormy expression, as if he wanted to tear her from Vladimir. Then why didn't he act on it? She wouldn't stop him. Did the Czech prince really have a claim on her?

She scanned the other men in the room to determine their relationships with her. She registered that they were her guards. She twisted away from Vladimir. "Why do I need to be guarded by so many men? Am I in danger?"

"You're safe with me," Vladimir said.

Ashburn sneered. Lucienne turned to him with a half smile. She didn't like the prince's answer either. His conceit didn't sit well with her, so she decided to pointedly ignore him.

"Do you like my red dress, Ash?" she purred, flaunting her feminine charm. But her dazzling smile only brought out misery in his eyes. What was wrong with him?

Vladimir, however, immediately tensed, his muscles bulging on his arms and beneath his black designer shirt. His jealousy was tangible and entertaining.

"I like anything you wear," Ashburn said, but he wasn't flirting.

Vladimir shifted his weight and blocked her sight of Ashburn again. He laid his hand against the small of her back, using a firm touch to draw her attention back to him.

"You must be hungry, Lucia," Ashburn said. "Aida made you your favorite omelet."

Amusing. Ash was using the primary human need—food—to get her leave Vladimir's arms.

These boys each wanted to pull her in his direction, but she would show them she was in charge. Then her stomach unexpectedly grumbled. That wasn't lady-like. She brushed aside her embarrassment. She was hungry. She shoved Vladimir aside and went back to her seat.

Ashburn gave her an encouraging smile as she cut a piece of omelet and put it into her mouth. It tasted good. Ashburn and Vladimir sat across from her, but neither touched their dishes. Lucienne flicked her gaze between them.

"They stare at me as if they want to eat me, Aida." She addressed her nanny, her gaze locked on the boys. "I must be delicious." She giggled again and flung a seductive look at Vladimir, then at Ashburn. Which one wanted her more?

But instead of showing desire, their eyes held identical pain and wariness. If it weren't for the undeniable tenderness dwelling in the depth of their sadness, she'd have thrown her plate at them. They made her feel like she was eating at her own funeral. Suddenly, the memories of attending the funerals of Orlando, Marloes, and her other loyal warriors flooded back. With that piece of memory, grief struck her. *No!* She wasn't equipped to deal with that amount of sorrow and guilt. She must put them in a box, as Kian had advised.

"Where is the box?" she demanded. Grief kept hitting her. It was too much!

Everyone looked puzzled, and then traded nervous glances.

Lucienne tossed her fork onto the table. It clanked. "You all look at me as if I'm crazy," she hissed. She was also humiliated that the boys didn't desire her as she'd wanted. "Did I ask any of you to pity me?"

"It's not pity, Lucia," Vladimir started. "I—"

"You're a liar," she said.

"Lucia." Ashburn reached her. "I don't know about him," he said over Vladimir's growl, "but I've never lied to you. Look at me and see the truth."

She peeked into his eyes. Their color shifted from ice blue to silver gray with thick emotions, which made her pulse quicken. His young male musk distracted her more. It was calling her to him, tugging her toward him. Her eyes brightened. There was something between them, and it was lovely and lush. She put her palm against his face, her anger whiffing away. "I want you, Ash," she said.

Ashburn sucked in a breath. She knew he shared what she felt. He wanted her even more than she did him. Then what was he waiting for? Shouldn't he start kissing her?

Vladimir shoved Ashburn away and cut in between them. "Lucia, you're tired," he said. "I'll take you to your bedroom."

"No, you won't take me anywhere." She didn't even look at him, her eyes fixing on Ashburn. "And I'm far from tired."

Vladimir turned to Ashburn and gave him a blunt order, "Leave."

"Like hell I'll leave her in your incompetent hands," Ashburn shot back.

"She isn't herself," Vladimir said through clenched teeth. "The thing in you is making her worse."

Ashburn turned to Vladimir, eyes narrowed in fury. "The thing in me?"

Lucienne also glared at the Czech.

"You know exactly what I mean," Vladimir said.

"Who caused her to be like this?" Ashburn asked.

They talked about her as if she weren't here, as if she were a weak girl. How dare they! She was …. Who was she? The vague recollection of her role came into focus. She was the Siren? Yes, and a terribly powerful one. She must show them that, but how?

Something in her consciousness twinkled, but then slipped through her grasp. She studied the boys closely, desperate to find clues. The veins in Vladimir's temples jumped. Guilt and self-loathing darkened his hazel eyes, diminishing the remaining light in them—it was scarce already. *The guilty one*, she realized. Ash had said Vladimir had caused her harm. If so, he deserved to be punished, but she needed to find out what kind of harm he'd done her.

"She's better off without you," Ashburn said. "Why don't you do us all a favor? Get off this island and disappear."

"Want to get rid of me?" Vladimir laughed viciously. "It won't happen. I stick to her. You, on the other hand, should get lost."

Earlier on, she'd worried that none of them found her attractive, but that had been baseless. Look at how they were fighting for her! She couldn't help but curl her lips in a grin.

"I know all about your dirty secrets," Vladimir said, a menacing smugness flashing in his eyes. "Yes, I know what that *thing* in you has been doing to her. Even now you're influencing her. Remove yourself this second, or I'll remove you myself."

The thing in Ash? What was the Czech prince talking about? She did feel an unnatural pull from Ash. Was he trying to do her harm too? Both of them? Her breath shortened.

Rage turned Ashburn's eyes to stormy gray.

Oh, this one is so pissed. Was he going to leave? Lucienne leaned toward Ashburn. If he exited from the scene, she'd lose a suitor. The Czech boy was starting to grate on her nerves.

Her movement brought back the attention of both boys. The Czech prince gazed at her, almost pleading. The vast gentleness in his hazel eyes failed to melt her heart. Lucienne was no fool. She didn't fall for pretty, dangerous men easily. No, he was the fool to hope she threw herself into his arms while all she had in mind was to punish him for his rudeness. A cruel smile tugging at the corner of her lips, she shoved him away. The tremendous hurt in his eyes appeased her sense of justice. He'd hurt her first. Ash had spelled out the truth.

"Let's go for a walk, Ash," she said, reaching for his hand and leading him out of the sun room and down the long hallway.

Ashburn clasped his hand around hers tightly. Vladimir and the guards fell in behind her. The Czech prince's jealousy and anger were sizzling. Lucienne rubbed her face against Ash's shoulder briefly to make the prince even madder. How easy it was for her to wrap them around her fingers. Lucienne was pleased with herself, but she hid her smirk.

The air was crisp outside the mansion, and the red forest ahead promised a good walk. Giddy, Lucienne quickened her pace, her hand still interlinking with Ashburn's. The touch felt luscious. If she lured Ash deep in the woods, away from these prying eyes, he might kiss her.

"Are you cold, Lucia?" Ashburn asked.

"I've never felt better," she said.

"Lucia," Vladimir called after her, demanding her attention, but she purposefully ignored him. She allowed him to tag along just to torment him. She let her hip brush against Ashburn's with each gait.

Like a flash, Vladimir darted to her other side. She'd seen him limping. How had he moved this fast? "Lucia, come to see my collection?" he coaxed, wrapping an arm around her shoulder, trying to turn her away from Ashburn. "I've acquired a rare sword—"

"Do I look like a tomboy who's into weaponry?" she scoffed. "You're crazy." Why did everyone wince when she said the word 'crazy?' She shook off the prince. And what kind of idiot would want to win a girl with a display of swords? She was disappointed in his courting skills. "And you should have a doctor treat your face. You don't look good!"

Pain welled in Vladimir's eyes, and beneath it, a dangerous glint. Would he challenge her then? Danger served as her companion since childhood. She gave him a defiant glare before turning back to Ashburn, whose eyes brightened at watching her scorn his rival.

His delight brought something alive. As energy rippled in the air, an unseen cord formed, chaining her and Ash together. The Lure. She recognized it. It wasn't a stranger. It always gave her a high. Time to ditch their audience. "Bring Spike, Ash," she said. "We're going for a ride."

"But—" Ashburn said.

"You will not take her." Vladimir advanced to Ashburn's side, blocking him with a threatening look. "You know better."

What a continuing nuisance! "You just have to go against me, don't you, Blazek?" she asked. "From the day I met you, you were plotting against me."

"I plot against you?" He narrowed his eyes, as if he'd had enough. "Darling, you do have a selective memory." He fixed on Ashburn again, as if he wouldn't want to bother with her. "Take her back to the house. Now. She isn't well."

Ashburn's eyes turned metal gray. "Back off, Blazek," he said.

"Yes, piss off, Blazek," Lucienne joined in. "I don't appreciate your attitude!"

Ash had been hesitant to take her for a ride, but that was before the Czech prince had enraged him. All she needed was to give Ash a nudge. "Please, Ash." She conjured up her damsel-in-distress voice. "It's suffocating to be inside that white prison. Don't you want to make me feel better?" She batted her eyelashes. "We used to go watch the sunrise in Nirvana, remember? That was a good time."

Ashburn grimaced. Then Lucienne recalled that it hadn't been a wonderful time for him. She's drugged him when the orange sun leapt from the rings of the silver mountains of the futuristic town. When Seraphen had arrived to pick a fight, she'd pondered whether to kill Ash to win the battle. What was she thinking by bringing up the irony of it?

"Well, I'm so sorry for what I did to you last time, sincerely," she said. "Take me for a ride, Ash. Let me make it up to you."

"You. Will. Not. Take. Her. Away!" Vladimir said with all the menace in the world.

Ashburn gave Vladimir a look of full disdain before he whistled to summon Spike.

Lucienne's eyes lit up as Spike, the machine of light, beamed into existence beside her.

"Ashburn, you can't do that." Duncan, the guard, stepped forward. "You can't take the Siren off Sphinxes."

"You see that, Ash?" Lucienne grabbed Ashburn's arm. "My jailors watch me twenty-four/seven. They say I'm sick and try to lock me up in the house. You're my only true friend, Ash. Will you let me taste freedom again, even for a few minutes?"

"Send the darn machine away!" Vladimir demanded.

"Chief McQuillen will have your head, Ashburn, if you do this!" Duncan added hotly.

"Then let him have my head," Ashburn said.

The guards and Vladimir lunged at Ashburn in unison. Ashburn raised a hand and shot out dark lightning, sending Vladimir and the guards flying to the trees.

"They had to learn the hard way." Lucienne giggled. "Good for them. They'll think twice next time if they decide to go against me— us. But you must teach me how to throw lightning so I'll have them taste mine if they bully me again." She climbed onto the seat of Spike, and Ashburn slid behind her in a second.

"She needs this." Ashburn turned to the guards. "I'll bring her back safe in an hour. I promise."

As Spike took off, Lucienne turned to look down at Vladimir and blew him a loud kiss.

His suffering was her joy.

Spike zoomed out of Sphinxes and soared higher until Earth was a blue marble, half covered by clouds of different shades. The artificial lights on the land were like numerous tiny fires. And a wild fire lit in Lucienne.

"Fascinating," she said in amazement, nestling her head against Ashburn.

"I'll take you to the moon one day," Ashburn said.

"Why not now?"

"We don't have enough time. Your people worry about you. Even now, Dragonfly is tracking you."

"They should stop bothering me," she said in irritation. "All I want is a little fun."

"We've had fun flying this high. We should go back before they panic."

"Not yet! I have a better idea."

Ashburn's body tensed as if he were afraid of her idea.

"How about we visit your mom and dad?" she said. "They'll be thrilled to see us. I like the jasmine tea Clement made."

"We'll visit them another day."

Lucienne leaned away from him. "Are you ashamed of showing me to your parents?"

"Ashamed of you? You've visited them a hundred times already."

She arched an eyebrow. "Then what's stopping you?"

"I haven't seen them in a while. I don't want to visit them empty-handed."

"Then let's buy them gifts, as many as you want."

"I have no money on me, and neither do you," he said. "I insist we visit them next time."

"But—"

"You see that place, Lucia?" Ashburn pointed at the landscape far beneath them.

"Where?"

"There, the greenest forest on earth."

"Yeah, very green," she said indifferently. Her interest was Ash, and she wanted him to reciprocate.

Spike abruptly descended from space, plunging toward the forest. Lucienne didn't blink an eye at the speed. The air and wind whooshed by, but didn't affect them as Spike's force field shielded them. Lucienne's eyes widened in excitement as the lighted machine pierced the clouds. She stretched a hand to touch them, but Spike's power blocked their icy mists.

As they left the clouds and upper atmosphere behind, a gem of ocean expanded beneath them, reaching out to the horizon, then blurred as Spike whisked by. The machine dove toward the trees. An instant later, it glided over an endless sea of rainforest.

It was spectacularly beautiful, Lucienne had to admit, but it wouldn't be a romantic getaway for her to seduce Ash and have her way with him, even though this jungle would be the last place anyone would ever come to interrupt them.

"This is the most dangerous, uncharted jungle in the world," Ashburn said. "A beauty it is."

She needed to distract him from this dangerous beauty and return him to hers. She twisted her body on Spike and gave him a sensual smile. The Lure responded to her desire, pulling Ashburn toward her. He gazed down at her lips subtly parting for him. With a swallow, he glanced away.

"In this forest dwelled the most deadly species that," he muttered, trying to get back to his former subject, "humans —humans haven't known about."

"Ash." She pouted. "Must we forever discuss hazardous species?"

He gave her a look, then pointed toward the yellow mountains at the far end of the rainforest, separated by a vast river. "See the mountains?"

At last she realized where he was going. He was stalling. He pretended to be oblivious to her feminine charm, but was doing a poor job of it. His racing heartbeat betrayed him.

An amused smile crossed her lips.

"Within three months," he continued, "that volcano is going to erupt."

Lucienne didn't care about volcanoes or rainforests or yellow mountains. She must end his silliness and take the lead when it came to romance. "We've seen enough of jungles and mountains, Ash," she purred, knowing the effect her silky, honey voice had on men. It always worked wonders on the Czech prince. "Can we go to Ghost House? We won't visit your parents, but we can sit on the roof and talk and do something really fun."

Ashburn studied her with uncertainty, but Lucienne knew he was tempted, especially when she pressed her face against his chin. The Lure approved, rewarding her with a distinctive pleasure. Ashburn grew tenser, but he bent toward her despite himself.

She knew she had him. He could no longer keep her at bay. "Please, Ash," she whispered in his ear, her warm breath caressing his skin. "I haven't had a good time in so long."

He caved. "After that, we'll go straight back to Sphinxes, where you won't come up with another idea."

"Deal," she said, her cheek gently rubbing against his jaw one more time before she turned back and hid a smug smile.

Spiked pulled up to the high sky at a 45° angle. When it dove again and touched down, Lucienne was on the rooftop of the Ghost House.

Lucienne swung her legs off the machine in giddiness.

Nirvana stretched under her feet like a garden of gems. It was nowhere near its glory day when she'd first spotted it several months ago, but it was still one of the most beautiful, sheltered towns, thanks to Ashburn, who powered it with TimeDust. Lucienne knew Ash had no love for the king, the queen, or its residents, but he maintained the town for his adopted parents. Once they passed away, Ash would extract his power, and this legendary lost city would be overcome by harsh climates and erode through by time.

Her memory was doing a funny thing to her. Until this moment, she hadn't connected his great power to Nirvana's survival. She breathed out a deep sigh. Soon this gorgeous, powerful man would be hers. She was the luckiest girl in the world!

Lucienne sprawled in the center of the roof and flashed Ashburn a lazy, disarming grin. He stayed on Spike, watching her every move, smitten, yet careful. She adjusted her position to lie on her side, her leg bent slightly, showing her curves to him.

The rooftop appeared to be made of ice, giving the illusion that she could fall through, but she knew it was more solid than anything built on earth. She glanced at the distant ring of silver-capped mountains before sliding her gaze back toward Ashburn—her true target. Her eyes invited him to come to her, and evidently drawn by the Lure and her wiles, he left his machine and jogged toward her.

He sat down beside her, his body taut.

"Lie down and you can see the faint moon," she coaxed. "I won't bite."

The Lure, a tempting mistress, worked with her. As he lay on his back, it wrapped them inside an invisible, enchanting dome. Lucienne wondered why she'd ever fought it.

She eyed the two and half feet between her and Ash, and inched closer to him.

He tensed with expectation and wanting, yet opposing it all the same. "Lucia—"

She set the distance between them to a foot and angled her body toward him, elbow on the roof, chin on her palm. "Yes, Ash?" She gazed at his perfect, symmetric features and his bright silver eyes.

The magnetism between them crackled in the air.

Ashburn turned his face toward her, looking at her sideways through his silver lashes. As Lucienne slowly edged herself toward him until there was only half a foot between them, he became very still.

This chase was fun. "I'm so glad we're finally alone," she said with a honeyed voice.

"Yes, I'm glad too," he murmured, having a hard time focusing.

Lucienne eliminated the space between them and pressed a hip against his thigh. His heat radiated to her. Eyes glinting, he rasped. Still, he didn't move, but managed to turn his gaze away from her to stare at the sky to mask his emotion. That didn't discourage Lucienne; it only drove her on.

"Ash?" she whispered.

"Yes?" he answered, holding his breath and not looking at her. As if by not gazing into her eyes, he wouldn't fall into them.

It wouldn't work. She saw through him. He was so hot for her. She could feel it as if it were burning inside her. She lifted her head and smoothly laid it on his broad shoulder. They fit perfectly. She placed her hand against his heart. It beat into her palm so fast and powerfully that she felt she was holding his lifeline in her hand. Her heart pounded just as equally strong.

"We probably … should head back," Ashburn said with great difficulty. "Kian is yelling at everyone. He's beyond mad and … concerned. He swears he'll snap my neck himself at the first sight of me."

"Don't worry about him. I outrank him," she said. "I outrank everyone in Sphinxes." She felt her own warm breath on his face, as her lips were an inch from his.

The Lure went wild. Heat surged between her thighs. Lucienne moaned.

He stared at her lips, his eyes glowing the brightest silver, thick with lust. He managed a sentence, his minty, ragged breath mingling with hers. "I don't think this is a good idea."

"I'll decide what a good idea is," she said as her eyelids went heavy. "Do you not want me?"

"I'm aching for you," he said fiercely. "I wanted you the first time I laid my eyes on you. You have no idea of what hell it is to control myself. You're the only girl I've ever wanted …."

Too many words made her dizzy. She spoke with action. Lucienne climbed on top of Ashburn. A wave of electricity shot through her. Such pleasure!

Ashburn arched his back. The Lure rewarded him with the same bliss.

"Lucia, my love," he said.

"Take me," she said in her most sultry voice. "Give me everything you have."

He tore her red robe from her shoulders, pulling it down to her waist, and ripped her shirt aside. He stared at her exposed breasts, licking his lips.

Lucienne grabbed his hand and placed it over one of her breasts.

As his hand tightened while cupping her, Lucienne inhaled. The pleasure was like no other. She'd been such an idiot to deny herself this unmatchable carnal joy. She ground her hips atop him, feeling his body hard and taut as a bowstring.

He couldn't help but gasp. Then he seemed to collect himself, if only barely. "Lucia, stop." His voice was rough, husky. "If you don't, I won't be able to stop later."

"I don't want you to stop, now or later," she said, pressing herself harder against him, desperate to remove any negative space between them. "Nothing can stay between us now. Undress me completely."

A ravenous hunger twisted his face. He pulled her robe above her head, followed by the torn remnants of her shirt, tossing them onto the ice-like roof.

"This long pent-up passion is killing me," she said. "Release it."

"Nectar, your perfume," he murmured as if drunk.

Lucienne bent down. Just before her lips touched his, he pulled her face up and held it there. "When you become yourself again, you'll hate me as much as you'll hate yourself," he said. "And I'll never forgive myself for taking advantage of you."

His talk of hate and consequences was like unexpected cold water spraying on her face. However, that ounce couldn't quench the fire inside her. "I *am* myself," she said, "and I'm yours to take and savor." She fought to get free of his hold. Once her mouth moved over his, he'd never resist her again. But he was stronger. He was as strong as any of her warriors, and that surprised her. "You said you want me!"

"You have no idea how much I want you." A low, hoarse laugh escaped him. "I want to make you belong to me and only me forever, but I'll hate myself for taking you like this. Not like this." He jerked up and sat straight, so she fell on his lap.

She pulled him toward her again, but he grabbed her wrist. "Don't do this, Lucia," he said with a ragged breath. "I love you. I can't leave a chance for you to despise me. I want this to feel right, so that we'll have no regrets."

The muscles along his jaw twisted. Agony spread in his light gray eyes. The Lure's penalty had descended on him.

"Stop resisting it and the pain will go away," she said. When he didn't abide, she cast him a withering look, bracing for the same pain to run through her. It didn't come this time. But the pleasure it had bestowed deserted her, as did the heat between her thighs.

He held her bitter gaze, heartache brimming in his eyes. It was the same ache she saw in Kian, her nanny, her guard, even her jolly friend Ziyi. She wanted to escape it. She brought Ash here to escape it, and yet he brought it right back to her.

Lucienne felt drained.

When Ashburn picked her up and put the tattered shirt and red robe back on her, she didn't fight him. When he carried her toward Spike in staggered steps and placed her on it, she remained passive. He mounted the machine behind her.

"Thank you for sending me back to my prison, guarded by the Czech prince and the sentinels assigned by Chief McQuillen," she said when Spike banked away from the ring of snowy mountains.

He didn't say a word but fastened an arm around her waist.

While the taste of bile and the humiliation of his rejection lingered on her tongue, the world suddenly shifted.

A veil of mist lifted from her.

Where was she? And why was she with Ash, traveling above the ocean at such tremendous speed?

She looked down. She wore a red robe, with a wrinkled, torn white shirt inside.

As she cringed close her eyes, everything that had happened since she'd woken up this morning flooded back to her. It was like watching the reflection of another person act inside her body. She remembered it all this time. However, being able to recall the day's events added only misery.

She untied the red robe, shrugged it off, and tossed it down to the endless water beneath. It twirled downwards in the wind and fell onto the sea like a splatter of blood.

Chapter Three

DUEL

The first thing Lucienne looked at was what she wore when she awoke the next morning. The white gown clinging to her body didn't improve her mood. Yesterday's shame stuck with her like a bad hangover.

She'd been cruel to Vladimir. She'd called Aida her servant. And she'd chased Ash like a feline in heat. If he hadn't fended off her advance, they'd have—

The worst part was not knowing what she'd do to hurt others and shame herself when she sank into her next bout of insanity.

She didn't want to get up. She made up her mind to skip breakfast. There was no way she could face Vladimir or Ashburn today. Not today. Maybe not ever, though that day would come.

Aida sat on the edge of the bed. "None of them are in the house. They didn't even show up for breakfast. We have a quiet morning for a change."

"Where did they go?" Lucienne asked sheepishly.

"They're boys. They can't stay in the house forever."

Lucienne sighed. "They've been restless."

"The boys are caged cubs in puberty."

"What does that mean?"Lucienne let out a low laugh. The next second, deep sorrow arrived like the cold rain. Neither of them could have a future with her.

After Lucienne had a quick shower, her nanny combed her hair. "Anything you want to do today, my sweet girl?" Aida asked.

"Good question," she said.

Although every day had become a test for her and everyone around her, Sphinxes' post-war operations needed to be smoothed out. Weakened defenses needed to be shored up and allies kept in place. Lucienne had to face a day of project reviews, stacks of documents waiting to be signed, and meetings. Endless meetings ....

She batted those thorny issues aside, but one of them pricked at her, demanding her immediate attention—she needed to stop the fighting between Vladimir and her men.

After Aida brushed her hair, Lucienne stepped into the adjoining sitting room. Her chief had the crew turn a small portion of her former bedroom into this waiting area. She could still have some of her privacy while the on-the-clock guards watched out for her here.

Thaddeus raised his head at her approach. He was eating the pancakes that her nanny had brought into the sitting room for her. "How do you feel, cousin?" he asked good-naturedly.

Aida hissed, "That breakfast isn't for you!" She scurried to his side, gave him a bang on the forehead, and snatched away the plate. Only two pancakes remained.

"Ouch, Aida," Thaddeus said.

"None of the guards dare eat Lucienne's food—unlike you!" Aida said.

"I'm not just her guard," Thaddeus said. "I'm family."

"Then you should care for her health rather than steal her food," Aida said.

"C'mon, Lucia can't finish all those pancakes," said Thaddeus. "She's to be a queen. A queen must be on a diet to keep her good looks. That's the part of her welfare I'm looking after."

"You have a slick tongue, like the Czech!" Aida said.

Thaddeus spit out his half-eaten pancake. "You do not put me and him in the same sentence!"

Like the others, her cousin also blamed Vladimir for Lucienne's fall. Her men lost reason after she'd been poisoned. If she couldn't kick some sense back into them, then she must make them see the consequences of their violent actions against her boyfriend.

"Stop," Lucienne cut in. "Will you two let me have a few moments of peace?"

They quieted.

"Sorry, cousin," Thaddeus said. "I won't eat your pancakes again."

"Eat my food all you want," Lucienne said, "just don't fight. You are all my family."

"But families usually fight," said Thaddeus.

Right. Her charming family—the Lams—didn't just fight. Two-thirds of them had once wanted her dead, and one-third of them had acted on it.

"Where's Kian?" she asked. He hadn't visited her today, which was uncharacteristic of him, in particular given her performance yesterday.

"He's having a meeting with the generals in the castle," Thaddeus said. "They don't ask for your presence anymore. You should pay attention to what they chat about. If they conspire against you—"

"They don't conspire," Lucienne snapped. "They're my loyal officers."

"That was before," Thaddeus said. "You were a powerful Siren; now, you—"

Lucienne gave him a chilly look, and Aida sent him a death glare.

"You always like it when I speak my mind," Thaddeus said. "I'm not going to look the other way like everyone else. You need to see the truth before it turns around and bites your butt. The damned poison is still in you. Half the time, you can't function. Your body is weakening, as is your mind. Everything but your will. But no matter what becomes of you, you never need to worry about my loyalty. You're my Siren. My queen. I've sworn a blood oath to you, and I love you as a worthy warrior and my true family. Claude and Kian are on your side too, but you can't trust everyone like before. We must act first and take out whoever tries to undermine you. You trusted the Czech with your heart, and all he's brought you are pain and disasters."

No more than I brought him. "It's not Vladimir's fault that the Sealers got me," Lucienne said. "You need to get this straight, Thaddeus. If I find that you had a hand in beating him up, I'll throw you out."

"I knew that!" Thaddeus said. "I have a big mouth, but I'm not an idiot. I pissed you off in the Red Mansion, and I lost two teeth!" He pointed at his face. "See the scars? I'm no longer handsome, thanks to the marks you left!" There was no bitterness, but pride in his voice, as if he regarded the scars as a trophy.

"You were never the nice-looking one before the scars," Aida said. "Do not blame Lucia for your ugliness."

Lucienne slid onto the couch across from her cousin and picked up a pancake. "I behaved badly yesterday, so Ash and Vlad refused to share a meal with me today. Do you know where they are?"

"They argued outside the house early this morning," Thaddeus said. "I gave them a piece of advice: take it out like men. Stop quarreling and squirming like chicks."

Lucienne gave him another hard stare.

Thaddeus shrugged. "The house is peaceful without them in the same room. Isn't that what you want?"

"The house is peaceful without all of you," said Aida.

An uneasy feeling settled over Lucienne. "I hope they didn't take your lousy advice." She sighed and strolled toward the door. "I'm going to see Kian."

Thaddeus rose to his feet and collected the other guards.

"Lucia," Aida called. "At least finish your milk."

"Later," Lucienne said, exiting the room.

Thaddeus voice commanded a jeep to start at the driveway. When Lucienne hopped in the passenger seat, he told her, "Kian almost bit off Ashburn's head yesterday."

Lucienne raised an eyebrow, wanting to know more.

"I don't know the details," Thaddeus said, "but I'd rather deal with that jackass Blazek than be near Ashburn. That guy can read people's thoughts like reading his own dear diary. I, for sure, don't want him in my head."

"One, Ash doesn't write a diary," Lucienne said. "Two, Ash can not only read all of your embarrassing memories, he stores all of them in his permanent databank. One of these days, we can review them together while you eat my pancakes."

Her cousin gave her a sour look.

Kian McQuillen's office was across from the underground Defense Room. If the Sphinxes' compound was ever compromised, the Defense Room would back up operations. Pressing her palm on the scanner, she waited outside Kian's office. The computer immediately informed Kian's aides of her arrival.

As the door clicked open, Lucienne gestured for Thaddeus and the guards to wait outside. She then stormed into the office that smelled of strong espresso and cigars.

Admiral Enberg, General Fairchild, and Director Pyon, wearing Sphinxes' gray and blue uniforms, stood up and saluted her. Lucienne nodded but gave them a stern stare. The gentlemen tried to look nonplussed at her sudden appearance, but Lucienne caught their first glances at her outfit. Yes, she was wearing white. That should calm their nerves.

She knew they were talking about her, her illness, and Sphinxes' future. They'd been watching her every move, especially after she'd taken the ancient poison home. Her recent flight with Ashburn only gave them more reasons to doubt her leadership.

There was no need to pretend they didn't know about her condition. She'd had two episodes in the castle—the first while she'd been studying the ancient scroll with her decoding team; the second while having tea with Ziyi in the French café in the ward. As a rule, bad news travelled fast.

"How are you holding up, Siren?" Admiral Enberg asked softly.

"I'm doing just fine," she said. "Thanks for asking. Excuse us, gentlemen."

Silently, the officers filed out. General Fairchild picked up his cigar box on a vintage whiskey-barrel table and gave her a solemn glance before heading out with the rest.

Lucienne stood in the center of the room, staring at Kian, her arms folded across her chest.

"Can I get you anything?" Kian asked. "Almond milk?"

Now everyone was offering her milk. What was she to them? A baby? An invalid?

Kian remained in his seat, regarding her wearily.

She'd given him the scare of his life taking off like that yesterday, but he hadn't yelled at her. She couldn't be held responsible for her actions whenever her insanity kicked in, so everyone raced to blame themselves. Even Director Pyon had cursed himself for his intelligence errors and inability to discover the true nature of Nexus Tear in time. She'd explained to them that no one could predict and stop a revenge set in ancient times, but they didn't want to listen. They wanted a scapegoat, and they found one—her Czech boyfriend.

"Your men ganged up on Vladimir again." She went straight for Kian's throat.

"You came all the way here to talk about him?" Kian asked, his voice dismissive.

"He's no less important to me than you are." Her voice also dropped a few degrees in temperature.

"Blazek also isn't that innocent. You know how provocative he can be."

"He has a foul mouth now and then, but that doesn't give your men the rights to maul his face."

"Then ask him to restrain himself."

Kian was unusually angry. He was like this when he felt he couldn't protect her or failed her. So instead of solacing her, the alpha male in him lashed out at everyone, including her.

"If you do not stop this, I will," she said. He knew she'd never made an empty threat. "And it won't be pretty."

"Lucia," he sighed, "the men, including your guards, won't forgive him for what happened to you."

"You know it *isn't* his fault."

"Part of it *is* his fault, and he didn't deny it. But mostly it's my failure."

"Can we end this game of pointing fingers? If you all need to find an outlet, let me be it. I brought this on myself."

There was a momentary silence between them. "They won't take his life," he said. "That I can guarantee you."

"But it's okay they maim him?" she asked incredulously. "One day he'll come to me inside a body bag."

"It won't come to that, at least not from my men. But sometimes we need to let them vent their anger."

"Their anger or yours?" Lucienne's voice was absolutely cold.

"I can't help you!" Kian shouted. "I can't rid the poison in you!"

"So you use my boyfriend as a punching bag for your frustration? Tell your men to suck it up, and you too. If Vladimir comes back to me with bruises again, I'll avenge him."

"Are you going to take us all out?"

Lucienne's eyes burned dark. She knew that the moment she'd been poisoned, Kian's wrath would have rained down on Vladimir. Her protector refused to see reason when she was harmed, but she wouldn't allow him to make Vladimir his victim.

"I'll pick the ringleader next to you," she said, "and set him as an example. Finley, isn't it? You have two hours to get him off the island before I hang him."

Kian stared at her for a long moment, and she held his eyes with an uncompromising glare. She needed to be hard with Kian, or one day they'd truly deliver her a body bag with Vladimir's corpse inside.

"It's time to let go of your anger," she said. "I'm not going to get well soon, and you'll have to brace for that." She sighed, her voice turning wistful. "Every day I have to swim across the ocean to get to the shore of normality. I need you to be in the boat to pick me up when I need it."

"I'll swim with you. I won't let you drown, kid."

"You mustn't let Sphinxes drown either," she said. "For Sphinxes to survive, we need a new motivation. Your military needs discipline. We aren't what we were two years ago. We're about to form a new nation, for pirates' sake."

Kian inhaled sharply, and his eyes sparked. "You're warming up to the idea of making Sphinxes a nation?"

Forming a nation was a necessary move. The war with the Sealers in the Polynesian Triangle made many nations nervous about Sphinxes' growing power. Sphinxes wouldn't want to become a rogue nation.

"Our people need new hope," she said. "When there is no vision, the people perish."

She'd have given them Eterne, a future of evolution, but she could no longer keep the promise. Eterne would have to be pushed back years, or decades, if she ever survived.

"You're right about disciplining the men," Kian said. "I can be shortsighted sometimes."

Lucienne agreed. "Sometimes."

"You lose sight whenever you think she's not safe, Kian McQuillen," Jed had once scolded a twenty-four-year-old Kian when an assassination of Lucienne had nearly succeeded. *"You need to learn to detach your emotions in order to protect her."*

"I'll transfer Finley to the Illinois op," Kian said. "He'll assist Claude Lam."

Kian would make it look like an assignment, not an exile. "I don't care if you promote him," she said, "as long as he stays away from Vladimir."

"Blazek doesn't want you to intervene. He has nothing but pride now."

"He has more than that, but make sure he knows nothing about it."

"He likes to dig. He'll find out."

"Then he'll have to suffer me."

"Ashburn proposed something," Kian said, handing her a bottle of sparkling water instead of the almond milk he'd originally offered.

Lucienne drank from the bottle. "After you threatened him last night?"

"This world has rules. If he wants to stay close to you, he must learn to follow them. If he hadn't saved you in Polynesia, I'd have shot him between the eyes yesterday for sweeping you away like that."

"He's as fearless as Vladimir, you know."

Kian shook his head. "The boys you pick are giving me a stomach ulcer."

"No more than me." She gave Kian a faint smile that didn't hide her sadness. She'd once believed that she'd solved the problem by stringing them along. She was now dragging them down with her, but she couldn't let them go. "What did Ash want?" she asked.

"The last scroll."

Lucienne's jaw dropped. He would leave Sphinxes then. He would leave her behind.

"None of the expedition teams you hired to search for the last scroll returned." Kian studied her sulky expression. "You wouldn't risk Ashburn, and he didn't want to fight with you, so he came to me."

"He can't avoid a fight by going to you."

"We need the scroll, Lucia. It might be our only chance to find the antidote. I'll send our best men to go with him. He'll be well protected."

"Jekaterina has the scroll, but Ash doesn't know her whereabouts," said Lucienne. "There's no point in sending him out."

She wondered if her mother had foreseen the trap in Schmidt's lab through the prophecy on the last scroll. *"Your mother sent me to protect you. She knew this day would come, and many more would follow."* Captain Marloes had showed Lucienne her last thoughts before her last breath.

If so, Jekaterina must have known about the ancient poison, but hadn't bothered to warn Lucienne. The woman had simply taken the scroll that might have the last piece of information regarding the cure and vanished into the thin air again.

What was Jekaterina's connection to the Sealers? How could she block Ashburn's sight as no one else could, except Lucienne?

"Jekaterina is dangerous," Lucienne said. "I don't want Ash anywhere near her."

"I believe the team can handle one dangerous woman."

"We wrecked the Sealers' headquarters, but their followers are everywhere. They've infiltrated every high circle in every nation. If they know what Ashburn can do, they'll come to tear us apart to get him. We can't fend off every nation. So I'm asking you not to risk exposing Ashburn."

On top of that, lay her personal reason. She didn't want to use Ash as a crutch, but he was her chance to fight her increasing insanity. She needed to keep him at her side.

"Let's not get paranoid," Kian said, then seeing her look, took a softer tone. "Ashburn can see danger before it arrives. I say we give him a chance to prove himself."

"He's proved himself."

"You can't keep him here forever. One of these days, one of them will eventually leave."

Lucienne's lips thinned to a line. "You don't need Ash to go after Jekaterina. You and Director Pyon can send the best men to track her down."

Then her encrypted phone vibrated. The screen read, *extremely urgent*. Lucienne picked it up. "Yes, Ziyi?" As she listened on, her face paled.

"What is it?" asked Kian.

She hung up the phone. "Vladimir and Ashburn are engaged in a life-and-death duel."

Lucienne sprang out of the office as Kian cursed Vladimir and Ashburn, then Ziyi.

~

On the training field in front of Vladimir's red-brick house, Ashburn and Vladimir were crossing blades viciously. A few months ago, when Ashburn had fenced with Lucienne, he'd expressed his distaste for violence, and now he was slashing a Viking sword at Vladimir's head.

The Czech warrior parried with a scimitar of two-parallel blades. It was from his valuable collection. The weapon had a sculpted gold pommel that had been made in two halves, as flamboyant as its owner. Vladimir went on the offense. He was much more experienced than Ashburn, and as a gifted swordsman, it didn't take him long to gain an edge over his opponent, even though Ashburn had TimeDust to aid him.

As Ashburn staggered a foot back, Sphinxes' warriors formed a ring to shout tips at him. They wanted Ash to end Vladimir. Finley, their leader, shouted and jumped as if wanting to cut down Vladimir himself.

Lucienne's jeep bumped along the dried grass and broke the ring of men. "Off you go," she ordered them sternly before leaping out of the vehicle. The soldiers scattered reluctantly. Finley was the last to depart. He bowed his head when Lucienne locked her gaze on him.

Lucienne stalked toward the duelers, but neither boy spared her a glance. A white blade clashed against a dark one, locked in a death grip. Grinding their teeth and leaning forward, the combatants added their weight to their hilts, determined to push the other back.

"You won't win the fight this time, Blazek," Ashburn said.

"I win every time," Vladimir spat. "And you'll pay for endangering her."

"Endanger her?" Ashburn said spitefully. "Aren't you the expert at that?"

With a furious yell, Vladimir threw Ashburn off and immediately lunged, swinging his blade and bringing it down toward Ashburn's head. Ashburn sidestepped, faster than a flash, and met the assault with his dark blade.

They both winced at the impact, but neither withdrew.

"She picked me this time. It hurt, didn't it?" Ashburn let his gloating sink fully into his voice, aiming to infuriate Vladimir even more. "If you accept the simple fact that she doesn't need you and get the hell out of here—"

Vladimir could always get under Ashburn's skin, but their roles had reversed. Whenever Ash taunted the Czech prince by reminding him that he caused Lucienne's dire condition, Vladimir looked like he'd been rammed by a runaway train. Lucienne knew he was barely hanging in there, but he hung in there every day for her. He no more backed down to her men than he did to Ash.

She would have a serious talk with them both after she ended their mindless duel. Vladimir needed to shake off his guilt, and Ash must stop taking out his anger on Vladimir. When had Ash become malicious?

"I'll never leave her," Vladimir shot back. "Don't think for a second that you can steal her from me."

"Stop it," Lucienne called. "Both of you!"

They crossed swords again, more aggressively than before. Her presence only fueled their hatred for each other.

"I told you to stop. Now!" she said again, face paling, her whisky eyes darkening with fury.

They ignored her.

Lucienne turned to her cousin behind her. His samurai sword was out of its sheath. Thaddeus held it tightly, ready to defend her, as if she needed his protection from her suitors.

"Thaddeus," Lucienne called, "lend me your sword."

"But it's the Chiyoganemaru sword, made by Ryûkyû himself," said Thaddeus. "I've never let anyone touch it."

Lucienne gave her cousin a potent glare and stretched out her hand.

Thaddeus offered, "I'll help you break them up."

"Thaddeus!" Lucienne said impatiently.

Reluctantly, he handed her the hilt of gilded black lacquer.

Lucienne summoned the Forbidden Glory. She hadn't a clue how it would respond as it was half mad as her, but she needed its power to break the boys' death lock.

She felt a stir in her. *Good.* Forbidden Glory still loved to play.

Lucienne swung the samurai sword from beneath the crossed blades of Ashburn and Vladimir. Her power came through the steel she brandished. One strike, and it broke the lock of the two blades. Vladimir and Ashburn staggered back, turning to Lucienne with an identical, stunned expression.

She'd gotten their attentions. With the sword tight in her hand, she cut in between them. "How long has it been since you swore to be civil to each other?" she asked. "Is it that hard to keep a promise to me?"

"I wasn't planning on killing him," said Vladimir. "I was only teaching him a lesson."

"Teach yourself," Ashburn said. "I can end you anytime I want."

"With those nasty black blots of yours?" Vladimir snorted.

"I'm tempted." Ashburn narrowed his grey eyes. "As soon as she realizes she doesn't need you anymore, you'll eat plenty of them. In fact, one will be enough to end this pathetic, useless life of yours."

"Bring it on," Vladimir said, two darts appearing in his hand and rotating between his fingers. "Before you throw your crap, you'll definitely get one of these."

It felt like déjà vu. They were the scene in the Hungarian café. Why must they torment her? Lucienne exploded.

Redness dove toward her like a vulture from the dark clouds. It hit her hard.

Lucienne spun toward Vladimir and slashed her sword at him. He ducked by reflex. Her sword narrowly missed his left ear. She missed? And why did the world look so twisted, like a mirror that didn't reflect images correctly? She lunged at the Czech prince again, stabbing the blade straight at his chest. He parried in a hurry.

"Lucia?" he called, looking stupefied.

Ashburn snickered. She wheeled toward him. Was he mocking her, or was he delighted by her aggression toward his opponent? She couldn't tell, but she didn't particularly care for his low chuckle while she was in the middle of action. She swung her sword toward his neck.

Behead him? Wasn't that a bit extreme? But Forbidden Glory longed for wild fun. It'd been trapped for too long.

Ashburn froze there. He couldn't read her mind. He hadn't expected this move of hers. If his head fell off, his shocked expression would be permanent. But his beauty would never fade. Before the edge of her blade reached his shoulder, another sword rose and met hers.

"Lucienne!" the Czech prince warned. She'd forgotten how fast he could move. But why did he save his silver-haired enemy? Hadn't he engaged in a death match with Ashburn a moment ago? Men were full of contradictions.

This is wrong. A ray of light seemed to break into the haze of her mind. For a second, Lucienne gained clarity, but it was slipping. Forbidden Glory had chosen to embrace her insanity. The poisoned aether now dominated the other four elements. *Get a hold of yourself,* she demanded, but all she saw was her reflection on the samurai blade—liquid rings of flaming red formed around her dark irises. They were steeped in madness, and they were beautiful. The wild fire would soon shove the Siren Lucienne aside and burn everyone close to her.

You did not play with fire. Its nature was to burn.

Fear grasped Lucienne.

"Run!" she shouted. "Run. Away. From. Me."

Vladimir and Ashburn, shoulder to shoulder, stood their ground, staring into the flame in her eyes. They didn't flee. They didn't intend to, even when a raging goddess emerged.

Brave, yet foolish.

"She's—out of it again," Vladimir cried.

Lucienne brought down her sword toward the Czech prince, then hacked at Ashburn the next second. They parried. "Now you combine forces to fight me?" she scoffed, delivering another strike. They staggered back a few steps. *Good.* But she wasn't pleased with their dismay at her ferocity. She didn't want their apprehension. She wanted their admiration first.

"Remember who you are, Lucia," Ashburn called. "Please remember."

"Like she's going to listen," Vladimir snapped, his blade holding hers. "Haven't we tried that already?"

"She's still out there, somewhere," Ashburn insisted. "We just need to get through to her."

The way they talked to her and about her was as if she were a rabid feline. These two boys had no respect for her. *"Remember who you are?"* She mimicked Ashburn's tone. "I know who I am. I am the Siren, the greatest among all!"

"Get out of the ring," the Czech prince ordered his companion. "You can't read her thoughts and you aren't a skilled swordsman. She'll cut you in half."

"I can help her," Ashburn said.

"You'll just get in the way!" Vladimir said.

While Ashburn hesitated, Lucienne kicked Vladimir in the knee and brought her weapon toward Ashburn. "Going somewhere, gorgeous? But the fun has just started."

Vladimir blocked her sword from the side. "Now's the time to use your bolts," he instructed Ashburn. "Stun her only."

"My lightning shocks you, not her," Ashburn said. "My power won't hurt her."

"Then find a way to incapacitate her while you're doing nothing," Vladimir said.

"Then you show me how to get it done!" Ashburn shot back.

"There's nothing you can do, boys," Lucienne purred. She moved like the wind. The power coursed through her, making her feel so free. She scored twice. The tip of her blade grazed both boys' cheeks.

My mark.

The blood flowing from their wounds excited her. "This is only a tease," she promised.

"Lucia!"

"Lucienne!"

"Lucienne Lam!"

Why did so many people shout her names? What did they want? So annoying.

"She can't hear you," said Ziyi.

The Chinese girl had joined her audience, but she was wrong. Lucienne could hear everything. She was just fed up with answering everyone. From her experience, they always wanted something from her. Always demanding.

"You must stop her," Ziyi said. "If she returns to herself, only to realize she hurt either of you badly, she'll never recover."

"Very cute, Shorty," Lucienne said. "But if I were you, I'd shut up. You don't want me to fix my attention on you today." She glanced at the girl, who opened her mouth agape at the threat. "But if you want to join the rank of these two insolent boys, be my guest. But you're basically useless when it comes to fighting."

Ashburn blocked a blow meant for Vladimir while she was distracted by that super-annoying girl. "You two just keep returning each other's favors?" she asked them. "*My enemy's enemy is my friend.* You two are learning."

"We're not your enemy, láska." Vladimir drew a breath. "We're your friends. More than friends."

"Now you want to be my friends?" Lucienne laughed her silky laughter and swirled to the side. It was a feint. She cut a strand of silver hair from Ashburn. *Souvenir.* She put the hair under her nose and sniffed it. At the same time, her sword hand swept the weapon upward to fend off Vladimir. The sneaky Czech was trying to disarm her while she pretended to be sidetracked. "Take advantage of a girl?" she asked. "You're excellent at it, Blazek. But I, Lucienne Lam, don't allow anyone, especially men, to walk all over me." She dashed aside and lunged, her sword meeting Vladimir's double blade again and again. From a mixed look of appreciation and apprehension on his face, she could tell she was faster than any opponent he'd ever fought. But several rounds later, when she still couldn't bring him to his knees, she wasn't thrilled.

Lucienne sent Forbidden Glory through her blade.

"Let's see how good you are at taking this," she snickered.

Fire flared from the clash of steel. The Czech prince jumped back with a yelp. His eyes widened, but he didn't let go of the hilt of his scimitar.

The men, who had scattered, returned and shouted out cheers, awed by her power. Lucienne was pleased. Many of them had never seen her in action. Now they witnessed how terrifying and powerful their Siren was.

Behold! Behold the power flowing in my veins.

Her sword sailing, Lucienne cut off a lock of Vladimir's wheat-colored braid before he wheeled away. She brought the strand of his hair under her nose too. It smelled of rosemary, chamomile, and nettle.

"Russian Amber Imperial, isn't it?" she asked with a lopsided smirk. "You have expensive taste, prince. Ash uses only plain lavender soap."

Do not hurt them! Please. Who made the pathetic wailing? For a moment, she almost thought it was her own voice. "Someone tried to get in my head, begging me not to kill you," she said. "I've given it a thought. It would be a pity to rid the world of both of you. Maybe I should keep one of you as my pet. Who's going to be the lucky one?"

Ashburn thrust his Viking sword toward her from behind.

"And I thought you weren't the irritating one, Ashburn Fury." She parried backwards without turning. "I can blindfold myself and still beat you both."

Then she heard roars. *Oh, brother.* Kian McQuillen arrived. He threatened to punish the men with court martial if they didn't disappear from his sight in two seconds. *The buzz killer.*

The spectators were gone. Now there were only her opponents, Kian, and her personal guards. The petite Chinese girl in qipao also stayed, looking sadly lost and terrified.

"Lucienne Lam," Kian called, advancing toward her. "Put down your sword."

"Why should I?" She looked at him defiantly, a hand on her hip. "And who are you to order me, McQuillen?"

Kian narrowed his eyes. For the first time, they weren't warm toward her.

"Are you going to join them and fight me?" She sent him another challenge. They were prey. She could bring down all of them. She could take down an army, like she'd done in the Sealers' Temple of Lemuria.

"I'm on your side," said Kian.

"Then don't get in my way," she said.

"Fight me," said Kian, "and me alone." He gestured for Vladimir and Ashburn to step aside. They gave him a tentative look before obeying him.

"You're the shrewd one, Kian," she said. "You've taught me since I was little. You know my every move."

"Not every move," Kian said coolly. "You picked up a few tricks on your own."

Lucienne laughed. But why did her laughter sound strange and coarse to her own ears?

"I'm unarmed." Kian raised his hands in the air. "You've crossed swords with two despicable boys and won. Why don't you and I go for variety? A fistfight. I promise it'll be more fun."

"Clever," Lucienne said. "You want to strip away my weapons. No matter." She tossed the Chiyoganemaru sword aside, and Thaddeus at once lurched toward it, removing it from her sight. "What are the rules, old man?"

"Three rounds. Whoever loses won't pick another fight, but will go home quietly."

"And the winner will do whatever he or she wants," said Lucienne.

"Deal." Kian adopted a boxing pose, gesturing for Lucienne to make the first move.

"I can never win in a boxing match against you," Lucienne said. "But you forgot one thing, Chief McQuillen." She flashed him a devious grin. "I don't need a weapon. I *am* the weapon." She stood where she was, five yards from him, and raised her hands in the air. Energy burst from her; the wild wind manifested itself, sweeping Kian off his feet and sending him flying several yards away. Until he crashed to the ground.

"Chief McQuillen," Ziyi rushed toward Kian with a wince, "can you stand? She didn't mean to hurt you."

Kian was up in a second, waving the girl away. There was no anger in his hard sapphire eyes, but a mosaic of sadness, pride, and heaviness.

"I wouldn't really hurt Kian," Lucienne said. "I love the man. I just need to show him my power, so he won't always stand in my way. However," she turned to point two fingers at Vladimir and Ashburn, "these two show me no respect." She watched their disagreeable expressions. "Have you seen the looks they just give me? They talk about teaching each other a lesson. Now they're going to learn that lesson for their insufferable arrogance." Slowly she pulled a hunting knife out from her boot. "But which one should I stab first?" Her gaze flickered from Vladimir to Ashburn, back and forth.

They stared at her grimly.

"Ziyi," Lucienne called, "I'm having a hard time here. You're my genius. Help me decide."

Ziyi scrambled to Lucienne's side in her stilettos, but kept a safe distance. "Stabbing is no fun. What about slapping them? It's more insulting." She made a dash toward Vladimir. "I really want to slap this one."

Vladimir grabbed Ziyi's wrist in the air.

"Play along," Ziyi hissed at the Czech prince.

"I don't care," Vladimir said. "No one slaps me, not even her."

"You'd rather be stabbed?" Ziyi hissed.

"You know, I have super hearing." Lucienne shifted her attention toward them. "And good job, Ziyi. You just helped me find my target." She stalked toward Vladimir, eyeing the scimitar in his hand.

Vladimir tossed his sword at her feet as he held her gaze. "I'm yours," he said. "Do whatever you want with me." He shoved off his leather jacket, flung it away, and tore open the black shirt that hugged his torso, exposing his bare, hard-muscled chest before her.

Lucienne stared at it for a long moment. It would be nice to lay her head on that chest. Vladimir rasped under the weight of her examination. He was turned on by her, but she wouldn't be seduced. She removed her gaze from his chest and peeked into his hazel eyes. They weren't as bright as she'd remembered. Anguish dulled them. Who caused such tremendous pain in him? But under its dark layer was an ocean of tenderness and love.

This one had a great capacity to love, and no amount of ache could kill it. Was that love for her or for someone else? It couldn't be for her. He knew she wanted to knife him. A pang of jealousy struck Lucienne, and she didn't expect that. She looked down at her knife, its tip pressing against his heart.

Kian moved toward them. "What are you doing, idiot?" he snarled at Vladimir.

"I need her to see the truth about herself." Vladimir sent out a warning look: do-not-interfere. "When she does, she'll make a comeback."

What truth? She didn't know the truth. They must have kept it from her. Anger spiking in her, Lucienne slowly sank the sharp tip of the blade toward Vladimir's heart. It punctured his skin, drawing a sequence of droplets.

Red excited her. Two more inches, and the blade would pierce the warrior's heart. She could almost hear it fluttering, like a bird's struggling wings. Lucienne peeped into his darkened eyes again, expecting to see his sizzling hate beneath the pain, but all she saw was unfaltering, undying love.

This boy allowed her to take his life. His vow to her rang in her ears, "I've given you my heart and I'll never take it back. I'll never love another except you."

She had a vague feeling that if she cut out the heart of this boy, it would be the end of her as well. The dagger in her hand became an unbearable burden. Her hand haltered.

But Forbidden Glory didn't particularly care for the affair of the heart. It spurred her, demanding a blood sacrifice. *Since he's given you his heart, it's yours to take. The sacrifice of a great love will make us stronger.*

She'd been weak, she knew. She must be stronger if she wanted to survive. Fluttering her eyelids shut and feeling the ache in her own heart, Lucienne drove the knife toward Vladimir's.

"Lucienne Lam!" Kian grabbed her wrist above the knife.

She turned to Kian, the mad gleam in her eyes reflected in his. Was that how they saw her? But that wasn't really her. A trace of regret and bitterness and shame came over her.

"My power wants him. I was poisoned because of him." With that knowledge, anger returned. "Didn't I tell you not to get in my way, Kian McQuillen?" Her free hand shoved Kian's chest with the power of Forbidden Glory.

Kian staggered back. "Lucienne, stop this madness!"

How she hated the word *madness.* "All of you hate him, and many of you want him dead," she said. "Now I'm doing what you wish, and all of a sudden, you want me to stop it. Make up your minds."

"It's not for his sake," Ashburn said. "It's for yours."

"For my sake?" Lucienne snorted. "How sweet. Let's see what I'll do for *my* sake." Their disapproval only irked her. She wouldn't allow them to shame her. Seething, she twirled the knife in her hand, its tip pressing against Vladimir's skin again, at the same spot where his blood had streamed, ready to drive home into his heart.

"Go ahead, miláček," Vladimir said. He didn't flinch.

Miláček meant sweetheart in Czech. It was his term of endearment for her.

A feeling, unfamiliar and overwhelming, travelled through her. It confused her. Was that how it felt to be touched by love? Lucienne drew a shattered breath. Her hand shook pathetically. She was sweating. The hilt of the knife grew slippery and heavy in her hand.

"We'll have to use a tranquilizer," Kian said, his voice pained.

"Absolutely not!" Ashburn countered. "She might not come back this time."

"She'll be lost forever if she recovers and learns she killed the Czech idiot," Kian said.

They were openly planning to sedate her. Lucienne let out an icy laugh. "Try it, and I'll show you—"

Then, an unseen shock wave—sweet and seductive—reached her. Ashburn jogged toward her, his hands aloft to show he was unarmed. His desire for her in his silver eyes sent a pleasant chill throughout her body. "Siren," he said humbly, "I—we surrender to you, completely."

Finally they got it. A smile of relief grew on Lucienne's face, and her gaze grazed over Ashburn, as if truly seeing him for the first time. She was no longer interested in taking the Czech prince's heart.

Forbidden Glory grunted. She ignored it. She decided to satisfy herself first, with Ash. His nearness sent her a wave of electric pleasure—the Lure now battling Forbidden Glory—but the angel's Glory wouldn't give up easily. Conflicting energy and emotions, different in nature and temper, twirled in Lucienne like cyclones.

Fury, pleasure, love, and hate.

"They're tearing me apart," she moaned, then screamed, "Stop!"

Time stopped for her. And the world switched back.

For a moment, she was disoriented. Until she saw blood streaming from a hard, bare chest, a blade pressed against it—she was the one who held the knife still dripping Vladimir's blood.

She immediately released the weapon. It clattered to the ground harshly. She looked up at Vladimir's face in horror. He gazed back at her, a mosaic of emotions in his hazel eyes—pain, love, and triumph.

Shaken and nauseated, she looked down at her white dress. She blinked vacantly, then blinked again. Everything instantly came back to her, making her relive the nightmare. No, she was the nightmare.

She looked frantically around her. Vladimir. Ashburn. Ziyi. Her guards. Kian. They stared back at her, then called her all at once.

"Lucia?"

"Láska?"

She dropped her gaze toward the ground. She was a monster. She couldn't face them. She could never look into Vladimir's eyes again. Not Kian's. Not anyone's.

"I'm sorry." She didn't hear her own whisper. She couldn't beg forgiveness. Only shame, agony, and fear drenched her, dragging her down toward the deepest pit. This time she was going down alone.

"It's okay now, kid." Kian's exhausted voice brushed past her. "You're fine. We're fine."

She wasn't fine. Neither were they. They'd never be fine.

The sky was falling.

The earth moved beneath her feet. The ground opened up. Let it swallow her whole and never return her bones.

Falling through space, she lifted her gaze toward the light far above. She saw Kian reaching a hand toward her, his eyes glowing with warmth, as if it were reserved for her forever.

She knew she didn't deserve it, but she stretched her hands up toward him, like the baby she was when Jed had brought her to the Red Mansion. And when she'd spotted Kian, she drew out her chubby arms toward him and chose him to be her ultimate protector.

"Help me, Kian." She heard her broken voice.

Before Kian caught her, Lucienne blacked out.

Chapter Four

CONFESSION OF LOVE

Lucienne's breathing evened out when she saw herself in a white sleeping gown.

The sun settled into late afternoon. The curtain was half-closed. A man slouched in a chair near her bed, his clean-cut head buried in his big, calloused hands.

"Kian," Lucienne whispered.

He popped open his eyes, raised his head, and sent her a warm smile. "Hey, kid. Didn't know you were awake." He twisted open the lid of a bottled water and handed it to her, as if knowing her throat was parched. She drank the water in gratitude.

For the first time, the guards weren't hovering in the sitting room. She was alone with Kian. She put down the water bottle, now half empty, on the ivory bedside table and regarded him. His eyes were bloodshot. Unshaven stubble made his face look rougher. In his mid thirties, he already had gray hair mixed among the brown strands.

"You're a mess," she said.

"You're no better." He gave her another smile.

"It's getting worse," she admitted. "I think I'm losing it."

"You'll hang in here," he ordered.

She shook her head. "I can't grasp reality. I can't get hold of myself anymore. The last person I can trust is myself. I hurt everyone, and I'll hurt them again. I could never imagine I'd hurt *you* if it hadn't happened."

"But you didn't," he said. "You only threw me out of the way. It'll pass, kid. We'll get through this."

"No," she said. "I knew you and the generals were having a meeting about me when I stormed into your office. The men are right to worry about Sphinxes' future."

"You're still the heart and soul of Sphinxes. Its future lies with you."

"Blind loyalty won't get us anywhere," she said. "We need to face reality, especially you. I've become a danger to everyone and everything we've built."

"So you just quit?" He sounded like he wanted to shoot someone.

"I'm not quitting," she said, "but this battle I'll have to fight alone."

"You're not alone! You'll never fight alone."

"Kian, our army can't fight my war. Not this time," she said. "You have no idea of the dark place I've been. Even you can't go with me. No one can. I'd rather go down alone than drag you all down with me."

"The day you arrived at the Red Mansion, our fates were already tied together. You were just an infant in my arms biting me, but I knew you'd be at the center of this war. I've never regretted choosing to serve and protect you. You gave my life purpose that day."

Kian had been orphaned at seven years old. He'd watched his parents being slaughtered. Jed found him two days later, took him in as his own son, and gave him the best military training. Kian took off to track down his enemies. Half a year later, he returned with a bullet in his gut and a knife wound stretching from his left shoulder to his chest. News broke out the next day that a notorious gun smuggling lord and four of his bodyguards had died horrendous deaths. At thirteen, Kian had taken them out single-handedly.

He'd never been gentle and warm to anyone until baby Lucienne had clutched his face in her chubby hands and called him "Kia." That had been her first word. She'd also left her teeth marks in his chin. The power inside her had struck him, and Kian had been the first to recognize her as the true Siren. Their bond had been unbreakable since then.

"You sink, I sink with you," Kian said, "but I won't let you fall."

Lucienne gave him a long look. "Fine. But leave the men out of our struggle."

"That I can arrange," he said. "And kid, just so you know, this is just another battle we fight to win."

"And just so you know, we no longer fight the enemies we can see. We're fighting me. A war you and I might not win."

"Only when you surrender."

"I promise you I won't. But I'll relieve everyone around me, so they won't be in harm's way. There will be no house duties either, not even for Aida."

"That's a bit extreme, kid."

"Better safe than sorry."

"How about we give them a choice? If they choose to leave, then that settles it."

"You know they'll never choose to leave."

"Then you'll be insulting them by forcing them to abandon you."

"I'm doing this for their good."

"Let them decide what's good for them."

"Neither Vlad nor Ash should come near me again. I almost killed one of them."

Just then, Ashburn trudged in with a glass of almond milk. Why did everyone assume she should drink milk?

Kian also frowned at Ashburn. "I clearly told everyone, including you, not to disturb us."

Ashburn must have been watching them through the live feed of Kian's memories. "I have something important to share."

"I hope Blazek won't pop up in the next second and make this a circus show again," grunted Kian.

"He's in the medical center," Ashburn said. "Duncan dragged

him there."

Her knife had brought him there. Lucienne's stomach twisted in nausea and pain. She needed to check on him as soon as her companions left, even though she was too ashamed to face her Czech prince.

"That's what you wanted to share?" Kian flicked his gaze from Lucienne's anxious expression to Ashburn's hopeful look.

"I couldn't care less about Blazek." Ashburn turned to Lucienne. "I've been replaying the fighting scene from different angles, and I found something more about your lapse this time."

Kian and Lucienne stared at him.

"It wasn't the insane you who hurt the Czech," Ashburn said.

"Spit it out," Kian ordered. "These boys always talk like a clogged pipe."

"If you hadn't cut him off," Lucienne said, "he'd probably have finished his sentence."

"Lucia, did you summon Forbidden Glory when you fought us?" Ashburn asked. "You couldn't be that powerful without it. You couldn't have defeated both Blazek and me at once. You threw Mr. McQuillen into the air by simply raising your hands."

Remorse hit her anew at the memory of hurting them, but Kian squeezed her shoulder to assure her that he didn't hold a grudge.

"I called for my power," she said, "and it responded strongly."

"That's what I thought," Ashburn said. "Don't use it again before the poison is out of your system. It once helped you defeat your cousin when you were at the Red Mansion, but it almost controlled you. Your power acted erratically because of its lack of aether. Now, with the last element back but contaminated, Forbidden Glory is crippled. It can't connect to reason. When it manifested, it switched on your insanity, and the poison of Blood Tear makes you too weak to tame it. Forbidden Glory will take you over if you summon it again."

"Stay away from it!" Kian ordered Lucienne.

"Promise you won't use it again under any circumstances,"

Ashburn said.

"If you promise not to pick a fight with Vladimir again," she said.

"I'll restrain from provoking him," Ashburn said, "and I won't give in to his taunts."

Kian gritted his teeth. "Upset her again, and you're off Sphinxes forever."

"Yes, sir," Ashburn said. "You don't need to worry about that. Blazek doesn't exist. He's dead to me."

Hadn't he just promised he wouldn't upset her? Lucienne opened her mouth, but insurmountable exhaustion swept over her. Her heavy eyelids pressed together. She didn't fight it, knowing she was safe among her protectors.

When she awoke at midnight, her first thought was of Vladimir. She was supposed to visit him in the medical facility in the castle, but fatigue and shame had conquered her. She needed to see him now, to see that he was safe. No matter where he was, she'd seek him out.

As soon as she stepped out of her bedroom, Duncan rose from a chair in the adjoining sitting room. Relief washed over his face when he saw her white gown. "Lucia," he asked with concern, "you need anything? I'll fetch it for you."

"Where's Vladimir?" she asked.

Duncan hesitated for a second and said, "On the roof."

"Thanks," she said and scrambled along the hallway toward the stairs.

Duncan didn't object, but trailed after her. He'd followed her for years. He'd fought with her in many battles. He guarded her with his life but treated her more like a fellow warrior than fragile china, and she appreciated that.

On the rooftop, the starlight silhouetted a lone figure. The ocean wind flapped the corner of Vladimir's black trench coat. Lucienne loved to come here at night to search for a possible new home in the sky. Was her sanctuary also becoming the Czech prince's new haven? She didn't mind sharing it with him. They hadn't been alone since she'd returned from the Sealers' temple. Ashburn and Kian had made sure of that.

Ashburn wasn't around now. He must be sleeping. *God bless his sleep.* He needed it, and she needed this alone time with her Czech boyfriend.

Vladimir slowly turned.

The light from the lanterns in the nearby maple trees made his features darker and sharper. He had a strong face. He'd shed his boyish good looks during these two years on the bumpy road with her. Weighted by guilt, stricken by grief, and beaten by self-loathing, he still looked strikingly handsome. The ugliness of reality couldn't take away his aristocratic air and breed, even though it savaged him with an often worn-out, ragged appearance.

Yet this new version of Vladimir was closer to Lucienne's heart. God, she'd almost killed him. If she hadn't come back to herself, she'd have driven the knife two inches deeper into his heart, killing the warrior prince who loved her more than the world and himself together.

And he hadn't resisted her. He trusted her when she couldn't. But then, a dark thought dashed out of the shadows. Deep inside, had he wanted her to end his life? End his suffering?

Vladimir gave her a lazy smile.

Lucienne's breath hitched. It never got old. His doting, easy smile forever had that effect on her. But was he still hers after what she'd done to him?

No apologies could redeem her. If he chose to be free of her, he'd have her blessing. She'd made Kian swear that his men would let Vladimir go and never hunt him. The parting would break her heart, but she was no stranger to heartbreak.

She sauntered toward him, the hem of her gown gliding across the floor.

"A princess from a fairy tale," he murmured, his hazel eyes brightening as she approached. Lucienne immediately felt better.

"There's no fairy tale, and I'm not a princess," she said.

"You're more than a princess. You'll be queen."

I won't be a mad queen. But she didn't say it. It would only add salt to his wound. He would hate himself all over again for robbing her of a future.

"Don't believe everything you hear," she said with a faint smile.

"You'll get well, Lucia," he said fiercely. "I'll do everything in my power to make sure of it."

Just don't do anything stupid. Again, she swallowed her words. Since when did she have to hold her tongue around him? But it would come out wrong. She took the simple approach. "I'm sorry for hurting you."

"You're sorry," he asked incredulously, "after what I did to you?"

"When can we get past this guilt trip?"

"When you're well," he said. "And you never need to say sorry to me or explain your actions."

She raised an eyebrow. "I don't?"

He always loved her playful side. His gaze roamed over her with hunger, caressing her without a touch. Heat rose in her and her pulse quickened. The air was suddenly charged. She thought only Ash could do that with the Lure, but Vlad was doing it, all by himself.

He opened his arms. "Come here, crazy chick."

She blinked, then smiled. Ever since she'd returned from the war, everyone had tried to avoid the words "crazy," "mad," "nuts," "insane," and anything related to mental illness. These nouns had become the worst profanity in Sphinxes.

She entered his strong arms more than willingly, and he crushed her against his hard chest. He didn't treat her as if she were a fragile thing, and she liked it. One look at the starvation in his eyes, she knew he'd held himself back for too long.

"Only an idiot dares to call me crazy," she said, "and likes me when I'm half-crazy."

"Crazy or not, I love you just the same." He buried his face in her hair, inhaling her scent, as if it was long overdue and he was deprived.

When she finally pulled away, she pressed her palm gently against his chest, feeling the uneven bandages inside his shirt. "Does it still hurt a lot?"

"My heart always hurts when it comes to you," he said, "but it beats stronger when you're around."

She flicked her gaze toward the scar behind his left ear. When he'd been initiated into the Sealers' circle, her enemy had branded him with their symbol. The first thing he'd done when he'd landed on Sphinxes was remove the enemy's mark—an arrow piercing the Siren's all-seeing eye.

The irony was that their arrow had indeed found its target and pierced Lucienne, the last Siren.

But she wouldn't dwell on the past. She must move forward.

She touched his face. Though the light was dim, she could still see the bruises left by his fight with Kian's men. "If you want to keep this face attractive, you'd better stop fighting."

He broke into a grin. "So you think it's attractive?"

"I prefer a clean face, not a bruised, swollen one."

"Then I'll keep it nice and clean for you."

"A true warrior knows when to walk away from a fight."

"I'll walk away from every fight if that pleases you."

"What if I need you to walk away from me?"

His body instantly tensed, and the spark in his eyes went out. "Finally decide to get rid of me?"

"Haven't you had enough of my cruelty?"

"The only cruelty I know from you is when you push me away."

"I almost killed you. What if I truly kill you next time? I won't allow that to happen."

"You didn't kill me. You couldn't, even when you weren't yourself. You stopped."

"Kian and Ash stopped me."

"Even if they didn't meddle, you'd stop," he insisted.

They all had such faith in her—a faith she felt she didn't deserve.

"So you bared your chest and let my dagger sink to your heart to prove a point?" she asked.

"I did prove a point," he said. "I want you to see that you wouldn't really hurt me, so you won't keep pushing me away."

"Vlad—" Before she could chide him more, he pulled her into his arms. His scent of Sphinxes, her home, made her feel warm and solid. Her arms went around his waist, until he loosened his hold on her, as if remembering her frail condition.

"I'm unkind, but not delicate," she said.

"You're allowed to be unkind to me." He traced his knuckle along her cheek. "And I'm not unfamiliar with that." He chuckled at her widened eyes. "You made me eat mud when we first met."

"There was a good reason for that," she said coolly. "You were a jerk."

"I still am," he said, his eyes burning brightly. "But I love you, Lucienne Lam. Always have and always will. What you are and what you do won't change that."

"And I love you," she said.

A flutter stirred in her heart, then came the pain. And her heart thumped.

Was it the Lure?

Through her bond with Ashburn, she sensed his nearness.

She looked over Vladimir's shoulder into the darkness beyond the illumination of the lanterns. A shadow and light flashed by.

Ash, she thought in heartache.

Chapter Five
PARTING

Lucienne was under self-imposed house arrest in her mansion. It was bad she'd gone mental in public. It was worse that her soldiers had witnessed how dangerous she was. She'd thrown the chief of Sphinxes to the ground and almost knifed her prince boyfriend.

She'd talked to her guards, but they'd refused to be reassigned or promoted to other positions. As Thaddeus had put it, "You're our Siren. Like it or not, we're stuck with you. Even if you take a trip to hell, we're packed to go with you."

"If you pick hell," Adam had added, "we'll have to bring portable air conditioning."

"Lucifer won't be happy," Duncan had concluded.

Aida had gotten offended that her mistress would even suggest she move out.

If Lucienne couldn't make them leave her, she needed to get well. But the last ancient scroll that might contain the only information of the cure had vanished along with her mother. Even Ash didn't have a memory that would lead to her.

What would Lucienne do when she was at the end of her rope?

Then fate took pity on her. For a whole week, she hadn't had a lapse.

Lucienne stood by a full window, looking out. The ocean was turquoise, blending into the sky like a gem frozen in time. The breeze rattled the scarlet leaves dangling outside. How fortunate she was to have a view like this and a precious moment like now. It felt like everything was right and would be all right. Everything was fleeting in the mortal world, but Lucienne let this perfection sink into her memories, knowing and accepting that they would eventually fade.

Before she strolled toward the sun room, she checked her outfit one more time—a white flowery blouse and white pants with a wide hunter's belt. In a rare good mood, she couldn't wait to see Vladimir and Ashburn.

Sunshine bled into the room through the space between the branches of the red maples. Lucienne's brilliant smile dropped at the sight of the empty room. It had become routine that Vladimir and Ashburn shared breakfast with her. Last time they'd skipped it was to duel each other. She turned to her captain of the guards with a dark, questioning look.

Then Vladimir strode into the room with a tray of Jose omelets, ham, grapes, and crispy potato skins. "I'm your chef today," he said with a grin as he put a full plate and a glass of mulled cider on the table in front of her.

Lucienne blinked. "Where's Aida?"

"Jesus." Vladimir shook his head in slight disgust. "It took five horses to drive that woman away."

Her Czech prince was in an incredibly good mood. Everyone was celebrating. Maybe her insanity had passed. They could hope. Lucienne suspected that Vladimir's cheerfulness also had to do with Ashburn's absence.

Had he threatened Ashburn not to come because he didn't want Ash to try his cooking? Vladimir wouldn't be that petty. And knowing Ashburn, Lucienne believed he would ignore all threats made by the Czech prince.

Then where was Ash? She couldn't ask Vladimir. Was Ash still upset with her for the cozy night she and Vladimir had shared at the rooftop?

Three months ago, she'd decided to free one of them, so that three of them wouldn't have ended up in a wrecked ship together. Better to break one heart than two. She'd believed Ashburn had accepted her with Vladimir, but he hadn't. And her insane doppelganger had bared her feelings for him and insisted on seducing him. They were falling back into their vicious circle, her madness only making this entangled relationship more mixed-up.

Kian had said, not once, and not without sympathy, "In the end, one of them has to leave."

She would not betray Vladimir again, but how could she keep breaking Ash's heart?

Today, he was done waiting for her.

But she hoped he was still sleeping, either in her mansion or in his old room at the top of the castle's tower. She sent a mental prod toward their bond, but didn't feel it. She reached out again, and aching emptiness bounced back. Ash had left Sphinxes.

He'd broken his promise that he wouldn't leave Sphinxes without telling her. But could she blame him? He'd heard her confession of love to Vladimir, the person he hated most in the world. Who in his sound mind would stick with a half-mad girl who could offer him nothing but constant heartache? She should be amazed that he hadn't run faster.

Lucienne understood the logic, but couldn't order her heart not to bleed. And it bled.

Vladimir watched her. She hadn't been able to hide a fleeting, bleak look at the empty seat Ashburn used to occupy. She collected herself, ignoring her pang and pushing Ash to the edge of her mind. A mind was a terrible thing to lose. She wouldn't allow her grief to trigger another mental collapse. Not after she'd held on for so long.

She must survive every disappointment.

And she wouldn't ruin Vladimir's good mood, which was rare lately. Ash was gone—the thought of it brought another wave of ache—but Vladimir was right in front of her.

Lucienne sipped the cider and nodded at Vladimir. It was excellent. He looked pleased.

"So how did you persuade Aida to leave the house?" she asked.

"You don't want to know," said Vladimir.

Lucienne smiled sweetly. *Keep chatting with him. Keep up the small talks. Be more engaging.* But part of her wasn't there. It had left with

Ashburn. And that wasn't something she could control. She prayed that Vladimir wouldn't detect her subtle shift in mood, but from the look on his face, she knew he wasn't fooled.

He understood that she needed Ash. When she lapsed, Ashburn was the only one who could calm her. That pained him to a degree she didn't want to know, but he never asked her to stay away from Ashburn. Instead, he put up with Ashburn's every jab, until the day Ashburn had flown her off Sphinxes.

Vladimir was unapologetic for being self-serving, but he wasn't selfish when it came to her. He'd once told her that he couldn't stand any man except him to have her, and he'd counted that as his most self-interested act. He'd told her, "Even if you can move on, I can't. Call me selfish, call me whatever you want, but I'll not let any other man have you. You promised that one day we'd be together. I won't release you. I know you're a warrior of honor. As long as I stay true to you, you won't move on either."

"What do you want to do after breakfast, miláček?" Vladimir asked, dragging her back from the memory of sitting on his lap in the Hungarian café in Chicago.

She finished chewing and swallowed potato skins. Vladimir indeed had a talent for cooking. Who could imagine an eighteen-year-old fierce prince warrior loved working in the kitchen?

"I'll go spy on the generals," she said, "and see if they're still behaving."

~

Accompanied by Vladimir and her guards, Lucienne visited Sphinxes' air force base.

Soldiers saluted her wherever she went. They shouted that she was one of them, a worthy warrior. She promised them a nation to give them new hope and a legitimate home. It kept Sphinxes together in a difficult time. But what if, in the end, she failed them? She couldn't be their queen if this madness didn't leave her. A mad queen would be the worst sovereign.

General Fairchild, Admiral Enberg, Director Pyon, and other

officers joined her. Kian came as soon as he heard she was at the base. They all knew about her improved health and had high hopes that the poison had run its course.

She listened to her officers map out Sphinxes' future—nationalization, expanding the military, and investing more in scientific research and technology.

After the air force meeting, Lucienne went to inspect her navy fleets and troops. They cheered her enthusiastically, as if she were already their Siren queen. Staying with her people, she temporarily forgot the pain caused by Ashburn's leaving.

She'd achieved the goal of encouraging her army. At the end of the day, she was more exhausted than she expected, but she insisted on going to see Ziyi and the scientists before retiring to her mansion.

While Ziyi embraced Lucienne again and again, she didn't forget to send Vladimir glares. Ziyi had excused herself from helping Pyon's intelligence division track the remaining Sealers' forces. The girl deployed all her genius in the cyberworld to search for a cure for Lucienne, but she hadn't had much success and had become testy.

"Dinner tonight?" Ziyi asked hopefully. "I've been feeling lonely without talking to you."

"Lonely?" Lucienne raised a brow. "You have a short date with a different guy almost every night."

"How do you know?" Ziyi blinked. "You haven't stepped out of the house for a week."

"You have your ways of knowing things, and I have mine," Lucienne said.

"You know all about my ways," Ziyi said, "but I haven't figured out yours."

"Haven't you sworn on your Girl Scouts' honor that you wouldn't put your ears on my walls?" Lucienne asked.

"I tried a few times," Ziyi said with a pout. "I've accepted defeat by now. I guess that makes you the Siren, and me the one who works for you."

"I need your help." Lucienne excused her guards and Vladimir before stepping into the satellite room with Ziyi. Vladimir gave Lucienne's hand a gentle squeeze, ignoring Ziyi's glare, and took off.

When Lucienne and Ziyi were alone in the lab, Ziyi said under her breath, "Ash came to see me before he left." She paused, waiting for Lucienne's reaction.

Lucienne licked her lip as dryness suddenly filled her mouth.

"He said he must go back to the beginning," said Ziyi.

"What beginning?"

"I don't know," Ziyi said. "He wouldn't explain it. He asked me to tell you not to go after him. He said not even you could change his mind."

So she'd driven him away. Lucienne fought back the sting behind her eyes. "Why couldn't he tell me to my face?"

"Look at them," said Ziyi. "Both of them. Neither can think straight when you're around. If Ash told you that, you'd stop him, and he wouldn't have the willpower to do what he must do."

Lucienne's heart jerked. "What must he do?"

"Leave you to find the cure. What else?"

The last time she'd asked him not to venture out of Sphinxes to go after the scroll, he'd retorted, "I'm not a warrior, but I'm better than Blazek getting things done."

She'd shot back, "When will you stop this foolish comparison?"

"When you stop having so little regard for me."

"You know how I feel—" she'd said furiously, then caught herself, "—think of you. I don't want you to leave because—"

Ashburn had waited.

He was never secure with her. He could read every human's memories and thoughts, but not hers. The only way for him to know how she felt was for her to tell him. But how could she promise him a future together while committed to another? She'd once given him hope and then crashed it, when she'd learned Vladimir had never betrayed her. She wouldn't toss Ash around again.

So Lucienne had never told him that she'd lose it if she lost him. She'd never told him how his absence affected her last time. While he'd waited for her to say how much he meant to her, she'd wished he could read her mind and know her heart.

He couldn't, so he'd left.

"Oh, no, no, no," Ziyi cried. "Don't do that to me. Don't look like that! You must not turn." She then cursed herself before instructing, "Deep breaths, Lucia, deep breaths!"

Lucienne breathed in and out. The redness receded, but coldness swept over her. "I'm fine." She squeezed her friend's shoulder and forced a smile. "Let's have dinner another day."

Lucienne left the lab.

~

In the first few days, Lucienne's heart stumbled every time she rounded the corner, expecting Ash to show up. He never did. She couldn't go after him in her volatile mental condition. She could no longer afford to act like when she was fifteen and had run off to Tibet with Vladimir. She now had a burgeoning nation on her shoulders and a people she must put before her.

She also had Vladimir to consider.

At seventeen, she felt old.

In the morning, she awoke to find her pillow wet. Had she cried herself to sleep? She didn't recall. She never expected her bond with Ash to go so deep that his absence made it difficult to draw a breath.

She jolted up in bed. For a second, she sensed him through their bond, but then the connection stretched thin. He was gone again.

At nights, she often wandered alone in the red forest. The guards gave her a wide berth. Vladimir watched her silently. He gave her space, but he'd become as somber as her. She knew how unfair she was to him.

That day she went for a walk in the afternoon. Her white gown flitted across the leaves on the ground, making fluttering sound. As sunlight sifted through the leaves, she saw red. It was all red—the sky, the forest, the light, and the distant blur. She started hyperventilating, seeing that a slice of her insanity would hit in the next second. She wheeled around, stretching her hand to grab something solid, anything. But she was in a clearing.

Then Vladimir was at her side, holding her, anchoring her, letting her head rest on his solid shoulder. "I'm here, miláček," he whispered.

And she calmed.

"It's okay you miss him," he said. "Your feelings for him are part of you now. You don't need to hide any part of you from me."

Her breath caught in her throat, she turned to cautiously peek into his eyes. The forest's redness didn't get into his eyes, which were a well of clear understanding.

"I can't deny I'm jealous," he said, "but I'm not crushed by it. Not anymore. Even if you don't need me, I'll still hang round. I'm not going anywhere."

"I'm afraid one day I'll finally drive you insane, like me," she whispered.

"You already drive me crazy." He gave her a lazy, warm grin. "I'm crazy for you. But my love, for you, I'll hold on to my sanity."

She rested her face against his chin, her arms wrapped around his waist. His solid frame enveloped her. He was no longer that hotshot she'd fallen for two years ago. He became a man for her.

Chapter Six
MAD DANCE

Ziyi took a big bite of sausage before she could swallow a portion of bacon she half chewed, and inserted a spoonful of baked beans into her mouth.

"When was the last time you had a good meal?" Lucienne asked her friend in the sun room.

"Before you went to Polynesia." Ziyi returned to her food.

Sphinxes had won the war, but no one had felt like winners. Lucienne had come back poisoned.

"Swallow your food before you speak," Lucienne said.

Ziyi grabbed a buttery rowie from a plate and pasted more butter on it with a knife. "But you asked me a question." The sunshine painted her purple-streaked bangs a lighter hue. "I haven't felt good for so long."

"Should I know the reason of your fabulous mood?" asked Lucienne. "Has it to do with men?"

"I'm a postmodern girl. I don't need a man to feel great," she said, raising a finger. "First, you haven't had a breakdown in ten days. I think the poison has expired. Even Dr. Wren is positive."

"Thanks." Lucienne felt good too. "And Vlad hasn't come back with black eyes and a split lip. The men have behaved. Vlad hasn't picked a fight, either. Things are good between us."

Ziyi put down the bread and sighed. "Would you rather know the truth?"

"I'm not blind. The men still hate him, but they won't touch him, and that's good enough, for now."

"They stopped fighting Blazek because Ash told them that the Czech enjoyed being beaten. The more he hurts, the better he feels. So the men won't give him that. They won't beat the misery out of him. They want his own conscience to torment him. He's already in hell, and they want to keep him there. They take another path to avoid him and treat him like the plague."

Lucienne pressed her lips into a line, her fine mood gone. She could stop the men from hitting him, but she couldn't stop them from making him an outcast. Her dark gaze fell on Ziyi's face. "What about you?"

"I've had a change of heart. I can be nicer, for your sake."

"Then we try it now," Lucienne said. "Aida told Vlad that we need girl time this morning. He's been giving me space. I'd like to have him join us, if you don't mind. You and I will do a morning run together and then go shopping. We'll have a lot of girl time."

Ziyi put down her black tea and coughed into her hand.

"You all right, Ziyi?" Lucienne asked with concern. "Take it easy, will you? I won't take your food."

Ziyi kept coughing and her face reddened. Lucienne went around the table to pat her friend's back. When Ziyi calmed, she stared at Lucienne, wide eyed. "You—you don't know?"

"Know what?"

"Blazek left Sphinxes last night."

Lucienne's heart stopped for a beat. "Did he say when he'd be back?"

"No one knew. I—I don't think it's a short-term thing," Ziyi said, watching Lucienne anxiously.

Vladimir had abandoned her too. Just when she'd believed he would have always stood by her no matter what, he'd deserted her. When she drifted closer to Vladimir, she drove away Ash. And when she couldn't help but miss Ash a little, Vladimir couldn't stand it.

She was now all alone. A rush of blood pumped in her eardrums, then the redness came. Lucienne didn't try to fend it off. "Are you truly my friend, Ziyi?" she asked.

"Of course I am! You know I'd die for you."

"Is that so?" Lucienne drawled. "Isn't this the second time you failed to inform me of his leaving? The first time he joined up with my enemies, and they used him to get to me. And now when I need him more than ever, you didn't bother to tell me of his parting again. I didn't even get to say goodbye. I might never see him again."

Ziyi's face paled. "It won't come to that."

The red wave surrounded Lucienne.

"No, no, no," she heard Ziyi cry. "Please, Lucia, please—"

Lucienne regarded the girl, whose dove-like eyes were pleading, her small hand tight on Lucienne's arm. This girl was her subject. "What do you want?" she asked. "To become a duchess when I become queen?"

"No, no," the girl said, tears in her eyes. "Please come back, Lucia. They didn't leave you. They all went to find a cure for you."

"A cure? Why do I need a cure?"

"Please don't do this," Ziyi begged, tears dropping from her eyes. "Please. I don't know how to deal with this you—and Ash isn't here right now."

Ash. Ashburn Fury. He'd also left her, and with that memory, an empty ache crashed her, followed by the remnant of the Lure. Ash wasn't around to fuel it, but he'd left part of it behind. The incomplete Lure was like a restless, half-awake, yet hungry beast. It had no one to prey on but her. It stirred heat in her, yet left her unsatisfied.

She couldn't find a release.

The cure.

Could it help her put out the heat?

"Ziyi Wen?" she asked.

"Ye—yes?" Ziyi answered timidly.

"Aren't you supposed to be my best friend?" she asked in a measured tone.

"I *am* your best friend," the girl said.

"Then why aren't you out there finding the cure for me?"

"I've been searching for it every waking moment." Ziyi wiped the tears off her face with the back of her hand. "I'm not good at guns or exploring the outdoors. My expertise is in the cyberworld. I—"

"Excuses!" Lucienne hissed.

The guards and Aida rushed into the sun room. One look at her, and they instantly tensed, as if facing the most hazardous species on earth.

Lucienne wasn't pleased.

"I—we were having a nice breakfast." Ziyi looked to the new group apologetically. "I upset her by telling her about Prince Vladimir."

"Vladimir Blazek, the traitor," Lucienne said, scanning the guards' faces. "Do you all know about his treason?" She narrowed her eyes on them. "No?" She shoved Ziyi aside and strode toward one of the guards. "We have an enemy among us," she regarded the guard sternly, then pinched his cheek hard with her thumb and forefinger, "and you look so robust and keep feeding yourself well. Have you forgotten your duty, soldier?"

"No," the guard said, standing very still, "not for a second."

"Then what's your duty?"

"To protect you, Siren!" the guard said.

"Well said, but empty words." Lucienne released the guard. "You let Blazek escape. He'll come back and drive the blade into my heart."

"He won't," someone said.

"Then why do I feel pain in my heart already?"

"Love hurts," Ziyi whimpered.

"Nonsense! No more love talk." Lucienne looked around the

room. "Where is Kian McQuillen? I need him to capture Blazek and bring me the traitor."

Thaddeus sauntered in. "Chief McQuillen went to the Continent."

"What for?" Lucienne demanded.

"To ensure the stability of all ops," Thaddeus answered.

"Why should he worry about the ops?" asked Lucienne.

"There are rumors," Thaddeus said.

"I know the rumors," Lucienne snorted. "They say that I'm insane. Even some of my high-ranking officers doubt my leadership. Do you doubt me like the others, cousin?"

"No, cousin, never," Thaddeus said. "You're my Siren, forever."

"What about the rest of the family?" Lucienne asked.

"We who swore a blood oath to you will stand by you till the end."

"But one among you is Judas," Lucienne said.

"Who?" Thaddeus asked, immediately tensed, a murderous look in his eyes.

Lucienne smiled coldly. "You'll know soon. I have a pretty plan for him." Then she let out a sigh. "I also trusted Kian, Ash, and Vlad, but look how they all left me."

"They'll come back, Lucia," Ziyi said.

Lucienne eyed her. "I know you mean well, but we're girls of independence. We don't need boys or men to feel better. Think of the Amazon warriors. Who needs men anyway?" With a swift, fluid movement, she leapt onto the dinette table. She twirled while singing a battle song of blades and ashes and bones.

"Come, Ziyi," she called in an interval, "sing and dance with me." Already bored before she finished the song, she jumped off the table and landed beside Ziyi like a powerful feline. She wiped her friend's tears. "Don't cry, silly girl. I was teasing you. I know you're loyal to me. I can read your mind. Now let me take you to my castle. We'll party all night."

She dragged her friend out of the sun room and into the hallway, still dancing. Then remembering something, she turned to the guards. "And you, yes, all of you, need to have a good time. You've been working too hard, good men. I'll make sure there are no enemies tonight to spoil our fun."

Ziyi, in a mist of tears, stumbled along in her stilettos and tight qipao, as Lucienne made her spin and spin.

Part Two

Chapter Seven

CAPTURE

For the first time in his life, Kian McQuillen had no idea where exactly he was.

His enemies had intended that with hard kicks on his head, feeling that the terrible pain from his broken ribs wouldn't be enough to dull his sense and judgment. Even tied, blindfolded, and drugged, Kian was aware that his tormentors had moved him across a few countries. He also knew they'd made a detour three times.

When agonizing pain woke him, Kian instinctively groped for a gun, but found himself chained to the damp ground in a cell of windowless walls and a steel door. His captors had plucked the knives from his boots, as well as anything that could be turned into a weapon. He knocked on the wall behind him. It had to be several feet thick, constructed of poured concrete. The light in the room was sparse, but Kian knew well that night-vision cameras were fixed on him.

He must be in Abaddon 5. They put only the most high-profile prisoners—people like him and Jekaterina—in the Sealers' most fortified prison.

He was where he needed to be.

It had broken his heart to see Lucienne battling herself.

They'd escaped many death traps. They'd beat the impossibilities. She became the first female Siren in an eon and achieved more than any of her predecessors. She'd obtained the Eye of Time, an ancient sentient being he was wary of but she was obsessed with. Together, they were about to form an elite nation.

Then she'd been poisoned.

How could he find the antidote to an ancient poison that was beyond human knowledge? Even the Fury kid said there was no cure. But as long as there was the slimmest hope, he would go through heaven and hell to find one. He wouldn't accept that there was no cure. He wouldn't accept this fate for Lucienne.

The answer lay on the last scroll—Lucienne's and his only hope.

When Kian had agreed to send Ashburn to find the scroll, Lucienne had exploded. That kid meant a great deal to her, and he was good for her. "Spare him," she had said. "You and Pyon can send your best man to track Jekaterina."

And who was a better man than himself?

So he'd done what he must do to find a cure for Lucienne.

~

Kian had left Sphinxes over a week ago to hunt down Jekaterina. Jed Lam, the former Siren, and his agents had failed to catch a glimpse of the woman for a decade. She'd remained off the grid. No one could pick up her trail, at least not until she had "accidentally" popped up in Ashburn's memory bank. The woman had flashed the last scroll as bait in Ashburn's face, then had vanished again.

Kian returned to use old school methods to find Jekaterina.

All the lookouts from Sphinxes' continental operations focused on any possible footprints she'd left, but there was no trace. No one even knew what Jekaterina looked like. The agents searched for any middle-aged Russian woman who looked remotely similar to Lucienne Lam.

Then Sphinxes Division of Intelligence obtained intel on a Sealers elder, Nickolas M. Poles. The twenty-five-year old, Ivy-League graduate had just risen to power. He had a square jaw and green eyes, with privilege written all over his boyish face.

The Sealers still maintained their traditional hierarchy structure. Twelve elders held the highest rank inside the brotherhood, except for the founder, a descendant of the first Sealer. Sphinxes' forces had destroyed half of the elders in the Polynesian war, but the founder had survived.

Kian's men hijacked Nickolas' private jet when he brought two blondes with him, heading for Hvar to enjoy lush vineyards and secluded coves and lots of sex. The men took him to the Berlin operation, where Kian impatiently waited.

Berlin op had two locations: one inside an upscale commercial building, running business as usual, the other disguised as an old warehouse away from the center of the capital city.

"Is he really an elder?" Hanz, the head of the Berlin op, asked in a slight German accent, eying the young captive sitting on a hard chair in the center of the warehouse.

"If I am not, why don't you just let me go?" said Nickolas.

"If you are not, we'll just have to kill you," said one of Kian's aides.

"In that case, I admit I've ascended to the elder position after you killed my father in the war. The eldership is inherited in the Brotherhood. You kill one elder, one of his sons or daughters warms the seat. If the elder's line has no direct heirs, then the bench goes to the nearest relative. So, am I betrayed by someone in my family? Who benefits the most if I am out of the way?" He pondered for a moment. "Two of my cousins." He looked up at Kian. "Who sold me out?"

"Let's pump him with truth serum and get some answers," Hanz said with annoyance.

"You don't need to do that," said Nickolas. "I have conditions to medication. I'll tell you whatever you want to know. They've already tossed me to the wolves—no offense—when I was in power for only a month. I want revenge. I have no personal grudge against the Siren, even after my dad was killed. I understand how war goes."

Kian gave his aide a nod, and the man plunged the syringe into the side of Nickolas' neck.

Nickolas yelped.

The injection was water, but the young elder didn't know.

The aide waited for a minute before asking, "What's your position and territory, Nickolas M. Poles?"

"I'm one of the Sealers elders. My territory is South Asia, but I prefer Africa."

"Did the founder sink with the fleet?" Kian asked.

"He doesn't sink. He never sinks. The legend says he has supernatural powers and can't be killed. Even if he is killed, we wouldn't know. And it doesn't matter much. His son or daughter would take his crown. You only blew up his messenger, Elder Emmanuel Thorn. He was the most powerful man next to the founder. I've never liked that pompous snake."

"Who replaced Emmanuel Thorn?" Kian asked, knowing the answer already.

"Thorn's only daughter, Bayrose. Rose, the submarine you airborned, was named after her. She's become the new speaker for the founder."

Kian's eyes hardened. The elder's daughter tricked Blazek into leading Lucienne to the poisoned Nexus Tear. He'd spill the girl's guts when he caught her next. "Where is Bayrose Thorn hiding?"

"No one knows. She's well protected," Nickolas said bitterly. "Perhaps she's the one who stabbed me in the back. She isn't a fan of mine, and the speaker has eyes and ears everywhere. This trip of mine was supposed to be highly classified."

"You can brood on your misfortune on your own time," said Kian. "Tell me about the cure."

"There is no cure," Nickolas said, "at least not from the reports I read. The ingredients of the poison don't even exist in this world. You need to find the founder. Maybe you can force the cure out of him, but he's a ghost in the machine."

"Then you're no use to us," Hanz said.

"I'm not useless," Nickolas said. "I can offer you my insights, profound, useful ones."

Hanz and an aide narrowed their eyes on the elder, not appreciating his stalling.

"You can't exchange me for the cure," Nickolas said in a calculating voice. "I'm an elder, but I'm still disposable. Even if there's cure, you probably won't get it. The Brotherhood didn't go through these elaborate schemes to destroy the Siren, just to hand her the antidote. Bringing down the Siren race has been the main goal since the Sealers was founded. Incapacitating the current Siren is our biggest achievement in millennia—"

The image of Lucienne stretching her hand toward him in blood tears, pleading, "Help me," flashed before Kian.

Hanz raised his hand to strike the elder, but Kian had beaten him to it. In a fit of rage and grief, he punched the elder's face.

Blood streamed from Nickolas' nose. "That's not cool, Kian McQuillen," the elder said. "I thought you'd appreciate my candor. Isn't that what your truth serum is for? I understand your rage, but I wasn't the one who poisoned your Siren. I should not inherit my father's sins."

"Is there a cure?" Kian demanded again.

"There's no evident cure for the Siren," the elder said, "but there is intelligence that will lead to an antidote."

"Say it now," Hanz said, "and you'll probably save yourself."

"I'll tell you about it in exchange for my freedom," Nickolas said.

"You're in no position to bargain," Hanz said.

"I'll release the liquid bomb in me," said Nickolas, "and you'll get nothing."

Before one of Kian's aides could reach him, the elder raised two fingers to stop his advance. "You can't get it out," he said. "The bomb is connected to the mind. Only the elders are granted this luxury to protect us from our enemies' torture."

Kian waved his aide to step back.

"Deal or no deal?" Nickolas asked. "I'm not afraid of death. I volunteered this information because I want vengeance. I won't be the sitting duck they made me."

Kian regarded him. "If your information is useful, your safety will be guaranteed."

"And you must free me," Nickolas said.

"I'll consider it," Kian said. "But what you say next will decide if you get to live or die."

"The ancient scroll foretold the poison and the Siren's fall," Nickolas said. "I paid tons of money to have that piece of intel. I was curious to know what the founder and Thorns were fussing about."

"Tell me the prophecy," Kian ordered.

"Samantha deciphered part of the last scroll," Nickolas said. "Without the other two ancient ones, she couldn't go further."

Kian's eyes flashed. Lucienne had the other two scrolls. With the third one, they would crack the full prophecy and find the cure for her.

"Who is this Samantha?" asked Kian.

"An enigma," Nickolas said. "Her territory is Russia and North America. She turned on the Brotherhood after the Polynesian war."

"Why?" Kian asked.

"Power struggle," Nickolas said. "And she took the ancient scroll."

Lucienne had mentioned that her mother Jekaterina took the scroll from the Sealers and then disappeared. "What's Samantha's last name?" Kian asked.

"She doesn't have one," said Nickolas. "At least not that anyone knew about."

"You ever meet her in person?" Kian asked.

"Once," Nickolas said. "She's the most striking woman I've ever seen. She looks to be in her early thirties, but I believe she's older."

"Find a sketch artist," Kian ordered Hanz, who raced to the other side of the warehouse and dialed his encrypted phone. Kian turned back to Nickolas. "You'll be digging a hole for yourself if you lead us on a grand hunt. We know Samantha disappeared with the scroll."

"I'm one step ahead of you, Chief McQuillen." Nickolas smirked. "No matter how good your spies are, they're not granted access to the most classified, immediate information. I'm one of the elders after all. Samantha tried to flee, but was caught. The founder put her in Abaddon 5—the most secure, undisclosed prison on earth."

The word was that Abaddon 5 was located in a North Korean military center. When the Sealers had first built it, they'd equipped it with a remote-controlled steel door armed with laser beams. A sixteen-foot razor-wire fence was its first line of defense. Over the years, the Sealers kept upgrading Abaddon 5 with all sorts of new technology.

As a sketch artist came in, escorted by one of the Berlin agents, Kian ordered the elder, "Describe Samantha."

"Six feet two-inches tall," Nickolas started.

Kian felt his heart skip a beat. The woman stood the same height as Lucienne.

"Almond-shaped eyes, whiskey-brown color." Nickolas said. "They say the color of her eyes shifts depending on her mood."

Like Ashburn Fury's.

"High cheek bones and full lips," Nickolas continued. "Her eyebrows have a striking arch—"

As soon as the artist finished the drawing, an aide brought it to Kian. He stared at the image. The woman bore an uncanny remembrance to Lucienne. Then truth struck home. Samantha was Jekaterina! After seventeen years, Kian was going to find Lucienne's biological mother, a woman who had evaded the world.

Then a change of plans formed in Kian's head.

What was the best way to get to Jekaterina? He was the most wanted, next to the Siren, on the Sealers' list. Once the Sealers had Sphinxes' number one commander, they would lock him up in Abaddon 5, where they kept Jekaterina/Samantha.

"Nickolas Poles, you'll arrange to have me captured," Kian said.

The room went dead silent.

Nickolas blinked a few times. "You want to get into Abaddon 5?"

"And you'll follow my instructions step by step," Kian said.

"Once you're in," Nickolas said, "you're as good as dead, Chief McQuillen."

The air was thick and gloomy in the warehouse.

"Send me, Chief," Hanz offered.

All the men in the room volunteered themselves without hesitation.

"Our enemy will send you somewhere else," Kian said, "or torture you until you're dead. They won't kill me. They'll put me in Abaddon 5."

Nickolas nodded. "But there are a few complications. No one gets out of that godforsaken place. They'll execute you before they let your army storm the prison. If you're as good as dead, I'll be too. Second, even if you get to meet Samantha, how will you make her hand over the priceless scroll? She fears no threat or torture, and drugs don't work on her."

"That's for me to worry about." Kian gave the elder a cold, tight smile. "You follow my plan, and you'll have your freedom."

"I'll do it," Nickolas said, "but I should mention one last thing: when the founder caught Samantha, he didn't find the scroll with her. She said she ate it."

~

Things went exactly as Kian and his men had planned. He'd ended up where he needed to be—Abaddon 5. His team divided into three task forces—the first would come for him as soon as he had the information for the cure, the second went to catch the new elder girl, and the third was already tracking down Vladimir Blazek to use as bait for Bayrose Thorn.

Now Kian must find Jekaterina in this fortified prison, where his cell didn't even have a window, and where the prisoners were kept isolated at all times. He surveyed his environment without turning his head as the realization hit him: even unchained, he could never find Jekaterina. He'd have to make his enemies bring her to him.

So he waited for them like an emotionless rock.

Time crawled by. Kian had no concern for himself. His concern was for Lucienne. Even the former Siren considered his granddaughter more important than himself. Lucienne was the first female Siren to be born, and she was to shift the world. He didn't need the ancient prophecies or i-Ching's oracle to tell him that. He didn't know the end game. He didn't know what kind of revolution she was going to start, but he was with her. He would always be with her.

It didn't matter that he couldn't make it out of this dump alive as long as he could deliver Jekaterina and the scroll to Lucienne, followed by the cure. He wouldn't allow himself to fail.

So he waited patiently for the new interrogator, the one who mattered in the Sealers' rank.

It was hard to tell if it was day or night. They didn't send him meals every day, but when they did, they slid a slice of bread coated with mold and a paper cup of stale water through a narrow slot in the steel door.

At least five days had passed, but the interrogator or tormentor hadn't come. His enemies were playing a new game with him. They weren't just using sensory deprivation, isolation, and starvation to make him weaker; they were deploying a time element to show him they had plenty of it while he—or rather his beloved Siren—was running out.

Anxiety and fear came to him like bubbling acid, but Kian contained it. If he opened his mouth first, he lost. So he kept waiting, immutable like hardened steel. No matter what his enemies did to him, they couldn't break him. The only one that could break him was Lucienne Lam. He repressed a nagging worry—once she found out he was missing, she'd come for him, and no one could stop her. He'd forbidden his men to activate the tracer in him before four weeks' time, but Lucienne wouldn't care about his orders.

Once she came for him, she'd mess up his plan.

He prayed the men would stall her as long as they could. He must make his enemies bring Jekaterina to him before Lucienne made a move. Before she tore the world apart to get to him.

So waiting became the hardest things he'd done.

Time was chewing him, but still, he waited.

Chapter Eight

COLD BATH

Lucienne bathed in cold water.

She spent most of her time these days in a bathtub made of Caijou gemstone. The ancients believed this gemstone stored over one hundred million years of healing energy from the earth and the universe.

Lucienne felt no healing energy—only a shattered spirit.

The artificial candlelight cast part of her shadow along the gemstone wall. She could see the perky outline of her breasts. She lowered herself into the water, shivering at its low temperature, and stared with dull eyes at the patterns on the ceiling.

Vladimir used to say that her eyes could reflect the slightest light. He wouldn't say that if he were here to see her now. Where was he? Where was Ash? Neither even bothered to say goodbye. They kept their whereabouts from her as if she'd chase after their tails and cause more damage.

She commanded herself not to think about either of them, but their images, in turn, twirled in her mind.

Even amid Ash's absence, the Lure loitered. It brought his woody scent and male musk to her nostrils, not sparing her, not wanting her to forget its other victim at the far end of the world. Even submerging herself into the frigid water brought no break. The Lure sent a strong heat wave between her thighs.

"Stop it," she whimpered. "Just stop."

Aida rapped on the door. The guards wouldn't dare come in during her bath, but they'd fetch her nanny if Lucienne was inside the bathroom over an hour. They watched her like hawks.

If she refused to respond, Aida would just enter, despite Lucienne's protests for privacy. "Get over it," the nanny had said more than once. "I changed your diapers when you were a baby."

Kian had ordered Ziyi to remove Lucienne's heat signature from the doors, so if there was an emergency, her guards could break in and reach her in time. With the new lock, Lucienne could no longer completely seal herself in.

"Lucia, you ready to get up?" the nanny asked outside the door.

"In a minute," Lucienne said, annoyed at the intrusion.

Then a knock came again, and Aida called, "It's been more than five minutes. I'm coming in."

Whatever. She decided not to leave this tub. Aida didn't have the strength to drag her out. Today there'd be a contest of wills. She'd show her nanny who truly called the shots.

Aida turned the lock and scurried in with a white robe in her hand.

Lucienne made a point of sinking lower into the water, closing her eyes, and leaving only her nose above the water to take in air.

Aida sat on the edge of the gemstone tub. "You're a fighter, my sweet girl," she said, her voice full of love.

That was unexpected. She'd waited for her nanny to push on. When Aida gently brushed her hair off her forehead, Lucienne let her face surface and leaned her head against the edge of the tub. "It doesn't matter if I fight," she said. "They just keep coming back."

"Then you rest," Aida said, "and fight again, and give them hell."

"I *am* resting, but you keep nagging me."

"You've been in the water for nearly two hours," the nanny said. "Your nice skin is wrinkled now, like mine."

"Who cares if I have wrinkles? No one will look at me."

"Everyone looks at you and looks up to you. You don't get to live just for yourself. I hated this life for you when you were first brought to the Red Mansion, but now I understand. You're the Siren, and a queen can never live like a normal girl. You have people who need you."

"I can't even take care of myself," said Lucienne.

"Then let me take care of you, and you take care of them." The nanny started drying Lucienne's hair with a towel.

"Oh, Aida." Lucienne drew her knees up against her chest and rested her head against her nanny's shoulder.

Aida ran a hand over her hair. "Men and boys come and go, but we—your people—will always be here."

Lucienne felt tears from her lashes. "Has Kian come back?"

"No. He should be back in a few days."

"He hasn't returned my calls. That never happened before. And the guards don't know where he is. I'll check with Ziyi to see if he's in some sort of covert op. Nowadays, everyone keeps me at arm's length."

"Kian knows how to manage himself," Aida said. "Now get up and get dressed, or I'll have to dry your naked body. You hated it when you were a little girl."

"I'm too tall for you now, anyway," said Lucienne.

"Then you don't want me to slip and break my old bones." The nanny kissed the girl's head, rose, and exited.

Lucienne put on her robe and came out of the bathroom. She selected a white leather tank top and a pair of jeans from the closet. Her guards looked reassured at her white outfit, but to Lucienne, wearing red or white made no difference when in such a sulky mood.

Duncan was among her watchers. He hadn't been around since the day before yesterday. His dark skin was pale. Was he sick? She had scarcely talked to her guards ever since Vladimir and Ashburn had left. "Have you eaten, Duncan?" She eyed him. "Aida baked a pie in the kitchen."

"Not hungry," he said, looking angry and anxious.

As Lucienne headed toward the library, he trailed after her with another guard.

"Where did you come from?" She gestured for him to walk with her, and Duncan fell into step beside her down the hallway.

"The castle," he said.

"Any news there?" she asked casually.

Duncan didn't answer.

Lucienne looked at him sideways, quirking an eyebrow. "Since you came from the castle, you must know where our chief is."

"Chief McQuillen is—" A pause that was more like a choke caught in Duncan' voice.

Lucienne waved her hand in exasperation. She was sick of it. She wouldn't put up with this nonsense that she shouldn't be bothered or burdened with the Sphinxes' affairs. She was still their Siren. She had the rights to know what was going on under her nose. "What about Chief McQuillen?" she demanded. "He doesn't pick up my calls anymore, and everyone refuses to tell me where he is. Am I a plague?"

"Chief—" Duncan's voice was still choked up.

Lucienne stopped short. A passage of cold air whirled around her. A foreboding sense speared her guts.

Duncan wasn't trying to stall her.

"What's wrong, Duncan?" she asked softly, yet with authority.

"Chief McQuillen was captured," Duncan finally got his words out.

Lucienne's mind went blank for a few seconds. "What?"

"The Sealers took Chief McQuillen over a week ago," Duncan said. "The chief's men didn't want you to know about it. Ziyi intercepted some intel yesterday."

Blood drained from Lucienne's face.

The air around her turned colder than ice. Sphinxes' weather cooled down fast at night. Was it night already? That explained why it was so dark all of a sudden. She rubbed her arm at the chill. No, this cold was unnatural, as unnatural as this sudden darkness. Had her thought manifested itself, like a dreaded nightmare that always came?

She looked around. She was in a barren terrain, the sun blocked by vast, red wings. She broke into a run when a predator dove toward her with menacing purpose.

It struck her, knocking her to the ground. The wings became an endless red, ensnaring her. Air, she needed air, but couldn't break through the thick net. Someone called her name. It was Kian, her protector! He called urgently at first, then his voice trailed off, as if saying farewell.

Kian! Lucienne's senses spiked. He was in danger, and she must go to him! But this darkness, this redness, prevented her from reaching him. *No!* She screamed. She'd burn it. She'd burn anything that stood between her and Kian. She raised her hand and summoned her power.

The dark, red predator fluttered away before her power came.

Lucienne blinked. She was in the hallway in her home with her guards.

They looked alarmed. Accompanying her was like walking with a tigress that could turn on them at any time. As her frantic breathing slowed, she nodded to them. "I'm okay now," and watched relief wash over them.

This was the first time she'd slipped into insanity for mere seconds and come back, all because of her determination to reach Kian.

"How did it happen?" She fixed her gaze on Duncan, keeping her voice calm.

"Chief planned his own capture," said Duncan.

"Why?" she asked, though she'd pieced everything together.

Kian had gone straight to the Sealers for the cure because she was running out of time. Who didn't want Kian McQuillen, Sphinxes' number one commander and the Siren's ultimate guardian?

She'd tried to prevent Ashburn from leaving, so she'd demanded Kian send his best man to search for the last scroll. Who was a better man than Kian? "I'll sacrifice everyone," he'd said, "including myself, for you."

She'd condemned him without realizing it.

Her every action caused catastrophe. Kian had once put it in the kindest way: "From the moment you were born, Lucienne Lam, you were at the center of the war."

If she hadn't hunted Ash for his TimeDust, Orlando, Cam, and the other warriors would have lived. The chain reaction also cost Captain Marloes her life. If she hadn't bested all the boy candidates and taken the Siren's seat at the age of eight, the decades of the Lam family war could have been averted.

Seraphen had called her the catalyst. He'd been desperate to erase her for the safety of the world. Maybe the creature had been right? But how could she not be what she was born to be? How could she not pursue Eterne and a new future for humankind after being molded into who she was?

For Ashburn's sake, she turned her back on her Siren's call, and all things went south. War kept finding her and her men.

She might stand at its center, but she would not cost Kian. She would never lose him. But she might have already lost him.

Lucienne commanded herself to stay calm—she needed a cool head more than ever—but she couldn't keep herself from trembling. When she stepped out of the house, in desperate need of fresh air, her guards had gathered outside, waiting for her command. News travelled fast. They'd all heard about Kian's capture. And she was the last to know.

Thaddeus moved toward her. He steadied her and let her lean on him. "We'll get him back, cousin."

Tears flowed from Lucienne's eyes. The tears were clear. She had her sanity in check. She'd succeeded, for the first time, in pushing back the red wave. She wouldn't allow herself to slip. Not while Kian was in mortal danger. She wiped her tears and stepped away from her cousin. "Chief McQuillen has been taken," she said, facing her guards. "I'm assembling a rescue team."

"We'll go on your behalf, Siren," said Adam, the captain of the guards.

"No, I'll lead the team," Lucienne said.

Heavy silence fell in the air until Adam broke it. "I'll round up a special task force." He knew no one could talk her out of this. She'd burn the river dry if anyone put it between her and Kian.

Lucienne collected her guards and went to see her generals. She outranked them, but she still needed to go through them to rescue Kian. She could no longer do what she wanted, when she wanted, like she did two years ago when Sphinxes was nothing near being a nation. It had a system now, and she had to respect it.

A heated argument stopped abruptly as Lucienne entered the castle's underground conference room. Admiral Enberg, General Fairchild, Director Pyon, and other high-ranking officers snapped to attention and saluted her. She waved a hand to dismiss their formality. "I see you're having an emergency meeting," she said as General Fairchild stepped down and let her have the head seat at the table. "I'm curious why I wasn't invited to your big boys' club."

After a slow, awkward silence, Admiral Enberg spoke, "We think it's best not to get you involved."

"You think it's best?" Lucienne asked. "Am I not your Siren anymore?"

"You're forever our Siren," said Enberg. "Because of that, we can't risk you."

"If you try to make me a figurehead," Lucienne said, "it won't work. Many have tried before you and failed miserably."

"We won't try, Siren," General Fairchild said. "You're our warrior queen. But while we're capable of fighting for you, we're more comfortable when you aren't on the battlefield where the bullets can hit you. If we lose you, we lose our cause for fighting."

The other officers agreed vehemently.

"Smooth talk and manipulation never work on me," Lucienne said, ignoring the few officers double-checking her white suit. She'd never talked to her officers like this, but they hadn't treated her as their leader ever since she'd started having mental collapses. They treated her like a dangerous, mad teenage girl who happened to be highborn. "What happened to Chief McQuillen?" she asked curtly.

"I assume you've heard part of the story," said Pyon.

"As I happened to be the last to know," she said, "I plan to be the first to bring him home."

"Chief sacrificed himself for you," General Fairchild said. "If you throw yourself at the Sealers, then his sacrifice will be for nothing."

"Who gave you the impression that I'm just going to toss myself at the feet of my enemy?" Lucienne asked. "And Chief McQuillen's sacrifice is for nothing! He won't get what he went for—the cure. There is no need to pretend anymore, gentlemen. You're wary of me because I can go mental in an instant, but you're forgetting I always come back. If you can't deal with a half-mad me, then you shouldn't stay in Sphinxes. The land is mine. The door is wide open. As long as you don't align yourself with my enemies, you won't be mine."

"You're right, Siren," Admiral Enberg said. "It doesn't benefit our cause that we keep pretending. Insane or not, you're our Siren and always will be."

"We're with you to the end," the officers swore, though not General Fairchild.

"How can you get your act together if there's no cure for your sanity?" Fairchild asked.

Admiral Enberg snarled at the general, but Fairchild kept his cool. "Our Siren just said there's no need to pretend. I believe she prefers we speak our minds."

"I do," Lucienne said. "However, I won't tolerate disrespect."

"I'd never disrespect you, my Siren," said General Fairchild.

"I'm not an invalid, despite my condition," Lucienne said. "I'll keep contributing and building Sphinxes. It's my home." She looked into the eyes of each officer in turn and let the power of persuasion roll off her. She'd had this power even before Forbidden Glory had marked her. She was extracting it from herself, so the unstable Forbidden Glory had no reason to turn on her right now and send her to the insane land in front of her officers. But she knew she was walking on thin ice. "We're going through this crisis because I was poisoned, because Chief McQuillen was taken, because we haven't vanquished our old enemies and the new ones have sprouted up. Now more than ever is the time to test excellent character and loyalty. Yours and mine. Without honor, we're nothing. I won't let any man without it serve in Sphinxes."

Lucienne saw awe on the officers' faces as they bowed to her. They'd felt her power.

"We'll walk through fire with you, Siren," the officers said.

"You have my loyalty, as well," Lucienne said. "We'll be one people and one nation."

This was the first time she officially promised them that they would be a nation. She must do anything to keep Sphinxes together.

The officers pressed their fists against their hearts. Before they renewed their loyalty to her, Lucienne said, "One condition. Sphinxes won't be a country without Chief McQuillen. Help me get him back."

"We'll use every power we have to bring our chief home," Director Pyon said.

"I'll head to Berlin with the team that accompanied me to Russia and Polynesia," Lucienne said. "It's time I pay our captured Sealer elder a visit." She gestured for one of Kian's top aides to collect her team outside.

Adam led the men in.

"Siren, I bid you to reconsider leading the rescue," Admiral Enberg said. "We have special task forces and capable team leaders ready to go in your place."

Lucienne swirled toward the admiral, eyes burning with fury. "Then why didn't you act when your chief was taken over a week ago?"

"We're waiting for his signal," Enberg said. "We're executing his plan."

"He didn't plan to come back in one piece," Lucienne said icily. "Before you get his signal, he could be dead!"

"Let our Siren take the lead," General Fairchild said. "This action can be good for Lucia's health. She needs to have something to do other than sit in the house."

Was her general being condescending?

"Fine, you lead the team," Enberg said, "under one condition."

"Are there ever no strings attached?" Lucienne said drily.

"You bring only two of your guards," Enberg said. "We'll handpick the best men from special forces for you. They're specially trained for rescue missions."

Lucienne regarded her guards. Everyone looked overzealous.

"You won't leave me behind, cousin," Thaddeus said, using the family card.

"I'm the captain of your guards," Adam said. "I go wherever you go."

"Wait!" Duncan said. "I've been with the Siren from the start. I'm going."

The rest of the guards eagerly gave reasons why the Siren should pick them.

"I'll bring Adam and Duncan," Lucienne said. Then over Thaddeus' look of betrayal and hurt, she sighed. "And my cousin. I have another use for him."

"The team isn't an issue," Pyon said, locking eyes with Lucienne. "The problem is we lost Chief McQuillen's whereabouts. The Sealers took out the tracer in him after they transported him to the third location."

"Where is the third location?" asked Lucienne.

"Egypt-Libya border," Pyon said.

"Hanz, the head of Berlin ops, said the Sealers sent the chief to Abaddon 5 in North Korea," one of Kian's aides said.

Abaddon 5? Lucienne drew a sharp breath, and fire burned in her blood. "I'll turn that communist country upside down to get Kian out."

"The Sealers have had a change of plans," Pyon said. "They were supposed to put the chief in Abaddon 5 since it's where they traditionally put their high-profile prisoners, but they moved him further away from North Korea. The enemy's intention is unknown. My best guess is they moved him to a military center on the border of Libya. The Sealers have close ties with jihadists."

General Fairchild pounded the table. "We'll bomb the terrorist army!"

"Send two rescue teams," Lucienne said. "Team A to North

Korea; Team B to Libya. Alert all continental ops. Kian can be anywhere. Wherever he is, we'll find him. I'm going with Team B. Set it up now. We don't have time to lose."

"Let's not rush into the fray," General Fairchild said. "We'll draw a solid plan, including bombing military bases. Sphinxes can spare hundreds of warplanes. We take out the jihadists' bases first."

"There'll be absolutely zero air-to-ground bombs," Lucienne said. "There'll be no rockets, no nerve gas, and no grenades. We do a conventional ground assault. You can level the place to ashes afterwards, but while Kian is there, we don't blow the place sky-high. I don't want any blast to hit him by chance."

"There'll be no air raid on these two holding facilities," Pyon agreed. "Our ops will attack the Sealers' thirty outposts and military bases, so our enemy won't know our true target."

"We have a plan," Lucienne said. "Let's act."

"Hold back a few more days," Enberg said. "We must give Kian time to obtain the intel for the antidote while he's in the enemy's keep. That's one part of the initial plan we need to stick to."

"I don't care about the cure," Lucienne exploded. "We need to get Kian out this very minute!"

"Lucia." Pyon, who stood at Lucienne's right side, placed his hand on her arm. His voice had a calming effect, almost like Kian's. Lucienne evened her breath. If she lost control, a slice of insanity would kick in. And if she had a lapse right now, the officers would fight tooth and nail to stop her from marching out of Sphinxes.

Lucienne swallowed hard and composed herself.

"We'll get him back, I promise," Pyon said, "but you'll not rush in. You won't put yourself and the teams in jeopardy. Can you do that, Lucia?"

Lucienne nodded.

"I sent a team to Tibet to retrieve Prince Vladimir," Pyon said, "but they haven't returned. I need Duncan to go to Tibet now."

Everyone had been avoiding mentioning Ashburn and Vladimir, afraid the topic would trigger her mental meltdown. She hadn't asked their whereabouts either, not wanting to hear one heartbreaking report after another. Unable to rein in her insanity had brought out her insecurity. So she'd assumed the worst—both Vladimir and Ashburn had fled from her.

"What is Prince Vladimir doing in Tibet?" she asked, her heart banging in her chest, her face a blank mask.

Pyon gave her a look. "Seeking the antidote."

"I doubt the monasteries have it," Lucienne said. "I was there searching for a different item a couple years ago."

She and Vladimir had taken the second scroll—the holy sentinel of Tibet. The Lama had declared, "When the One uses the holy scroll for his personal gains, he'll sweep away the old world and its traditions in a maelstrom. His power will increase, but the world will sink into the third Dark Age."

It wasn't he but *she* who had taken the holy scroll. Did the Lama realize that? None of the Khampa warriors had pursued her and Vladimir after they'd escaped, though they'd warned her that they were the army of light that would purge the world's dark power at all cost. Guess they hadn't made up their minds if she was light or dark.

"You can't blame Prince Vladimir for trying," Pyon said. "He was with the monks when he was twelve. He said the seven saints left behind the knowledge of a healing ritual."

Lucienne shook her head. It was another futile effort. "What do you need Vladimir for?"

"To lure the elder's daughter," Pyon said. "Miss Bayrose Thorn is the new speaker for the Sealers founder. She's the most valuable among all the elders. We'll use her in exchange for Kian if all goes south."

Vladimir had once sacrificed Bayrose for her. Would he do it again? The psychopath Schmidt had told Vladimir in the temple, "Miss Thorn didn't completely betray you, Prince. You used her first, but she's better at it. She knew you never truly cared about her. You'd hurt any girl for your one true love. We're much alike."

How far had Vladimir gone with the elder girl to gain her trust?

"And you count on Miss Thorn's feelings for Vladimir?"

Lucienne asked. "Feelings are a flickering thing. If you bet on them, you might fail to lure the Sealer girl." She was referring to Vladimir's fleeting feelings for her.

"We have to try," Pyon said. "And Prince Vladimir will do what we ask of him."

The subject of Vlad invoked such pain and longing in Lucienne that she fought to stay focused. She turned to the generals, her face remaining neutral. "The jihadists are well-trained fighters."

"Our men are better," Enberg said. "But we'll need to borrow a handful of experts from Operation Desert Storm Nine for this ground rescue. The US Navy in the Mediterranean has put their most advanced surveillance aircrafts into use for us."

"Our old friends, the tribal leaders at the desert, will be our guides," said Pyon.

"Good." Lucienne nodded. "My team and I are leaving for Berlin immediately."

"Siren," General Fairchild called before Lucienne made her exit, "there's one last problem."

Lucienne arched a brow.

"What if you lapse in the field?" Fairchild asked. "You can't control your medical condition."

All heads turned to Lucienne.

"Thaddeus will incapacitate me before that happens. I've taught him how," Lucienne said coldly. "I'll not jeopardize this mission."

Thaddeus would knock her out cold at the first sign of a lapse, before she could summon her power. She'd informed him that if he timed it wrong, Forbidden Glory would burn him. She was sorry that she had to ask her cousin to do this, but she was out of options.

"You can trust me, cousin," Thaddeus had said. "I won't let you down."

If only she could trust herself and not let Kian and her men down.

"Anything else, gentlemen?" she asked. Over their silence, she turned to Adam. "Captain, inform the base we're taking Valkyrie and Chameleon II. We're leaving in the next hour."

Chapter Nine
BERLIN

Lucienne stepped into the sitting room of the Berlin safe house, leaving her team and Berlin agents outside the door. Nickolas Poles was having afternoon tea and snacks and complaining about the teabag.

"Nickolas," Lucienne greeted.

He shot to his feet and bumped into the edge of the coffee table. His tea spilled. "Siren of the Lams? To what do I owe the honor?"

Lucienne motioned for the Sealers elder to sit back while she settled herself across from him.

Nickolas blinked before looking away, as if realizing his own mistake by staring at the sun directly. That was most people's reactions when they'd first met Lucienne. Like her ancestors of the Siren race, her power radiated off her.

"The tea isn't up to your standard?" she asked.

"Tea? Tea's okay." Nickolas gathered himself. "I'm just bored."

"Perhaps we should entertain you?"

Nickolas widened his eyes. "You mean torture?"

"Is that my reputation?"

Nickolas smirked. "They say you aren't nice."

"The glowing reviews they gave me since I was a toddler."

Nickolas chuckled. "They neglected to mention you've got a fine sense of humor and you're also a rare beauty."

"Do you realize the danger of flirting with me?"

"I'm willing to take the risk," Nickolas said. "It's once in a lifetime for someone like me to meet the Siren." Now he didn't take his gaze off her. "The ancient myth of the Sirens is as old as time. But for once, they got it right. The rightful Siren would be female, and you came. In the depths of your eyes, I see Siren's luring power. You might truly change the world."

"I didn't expect a Sealers elder to be a poet or a prophet," Lucienne said.

"One can be both when in the right element."

"Do you understand the position you're in?"

"Perfectly," Nickolas said with a relaxed smile. "My life is in your hands. My chance of living depends on how useful I am."

"Good."

"I'll give you whatever you want," Nickolas said. "Please don't use the truth serum as Kian McQuillen did. A second time will cause my panic attack."

"I don't need the assistance of drugs," said Lucienne.

"I know that," Nickolas said softly. "You have that effect on people. I didn't believe it until I saw you in flesh."

This one, who was only a few years older than her, hadn't made the mistake of underestimating her, but he made one by complimenting her. "I'm flattered," she said.

"I'm not fawning over you," the elder said seriously. "I'm a frank man who sometimes can't keep his mouth shut."

"Not as frank as you claimed." She'd dove into his mind the moment she'd stepped into the room. "Your ambition is higher than your rank in the Sealers. All the extravagance and indulgence, including the two blond knockouts, is but a smokescreen. Your dream is to take over the Brotherhood. It's too old school for your tastes. You're itching to reform it with your Ivy League touch. Unlike your founder and your peers, you lack a burning desire to erase me. You're an opportunist. Since my chief captured you, you've been brooding on this new idea of combining forces with me to dominate the world, especially when you see that I'm a female Siren. Why not share the power instead of shedding each other's blood? You'll propose that we take a more practical, logical approach—negotiate like two global corporations. I can go on."

Nickolas contained his shock. To his credit, he didn't ask a stupid question like, "How do you know about all this?" He cleared his throat. "The Sealers Brotherhood needs a new leader, one who is a visionary and realist."

"The Sirens' and Sealers' forces have been on earth since old times," Lucienne said. "We can't uproot each other completely. We kill one of your elders; the next one will replace him. And the next one can be worse."

Her army had sunk the Sealers' fleet and blown up their submarine headquarters, but their numbers kept increasing. It was like trying to weed out terrorists—they reproduced at an alarming speed.

"We're all expendable in the Brotherhood, except the founder," Nickolas said. "He's almost irreplaceable, like you."

Almost.

I have no heir. That's what he meant, Lucienne thought. *If I die, the Siren's line dies with me. I'm the first female Siren, and I can't be with any man except Ash, for now.* She wouldn't allow her enemies to know her Achilles' heel. "No one is indispensable in this world. Life goes on. My cousins are all lined up after me to be the next Siren. But you're right about the obscenity of the bloody war. You and I can do better, but your founder still wants my head on his altar."

"Not if we get rid of him," Nickolas said. "He can't adapt, but we're the generation of change. We're standing at the crossroad, where the quantum revolution is calling. You and I can bring the coming new age."

"I sank the *Rose*," Lucienne said, watching the elder closely to detect the slightest shift in his expression. She wouldn't risk doing another mind sweep on him. The previous one had exhausted her. "I heard that your father was in that submarine. I killed him. Aren't you coming for my blood?"

"The war killed him," Nickolas said. "I'm not heartless, but blood ties are overrated. My father wasn't a good man. I knew that much. After all, I was raised by him."

"The devil you know," Lucienne said. "If you take over the Sealers' club, at least we won't be so impatient to cut each other's throat."

Nickolas smiled. "I dream of the day."

"And this future depends on my chief's safe return," said Lucienne.

Nickolas's grin vanished. "McQuillen went for a suicide mission. I told him the founder would never exchange me for him. He's the Sphinxes' chief!"

"My plan doesn't involve sacrificing you since there's no need to," said Lucienne. "But you're going to tell me everything you know about the Sealers' ops, outposts, safe houses, prisons, and military bases."

"I don't have access to the whole operation," Nickolas said. "You do realize that?"

"I'm not making an unreasonable demand," said Lucienne. "You'll try your best. If you lie or intentionally forget something, I'll know."

"I've given your men all the locations, including the bases on my territory."

"You gave only fifty seven percent of what you have."

Nickolas inhaled.

"We'll get to that later," Lucienne said. "I intend to preserve your power in the Sealers, but now I'm anxious to locate my chief's whereabouts. Your founder had him shipped to Libya instead of Abaddon 5."

Nickolas drew a sharp breath. "That doesn't sound good."

Lucienne's heart plummeted. "Why Libya?" she asked. "Shouldn't all high-profile prisoners go to Abaddon 5? Samantha is there, isn't she?"

Nickolas looked distraught. "The founder won't keep your chief alive for long," he said. "The Muslim extremists will decapitate him to set an example, or just to show how much they despise you."

Unable to draw the next breath, as if shards of glass blocked her air passage, Lucienne almost dropped to her knees and rolled on the floor. But she sat still and forced herself to inhale and exhale slowly. Seconds later, she was the steel Siren again.

"I'm sorry," the elder said softly. "The only bright side is it's easier to break him out from the Libya military base than Abaddon 5."

Lucienne gave him a tight look and summoned Hanz, his agents, and her team.

A German agent brought her tea—premium tea leaves brewed in a teapot. Lucienne dismissed the agent and the tea, but Nickolas said that he'd like to have some. The agent looked to Lucienne, who gave him permission to serve the Sealers elder.

"We're ready to move on to the second stage," Hanz said, "according to Chief McQuillen's plan."

"We won't execute his plan," Lucienne cut in. "I'm overriding it. We're going to Libya. We'll raid the military base tonight."

"*No*, you're not." Pyon walked in. He must have taken off from Sphinxes right after her. "I *am*. I'll get Kian out without risking you, my Siren. My intel just came in. The chief is indeed held along the Libyan border. Desert Wraith Ops has been activated under my command."

Nickolas looked from Hanz to Lucienne to Pyon with a grin. He seemed to be the only person in the room who was having a good time.

~

Hanz's office was designed more for convenience than comfort. There were no documents on the desk, just a high-powered laptop and a bottle of hand sanitizer. The only personal touch was a collection of brandies inside the cabinet. If raided, the safe house would leave no records and no trails for their enemies.

Pyon sat on a large, luxury sofa while Lucienne paced from wall to wall, curling her hands into fists, then straightening them, as if restraining herself from pounding the concrete.

The elder had confirmed that the founder had no intention of keeping Kian alive for long. Her enemy knew what it'd do to her and Sphinxes if they took out Kian McQuillen. Fear cut deep into her bones. What was she going to do if she'd already lost Kian, her rock and her ultimate protector? She kept shoving that thought out of her mind, but it kept swinging back.

"If you keep pacing the floor like that," Pyon said, "you're going to increase the level of acid in my stomach. And right now, I need to stay calm and go over the steps of breaking into the enemy base."

She turned to Pyon. "I won't need to pace if you let me go to Libya."

"You're in no condition to rush in," Pyon said sternly, "and you know I'm right. You want him out alive, you need to be at your best and help me."

She looked at the director accusingly. "But you refuse to tell me the details of the plan."

"You agreed that Desert Wraith Ops is under my command," Pyon said. "I'm not going to lay out classified information in front of everyone."

Lucienne's eyes burned with dark fire. "I'm not *everyone*."

"To secure a successful mission," said Pyon, "I can't let you step on my toes."

"Why does everyone assume that I love to step on their toes?"

"Your history has spoken for itself more than a few times. You're a hothead, like Prince Vladimir."

Lucienne gave him a withering look.

"You do well when it doesn't involve those you care about, but when their safety is at stake, you throw yourself into the fire without considering how hot it is. And we—your people—can't afford to lose you."

Lucienne wasn't a fool who couldn't recognize truth. She slumped in a chair across from Pyon, grasping her head in her hands. Her inside was like the churning sea. She needed to act. She needed to get to Kian now. But she couldn't afford to screw up the rescue.

"I must establish the command chain here," Pyon said.

"You're the commander," Lucienne said. The best leader always knew how to best use the most brilliant men and women under her and not meddle with them while they were doing their jobs. She had no problem picking the best man—Pyon—for the task, but she couldn't restrain herself from a little meddling. For heaven's sake, Kian's life was on the line! "You won't act like the generals, in the name of protecting me. You'll let me in on every plan of yours, and I'll actively participate in the rescue."

Pyon regarded her warily.

"Or I'll jump into the fire my way," Lucienne said.

"Will you promise to obey my orders on this mission?"

"Yes."

"I need another guarantee."

Lucienne raised an eyebrow. "You want written words on paper?"

"No, Siren," Pyon said. "I need your promise not to use your power."

Lucienne stared hard at him.

"Yes, I know your Siren's mystical superpower," he said. "I've been paying attention. I knew about it when you were made Siren at a very young age. The power will consume you if you use it unwisely. Everything has a cost, especially a power as great as yours. Your condition is unstable, as is your power. I won't let you sabotage the ops. So, will you give me your word that you won't use your power?"

"I won't use it unless it's absolutely necessary," Lucienne said.

"I need you to trust me, like Kian has always trusted me."

Trust the men you use, or don't use them. That was Kian's motto.

Lucienne hesitated for a second and nodded.

"We need to give Chief McQuillen time to finish his mission, or his captivity will be for nothing."

"Kian doesn't have time!"

"You promised to trust me."

Lucienne bit her lip. "I'll give you two days. And then no matter what, I'm going in and bringing him home."

"I need a week."

"Any moment they could kill him."

"If they wanted to execute him that soon, they'd have done it already. An extra week won't make any difference to our enemy, but it does to us. Give Kian time to find out about the cure, which is most important to the future of Sphinxes."

"I don't care about the cure," Lucienne said. "I want Kian back in one piece. So, no, I won't wait another week. You have three days, Director Pyon."

"I want to bring him home as much as you do, Siren," Pyon said. "I'll oblige you. Three days it is. But here comes another tough task. I need you to play a role."

"You always drive hard bargains, Director," Lucienne said drily. "I'll play the role. You can count on me to fight as hard as any soldier on the team."

"Your role is not to fight, Siren. We'll do the fighting."

The veins on Lucienne's temples bobbed as anger flared in her. "You agreed to let me fully participate in the action."

"Participate in observing," Pyon said, "from a safe distance."

"That's very comforting, but know this: no one can stop me from going for Kian. Not even you. Not even him."

"Do you really want him back?"

Lucienne had a deadly look in her eyes, but Pyon was unmoved. "The men and I can't function at our best when we have to look over our shoulders," he said. "We can't worry about your condition and rescue the chief at the same time."

"I didn't realize I've become such a dead weight," Lucienne said.

"As I recall, before you came aboard, I was in the heat of every action."

"You aren't a burden, Siren," Pyon said. "You're a national treasure. You're the hope of the new world we hold onto. That's why things have to change. I'll bring Kian back to you, but you need to stay safe for him, for us. The closest place I can put you is our Greece op post. Greece is only on the other side of the Mediterranean Sea. You can observe and supervise how we attack the jihadists' base from there. You can do that, can't you?"

But what if Pyon failed?

Pyon met her dark gaze firmly. "I seldom lose."

"You can't afford to lose this time, Director Pyon."

"On my life, I'll make sure Kian comes home."

And Lucienne blinked back her tears.

Chapter Ten

BAYROSE

Bayrose Thorn was reviewing the interrogation on a recorded hologram.

Kian McQuillen, chained by hands and feet, was forced to sit on an iron chair bound to the ground. A dozen heavily armed jihadists positioned themselves along the walls and at every entrance and exit of the stone room as their leader, Mirrikh Schwartz, roamed around the captive, assessing him as if the Sphinxes' chief were a wounded lion, and a lethal one.

Mirrikh, wearing a tennis top and a pair of khaki pants, bit his fingernails when he stopped milling and looked into the lens of the camera with a wink. Bayrose had to admit that Mirrikh had the bluest eyes in the world, but she also knew he was a psychopath. As she grew up with him, she kept overlooking his dark side. She needed more supporters other than those she inherited from her father to establish her new reign, and Mirrikh was loyal to her, at least to a degree. Their families had once discussed enhancing their influences through their son's and daughter's marriage.

Mirrikh had succeeded his late father. With his new power, he unapologetically let menace and nastiness roll off him. But standing before the bloody, battered Kian McQuillen, he was like a small vicious bulldog. McQuillen's sapphire eyes were steely, yet his posture was carefree, as if nothing in the world could break him.

"No wonder the Siren's force has grown so strong," she murmured to herself. "She has men like Kian McQuillen." But Bayrose had the bitch's lion in her cage now.

Mirrikh stopped biting his fingernail and towered over the seated

McQuillen. "I'm Mirrikh Schwartz, the new elder of the Sealers."

McQuillen stared at Mirrikh as if he could pierce through him, and Mirrikh didn't appear appreciative of his captive's silent disdain. "My subordinates say you refuse to talk to any of them," he continued. Even as a boy, he'd been talkative. And he hadn't changed. "You wouldn't spit out a word even under the influence of the new drugs."

"Drugs and torture are child's play," said McQuillen.

Mirrikh sniggered. "I heard that you're the master of torture. Surely you know how to resist it. I apologize for not being able to arrive earlier. A man with your status shouldn't be touched by vulgarity. My subordinates will be punished. We need to set up a standard for gentlemen like us."

"You heard it wrong," McQuillen said. "I don't resort to torture to extract information."

"But you pump fear into men's heart. I admire that even more. Now that you're chained, can you still exact fear?"

"I did not come to evoke fear. I came to make a deal."

Mirrikh raised both eyebrows and said, "I'm intrigued."

"Find me the elder you put in your dungeon. Give me five minutes with her, and you'll have the second ancient scroll your Brotherhood has spent centuries searching for."

"You want to see Samantha." Mirrikh broke into a wolfish smirk. "What does she have that interests you so? Has it to do with the last scroll she stole from the Brotherhood? Or is it a physical attraction? She's formidable, but a rare beauty."

Bayrose's face reddened in anger. How dare he show this disrespect?

"You want the deal or not?" McQuillen asked.

"Even if I want it, I can't grant it to you." said Mirrikh, his smirk gone.

Rage flashed by Kian McQuillen's hard eyes, but he was in control of himself the next second. "Send me the one who can say the word," he said. "My business with you is finished."

"Our business is far from over, McQuillen," said Mirrikh. "You see, you've come to the wrong place. You're in a military fortress, thousands of miles away from where Samantha is held." He looked pleased at watching McQuillen suffer distress. "Now I know you staged your own capture, but your plan went awry. True, it's a tradition we put the most dangerous animals like you and Samantha in Abaddon 5, but the founder has a different vision when it comes to you and your little Siren. Don't look so disappointed. Even if we threw you into the North Korean prison, you wouldn't be able to see her. No one but the founder has access to Samantha."

Or the one who had the founder's ring. Bayrose flashed a ruby ring on her index finger, the original Sealers' symbol of an arrow piercing an all-seeing eye engraved atop the priceless gem.

"Inform your founder that I'll trade the second scroll for a talk with Samantha," McQuillen said. "Thousands of miles are nothing. Modern transportation can make the mileage as narrow as the space between your eyes. Bring her to me, or me to her, and you'll have the scroll."

Mirrikh shook his head. "We want the scroll, but Samantha is more important than that."

"I won't hurt her," McQuillen said.

"You won't hurt her?" Mirrikh threw back his head and gurgled. "She'll hurt you. That's how her reputation precedes her. When we put her in Abaddon 5, we had to take extreme care with her."

We? Bayrose rolled her eyes to the back. *You're not at that rank, Mirrikh Schwartz.*

"Isn't your founder interested in what I'm going to say to Samantha?" McQuillen said.

"You want the information about the cure," Mirrikh said. "What else?"

"Samantha's long-buried secrets." McQuillen leaned back in his iron chair. "But I'm done talking to you. You have no real power or access to the founder. Why don't you fetch me Bayrose Thorn, the new speaker girl?"

Bayrose felt her heart skip a beat at McQuillen's mentioning of her name, then winced as Mirrikh delivered a punch to McQuillen's jaw. McQuillen rattled his chains, straining to strike back, but he was bound completely. McQuillen spat blood at his antagonist, and Mirrikh kicked his captive in the chest. With a raging yell and a violent pull, Sphinxes' chief half broke free one of the chains. That was incredible! Mirrikh reeled back, and his jihadist guards sprang forward like a pack of mutts toward McQuillen, their weapons pointing at the prisoner.

Mirrikh picked instruments of torture from a nearby operation table and closed in on Sphinxes' chief again.

Bayrose jumped as a chortle rose behind her. She verbally commanded the hologram to turn off, and the violence in it faded out. She wheeled around, facing Mirrikh Schwartz with a syrupy smile. "Mirrikh!"

"You've arrived, my lady," Mirrikh said fondly.

Another holo-screen played a live feed of Kian McQuillen in his cell. He shut his eyes—one of them swollen— in meditation. The man obviously knew he was being watched.

"Since when must you call me that?" Bayrose chided Mirrikh, but she stretched her hand for him to kiss—a respect all elders paid to the speaker for the founder.

Mirrikh kissed the founder's ring. His mouth opened wider to wrap her ring finger in it. Bayrose shivered and pulled back her hand. Being licked by Mirrikh felt like committing incest.

"What are you doing?" she demanded.

"Showing my respect to the new speaker for the founder." He peeked into her eyes with a spark of amusement. He must have mistaken her shiver as pleasure despite her clipped tone. "Any words from the founder?"

Bayrose didn't answer him. "Our enemy has Nickolas M. Poles," she said. "Do you think they'll demand to exchange him for McQuillen?"

"If they do, they're kidding themselves," Mirrikh said. "Nickolas has no one but himself to blame. He trusted the wrong people. In this business, you can't count on your own family. His first cousin

Laura is next in line for the elder's seat."

"So McQuillen threw himself at us for nothing."

"He wouldn't be so desperate to give up his own life if his Siren queen wasn't running out of time. Didn't Prince Vladimir once act equally desperate for her? It's quite ironic that in order to gain back her grace, he actually delivered the poison down her throat."

Bayrose gave him a sharp look.

"He broke your heart, didn't he?" Mirrikh shrugged. "You'll have your revenge. They'll all die. First McQuillen, then the Siren of Sphinxes, and then the Czech prince."

"You'll not touch him."

"Still harbor feelings for the prince," Mirrikh sounded jealous and angry, "after what he did to you?"

"No more than I did to him," she said coldly. "And he'll be sorry when he meets me again."

"He's already sorry that he met you."

Bayrose's eyes narrowed to slits. If she had claws, she'd use them to ruin Mirrikh's vicious, good-looking face.

"His relationship with you cost him his Siren." Mirrikh placed his hand against the small of her back as if seeking to sooth the tension out of her. "He never imagined an innocent-looking girl like you could outsmart him. You were really sweet to him when he was around, weren't you?"

Sidling out of his reach, Bayrose fixed her gaze on McQuillen on the holo-video. He opened his eyes and stared ahead as if he could see through her via the camera lens. There wasn't any human warmth in his steely eyes. Bayrose shuddered, but soon collected herself. She could be that way too. She could be cold, hard steel, and no one could ever hurt her again.

Her world had shifted overnight when Vladimir had deserted her, and when the Siren bitch had blown up *Rose* with her father Immanuel Thorn inside.

She could no longer live a sheltered life full of roses without thorns. She'd been thrown under the wheel of a war machine thanks to the power-hungry Siren. The pain hadn't stopped for even a second since she'd lost her love. It would lessen when she had the Siren's head, literally. It was time for Bayrose to return the favor. Actually she'd had her revenge on the Siren with Blood Tear. She only needed to make sure there was absolutely no antidote for Lucienne.

Her enemy wouldn't last long. It was a wonder Lucienne hadn't died on Bayrose's ancestors' altar in the Temple of Lemuria after taking the ancient poison. The Siren's power preserved its host. Jimmy Lam, the Siren's biological father, had reported back that he'd never seen any power like that. His daughter had brought down the ancient force field and destroyed the temple after he'd escaped. Of course, his daughter had let him flee.

No matter, Blood Tear was the most potent poison, its antidote far beyond the reach of this world. Lucienne wouldn't escape the horrible ending she deserved. After she was gone, would Vladimir return to Bayrose? They had unfinished business. His careless laugh that had once drawn her heart toward him echoed in her ears, and the image of the mischievous light dancing in his hazel eyes swung back and forth before her.

He betrayed her, but she'd betrayed him first.

"You're moody today, my Lady," Mirrikh said, glancing at McQuillen on the holo-video. "Will you actually consider his bargain?"

"We don't negotiate with terrorists," Bayrose said. "We don't make peace with them. It's been our motto since the beginning. I'll dance on the Siren's grave. I'm only thankful she won't go down easily. The ancient poison will burn her inch by inch until she has no skin left. I hear it's already burning her."

"Who would expect a girl who looks so sweet and lovely to harbor such venomous hatred? Hell hath no fury like a woman—"

Bayrose controlled her urge to kick him in the balls. He must have seen the scorching look in her eyes, so he cut out the final word. "However," he said. "I adore your ferocity. The fire in you has finally ignited."

All it had taken was pain and loss, and Lucienne was the source of it all. Bayrose glued her eyes on the injured McQuillen. "How will the Siren react if I send her McQuillen's head in a box?"

"My lovely Rose," Mirrikh leered, "let's find out."

Chapter Eleven

DESERT WRAITH

Valkyrie flew across the Mediterranean Sea, then over the green and brown mountains of Greece.

Lucienne's blood ran colder every second she couldn't get to Kian.

When she arrived at the operation office inside a high-tech corporate building in Athens, Bansi Soni, the Indian computer genius, and his team had set up the network. She had him secretly shipped to Athens to aid her. And now she was sharing Pyon's encrypted communication channels.

"Director Pyon will execute me if he finds out," Bansi Soni said. When he was nervous, his Indian accent became thicker.

"Who hired you?" asked Lucienne. "Who picked you up from the dirt?"

"You," Bansi Soni said.

"Then who do you want to please—me or him?"

"You're nice," said Bansi Soni. "Director Pyon is a formidable man."

"I can be very formidable," Lucienne stared down at Bansi Soni. "I'm sweet to you 'cause you're my friend. I can drop all the niceties if you prefer."

"Don't drop them," Bansi Soni grunted. "I'll do what you want."

Through the satellite Dragonfly, Lucienne watched Sphinxes' force attack the Sealers' thirty outposts and military bases. General

Fairchild and Admiral Enberg led the global assaults.

"Director Pyon is on," Bansi Soni called.

"Stay with him and his team," Lucienne ordered.

The hologram showed the team landing in Libya's desert. They each wore a white robe and black cap outside a mosque, disguised as desert tribal men.

Blocked by the enemy technology, the satellite couldn't see through heated objects inside the thirty-seven acre military compound. The base had a remote-controlled steel door, two razor-wire fences, and anti-tank traps. Outside the last fence, a two-mile radius was laced with landmines.

As soon as the Desert Wraith team deactivated the minefield, a dozen TanTrks—a hybrid tank and attack truck—sped over the dark sand dune carrying Sphinxes' commandos. A minute later, dogs barked from the enemy's fortress. The alarm went off and gunfire broke out. Two enemy militants fell from the watch tower. Missiles and counter-missiles from both sides met in the air like a rain of fire. The militants shot several missiles toward the rows of TanTrks.

One TanTrk flipped in the air and toppled down.

Acid flooded Lucienne's stomach.

The rest of the TanTrks didn't break rank as they pushed toward the enemy's camp, leaving twists of smoke and a storm of sand behind.

Cameron III and two fighters—Hornet I and II—whirled above the war camp but didn't drop missiles or bombs.

Lucienne slammed her fist on her palm, wishing she could join the fight. Thaddeus, standing behind her, appeared equally restless.

"Lucia," Bansi Soni called, "news from Abaddon 5 just came through."

"Let's hear it," Lucienne said.

Bansi Soni switched the channel, and a mission leader reported through the encrypted communication channel, "The chief isn't in Abaddon 5. We suffered a great loss, but we caught the head warden. He swore they never admitted the chief. And Sealers elder Samantha escaped three days ago."

Lucienne turned back to the screen just as Hornet I dropped a chemical bomb. In a blink of an eye, the enemies' stronghold ceased fire and turned into a silent zone.

"Black Coma, isn't it?" Thaddeus said. "Cousin Patrick mentioned it."

Black Coma—designed to knock out any living thing—was a new chemical weapon Lam's Industry developed a few months ago. The Lams would get a huge contract after Pyon's Desert Wraith assault.

"Why didn't Pyon use the sleeping bomb earlier," Thaddeus asked, "so none of our TanTrks would have been hit?"

"Director Pyon must have wanted the enemy militants to be aware of the attack but not have enough time to organize an efficient counterattack," Adam said. "That way, Chief McQuillen would be alert and get ready."

"Black Coma is costly," Lucienne said. "We haven't put it into mass production. Pyon was only testing it. He wouldn't use it to knock out our chief unless he had no choice."

The steel gate to the enemy's compound swung open.

"Ziyi hacked into the terrorists' system!" Bansi Soni pounded the table with a cheer. "I told you that girl is good."

The Desert Wraith team, wearing special masks, passed the electric fencing and sped through the door without any resistance. Gray-haired Pyon was among them.

Lucienne's heart raced erratically as hope and fear took turns running through her mind. The scouts were inside the compound now. Every step they took led them closer to Kian. Until she heard a team leader's brief buzz through Pyon's radio, "Chief McQuillen isn't here."

Lucienne's limbs went icy cold, fear in her every vein. *Where is Kian?* Had she already been too late? A red wave rolled in. *No, not now!* That was why Pyon had refused to let her be in the field. She could jeopardize the men's lives if she went mental. *Fear is only as deep as the mind allows. I'll take ownership of my fear. I'll take ownership—*

Still, she couldn't exorcise the black fear stuck to her bone marrow.

"Cousin?" Thaddeus clutched her shoulders. "Snap out of it, cousin! Kian needs you!"

"He's not there," she panted, her voice muffled in her ears. "Kian isn't there. Where is he?"

"We'll find him," Thaddeus said. "Look at me, cousin!"

Lucienne looked into the warrior's eyes. His loyalty, bravery, and determination lent her the strength she desperately needed.

"The chief is alive," her captain said, "and we'll find him!"

The red wave passed through Lucienne and was gone.

Chapter Twelve

THE SHADOW

HOURS BEFORE THE ATTACK OF

DESERT WRAITH

Bayrose studied a half-conscious Kian McQuillen.

Once he went free, he'd become the Sealers' nightmare again. But he wouldn't become hers, because she'd be his.

"I've had a change of heart," Bayrose said. "I don't want McQuillen's head. I want the Siren bitch's, and I want it before the poison ends her. So I'm giving her back McQuillen in exchange for her head."

"And she'll be so grateful that she'll cut off her own head and hand it to you," said Mirrikh.

"I won't reciprocate your sarcasm," Bayrose said. "If we execute McQuillen, we'll only maim Sphinxes. Its arms will grow back. To win this war, we must cut off the snake's head. Of course, our enemy won't hand us what we request, so I'm going to take everything from them. We'll set McQuillen free, and he'll grant me access to Sphinxes. When Lucienne Lam expires, which won't be long, I need to be there for the harvest."

Mirrikh guffawed.

"You wouldn't laugh if you had a higher vision like the founder and I do," Bayrose said haughtily.

Mirrikh stopped.

"You aren't the only reckless one," Bayrose continued. "I can be bolder. Even *you* said that I have this innocent, sweet look. I once tricked Vladimir. I don't mind turning it on Kian McQuillen too."

"McQuillen's heart is the coldest, hardest rock, and completely black. I doubt anyone could touch him except his Siren queen. Besides, all of Sphinxes is calling for your blood. They've been out hunting you as we speak. Should I remind you that you poisoned their Siren, or do you prefer they do it if they can catch you?"

"I'll deny it," Bayrose said. "I'll convince them I'm also the victim of the founder and my late father. After I rescue McQuillen, he'll support me. Everything is perception, and perception changes. Sphinxes will view me as the hero who saved their chief. I'll worm my way into their hearts before Lucienne dies."

"So this isn't an impulsive whim. You want to turn fantasy into reality."

Bayrose gave him a scorching look. "McQuillen delivered himself to our door. Will we ever find a better opportunity?"

"You might fool them with your innocent, pretty looks and a plausible story," Mirrikh said, "but what makes you think Sphinxes— an emerging nation with battle-hardened warriors—will follow the lead of a sixteen-year-old girl?"

Bayrose's eyes burned with dark rage. "The Siren is only one year older than me. I'm no less than her. Her background isn't that different from mine. She inherited the Siren's seat just as I inherited the elder's."

"She fought through fire and blood and defeated twelve bright boy candidates who had a river of powerful supporters and resources, to reach the Siren's crown when she was only eight years old. At the time, she had only Kian McQuillen."

"Do you realize the consequences of underestimating and humiliating me, Mirrikh Schwartz?"

"I'm reasoning with you because I care about you." He'd once told her that she was the only person on this planet whom he cared about and she believed him.

"Then you'll watch my back when I'm gone."

"Haven't I always looked out for you?" He sent her a sidelong, amused glance before turning serious. "You're now the speaker. Will the founder let you take such a risk?"

"The founder is all about hunting down the Siren race."

"How does he sound?"

"You shouldn't ask, Mirrikh," Bayrose said, not looking at him. "You know the rule. It's dangerous to even speak of it. The founder has a way of knowing everything."

"My apologies," Mirrikh said. Bayrose could feel he stiffened as he looked around.

They stood silently, then Mirrikh said, "If you do this, you're on your own."

"I'm ready."

"A sheep thinks she can take down wolves."

"I'm not a sheep!" said Bayrose. "I'm not the little girl you used to play with. You need to accept that and adjust your perception of me!"

"Fine, you'll lead the wolves and guide them with wisdom," Mirrikh said with a smirk. "You look lovely and fragile, which makes any man want to protect you. Sphinxes is full of alpha males. Your plan can work."

For a fleeting second, Bayrose sensed that Mirrikh had his own agenda. But then he'd always had an agenda. "It'll work. It must work," she said.

She had the Shadow.

Blood Tear, Shadow, and Devourer were the three gifts from an angel. Her ancestors chronicled the encounter with the angel, whose gifts verified that the bloodline Bayrose inherited was the chosen one— only the Sirens hijacked their birthright.

The Scroll of the Prophecy—known to the Sirens as the last scroll—also confirmed the truth of the secret history. The Sirens were usurpers from the beginning. Bayrose must correct the error and take back what was rightfully hers.

Her line had been carefully preserved. After one of her founder ancestors had been assassinated nine centuries ago, her family had created the rank of twelve elders, but unknown to all, one of the elders—the speaker was actually the founder.

Bayrose Thorn was now the new founder of the Sealers.

Even Mirrikh, her closest ally, had no idea of the secret structure of the Sealers, nor did he know about the Shadow.

The Shadow wasn't from Earth. The angel hadn't told her ancestors of its origin. It had the appearance of a triangular leaf, and on each side overlapped two smaller triangles. Under a microscope, one could see intricate runes all over the delicate leaf. No one could decode the runes. All her ancestors knew was that the Shadow was the shield. It safeguarded the mind of its host from any supernatural force.

But there was a cost. The Shadow would eventually consume its host. No mortal could resist its will. In the end, the carrier would even have a shadowy personality. Bayrose wasn't too concerned about that. She had no sunshine left in her since the day Vladimir had left. The day the Siren's forces had reduced her daddy to scattered ashes at the bottom of the Polynesian sea.

Right after McQuillen's captivity, Bayrose had formed a perfect plan—she'd go deep undercover in the enemy's camp, just as Prince Vladimir had done to hers.

How would he react when he saw her again? Her heart hurt so much at picturing him. With the Shadow in her, she'd be safe in guarding her mind, and probably her heart.

When the leaf-like Shadow had first touched her tongue, it had turned into a hovering, dark mist before vanishing inside her. Then it had spread like a web until it had reached every cell of hers and taken residency. She'd crouched at the corner of room, alone and silent and sweating, until the panic attack had passed.

But when she'd risen to her feet, she'd never felt more powerful and guarded. The Shadow was the impenetrable wall around her, and cocooned inside, she was safe from the whole world except the Shadow itself.

Mirrikh murmured something beside her. She turned to him, a

coldness that she hadn't had before coating her eyes.

"I have a better plan," Mirrikh said, "which doesn't involve risking you."

For a cunning second, she knew his intention. Was it because of the Shadow? Had it already made her sharper? "Does it involve a massacre?" she asked.

"You've become razor-sharp, Rose," he said, and Bayrose detected a trace of nostalgia in his voice. "The sweetest little girl I played with has grown up overnight, and now she wants to take over the world."

"What's your game, Mirrikh?" she asked impatiently.

"I believe you know more of Devourer than I do since you're now the speaker."

Bayrose managed to stand very still. Was he baiting her? "What do you know about it?"

Mirrikh regarded her reaction. "All elders know we have this top-secret, ancient weapon that can vaporize the world's population in mere seconds."

Bayrose gave a one-shoulder shrug to make the matter lighter. "So?"

"It will be a magnificent sight when we unleash it," Mirrikh said, his eyes flashing a feverish light.

"It will be hell on earth."

"We should have brought hell on earth a long time ago," Mirrikh said, biting his fingernails. "Why didn't the founder use it in Sphinxes before the Siren's forces struck us in Polynesia? Have you ever wondered about that?"

She'd lost her father in that war. She didn't understand either why he hadn't used Devourer to completely vanquish their ancient enemy. Why had father gone through that elaborate scheme to poison the Siren at the cost of his own life? When he'd sunk with *Rose*, Mother had been nowhere near. Bayrose knew that Mom had always been the one who called the shots. So, had Mother been behind all this? Had she let her husband die and poisoned the Siren, but had refused to deploy Devourer?

Was Mother still in control of the Sealers despite Bayrose being founder now? Why hadn't Bayrose had the access code to Devourer? She must thoroughly search father's digital safety box to find the rest of the secrets he'd left her. She'd do it tonight. It would be a nightmare if Devourer fell into the wrong hands, in particular Mirrikh's.

"Devourer is our last line of defense," Bayrose drawled. "The founder won't use it unless our very survival is under threat."

"Our survival has been under threat since the rising of the Siren girl and Sphinxes."

"Unleashing Devourer is not for us to decide," Bayrose snapped. "And the Polynesian war was but a small sacrifice." *Was it really?*

Mirrikh turned to her with a piercing look. Bayrose didn't flinch, even though her heart stumbled. Had she let slip the truth? She couldn't afford to let Mirrikh or anyone suspect her true role.

"I've been wondering," he said in a calculating voice, "if the founder survived in Polynesia, or if the new founder is a he or she." His gaze could have bored a hole in her face. "Only you know, Rose. You're the only one who has heard his or her voice, or maybe even met the founder in person."

He was baiting her, but she saw through him. Somehow she had a confidence she'd never possessed before. Mirrikh could no longer manipulate or outmaneuver her. No one could. The Shadow had taken root in her. "Mirrikh, stop this!" she cut in with a note of warning. "Do not test me again."

"My apologies," he said. "But Rose, you haven't realized how important your role is as the speaker for the founder. You'll be his counsel. You'll gain more influence and experience in time. When the day comes, will you speak to the founder for all the elders, including me?"

"Of course I will. What is your request?"

"Set the Devourer on Sphinxes and erase the plague from this already polluted planet. We're tired of lurking in the shadows with secret handshakes. We're the new generation who deserve the limelight. Let the world see us as we truly are. All shall fear us!"

"We'll rid the world of the plague," Bayrose said, "but why destroy Sphinxes when we have an opportunity to add it as our extra resources? I'm going there to make it happen. Plus, we'll have to consider innocent people on that island before resorting to ultimate violence."

"You mean Prince Vladimir?"

"Prince Vladimir is everything but innocent." Bayrose kept her emotions in check. "And he means nothing to me. But as I said, I'm not a butcher."

"What if you can't win Sphinxes?"

"Then I'll talk the founder into unleashing Devourer onto that island."

"What about the innocent ones you mentioned earlier?"

Bayrose whipped around toward Mirrikh. "Are you really enjoying pushing my buttons?"

Mirrikh chuckled. "No, Rose, no. I just want you to see that you and I are more alike than you realize."

She disagreed. But one thing she knew—she was no longer the sweet Rose. And the Shadow had set her on the path of no return.

Carrying a paper cup of coffee and a pastry on a paper plate, Bayrose stepped through the door to Kian McQuillen's cell.

"Leave us," she told the guards. One of them held the steel door.

"My lady—" a leading guard said nervously.

"Don't make me repeat myself," Bayrose said, her stern voice at odds with her looks. It was as if a sweet child forced herself to be unfriendly.

"Yes, Lady Thorn." The guards withdrew.

Bayrose closed the steel door behind her and breathed out. She knew the guards weren't far off. "Light," she ordered.

An artificial light filled the room.

Still chained to the wall, McQuillen sat despite his injuries.

Is this man truly made of steel? Bayrose stood unmoved beside the door for a full minute as her mind went blank. She had no clue what to do next. Then she remembered the coffee in her hand. She walked toward Kian McQuillen, her hand shaking slightly, and the coffee swayed. Bayrose stopped, took a deep breath, and steadied the tray in her hands.

She bent down, put the food and drink before the man, and stepped back.

He didn't spare a glance at the coffee, but she knew how much he needed it. The jailers hadn't fed him for two days. He stared at her with a blank expression. With the Shadow in her, Bayrose could sense the burning lava beneath his expressionless mask. He wanted to tear her apart for the poison she'd helped deliver to his Siren.

But Bayrose refused to obey her instinct to recoil from him. She squatted in front of him and held his stare. "I'm Bayrose Thorn," she said softly and sadly. "I'm sorry they tortured you. I just arrived."

Lying was so easy now with the Shadow in her.

McQuillen picked up the coffee. Involuntarily Bayrose leaned back to give him a wide berth. The coffee was room temperature. If he threw it at her, it wouldn't hurt her physically, but it might hurt her feelings.

McQuillen took a big swig of the coffee, not wanting to waste it on her, then finished the rest in one gulp. He crumpled the empty cup and tossed it aside, not at her.

Guess he's still a gentleman, even though he wants to kill me. Bayrose tried not to flinch under his assessment. He exuded an aura of command and formidability, even chained in a dungeon.

"Mr. McQuillen," she said, her chin cocking toward the corner of the ceiling, "I've disabled the cameras."

McQuillen didn't respond, but narrowed his eyes on her with that unnerving look of his. Once again, she wanted to run away from him, but then a courage she hadn't known came from the pit of her belly. She would handle a legend like him. She was a ruler, born and tailored to inherit an ancient kingdom—a powerful shadow government on earth.

"We don't have much time." She kept going, afraid if she stopped, she'd lose her nerve. She gestured at the pastry in front of him. "It was supposed to be your last meal. They'll execute you in two hours. You're too dangerous to be kept alive." She saw a query in his eyes. For the first time, he was responsive to her. "That's why they didn't put you in Abaddon 5."

"Is Samantha in Abaddon 5?" McQuillen asked, his hard eyes still locked on her.

He's trying to detect my lie. "Was," she said. "She escaped."

"How?" he demanded, his voice rough and cold.

Bayrose had arranged it as instructed. She'd left a crack for Samantha to get away. She shook her head. "We don't know. Samantha is a well-connected elder. She has people everywhere. Her secret agents inside the prison must have aided her. The founder isn't pleased. Abaddon 5 is under tight investigation."

A mosaic of emotions flashed by McQuillen's eyes, but Bayrose had caught them. Sphinxes' chief was beyond bitter for missing an "appointment" with the woman he'd come for. He'd thrown himself at his enemy for nothing. He'd failed his Siren queen. His rage was terrible, but she wasn't as afraid of him as before. She had her own power. She felt joy at reading his emotions. She was certain now the Shadow didn't just shield her. It also gave her perspective.

She'd further crush McQuillen's hope. She hadn't been this vindictive, but she'd learned from the master—Prince Vladimir. His devotion to his Siren made him cruel to her, and thus Bayrose became cruel herself. They'd made her this way.

"Samantha went to Abaddon 5 voluntarily," Bayrose said. "No one can find her if she doesn't want to be found. I heard that it once took seven years for all of the elders, putting all their resources together, to just get the wind of her. That was before I was born." *So good luck, Mr. McQuillen. Your Siren doesn't even have a month.* The Shadow concealed her delight. "I'm very sorry, Mr. McQuillen." She controlled the urge to tell him that there was no antidote to the poisoned Nexus Tear on earth or in heavens. But she bit her tongue. It wouldn't help her plan if she snuffed out his last, doomed-to-fail hope.

For a fleeting second, she felt his broken spirit. Kian McQuillen wasn't untouchable after all. Lucienne Lam was his weakness. If Bayrose ever needed to strike him, she knew where to hit. However, he wasn't her target.

"What do you want, Miss Thorn?" he asked, his eyes harder than anything she'd seen. "Why did you come to bring me my last meal and tell me all this?"

"I must let you know it wasn't me who poisoned Lucienne," Bayrose said.

"Don't kid yourself," McQuillen said. "You had a red hand in poisoning my queen. You're *not* innocent."

"I didn't mislead Prince Vladimir intentionally," Bayrose said, holding back tears. "I even let him inject a liquid bomb in me to show that I was truthful to him before he went to extricate Nexus Tear. He wanted it so badly, and all I wanted was to make him happy." She paused to control her emotion. "Lucienne's father returned later and told the elders he poisoned his own daughter. The virus was added an hour before her arrival. I had no idea. I've grieved for her, for Prince Vladimir, for my father ever since. I grieve that the war cost good people on both sides. And I don't want the war to continue."

As Vladimir's name poured out of her tongue, an unexpected agony slammed into her. His cocky grin flashed by her eyes. *I still love him, despite his betrayal. I even love his flaws.* The realization brought her more misery, and she allowed the pain to sink in her eyes. She knew that McQuillen saw it. Being raw, real, and vulnerable was the best move in front of an alpha male. "The founder used my feelings for Prince Vladimir, and unknowingly I became a pawn in his scheme." Anger blazed from her eyes, and she tried not to be bothered by how closely McQuillen scrutinized her.

"You were a willing pawn since Lucienne is your rival for Blazek's affection," he said.

"I didn't realize that Lucienne was even in the picture," Bayrose said, and the distress couldn't be plainer in her eyes. "Prince Vladimir and I were—close. He was always tender and loving toward me. I pieced everything together only after he was gone and never returned. Even if I was aware that Lucienne was Prince Vladimir's—" she swallowed, "—true love, I wouldn't have won him over by hurting her. It isn't in my nature to harm people. And it wouldn't have worked anyway. I'm sixteen, but I am not that foolish." Sorrow passed over her face. "I'm terribly sorry that Lucienne is also a victim. If the founder and my father could have realized that no one would have gained from this war, then—"

"Your apology means nothing while Lucienne suffers from the poison," McQuillen said.

"I wish I was the one being poisoned instead of her," Bayrose said. *No, of course I don't wish that.* If she could, she'd shove the Blood Tear down the Siren's throat herself. Because of Lucienne, Bayrose had taken in the Shadow. There was no antidote for that either.

"It doesn't change a thing." Kian McQuillen remained untouched. "It doesn't matter if I believe that you're innocent or not. I'll be dead in the next hour."

"It matters to me very much," she said, "because I'm going to help you escape." She caught a fleeting spark in McQuillen's steely eyes before it vanished. She bet he'd give everything to see his Siren queen again, yet he didn't show a jot of desperation.

"I can't give Lucienne the antidote. I don't know if anyone has it," she said. "But I can give you back to her."

"Just like that?"

"I want something in return," she said. Only the naïve believed people did good deeds without an agenda, and McQuillen was the opposite of naïve. She must give her enemy a plausible intention. "If I give you back your freedom, you'll guarantee mine. I want no part in this war, but I'm an elder's only heir. I haven't been able to escape this horror since I was born. All my life I've been living inside a golden cage. Now I've become speaker for the founder. I'm to be put in a more decorated cage."

"You think I'm your chance of getting out of the cage?"

"I intend to go with you to Sphinxes."

"Don't you fear you might wind up in another kind of cage—a

crude one?"

"At least it won't be the one I've been trapped in for sixteen years and maybe forever," Bayrose said fiercely. "At least there'll be a change of scenery. At least the founder can't find me there." She let out a breath and slowed the rhythm of her speech. "I haven't had a chance to see the outside world and live a life I want. This is my only opening to be free of war and politics." She saw something flash beneath McQuillen's eyes. Pity? She was close to Lucienne's age. Did McQuillen think of Lucienne when looking at Bayrose? Pity or not, she must evoke this alpha male's urge to protect the weak.

"And I'm not naïve," she continued, giving McQuillen the impression that she was exactly that. "The war and the betrayal have changed me, but somehow I believe I can trust you a little more than the others. You sacrificed yourself for Lucienne. When I offered you an opportunity to get out of here, you didn't jump to make promises. Instead, you put a fearful picture in my head to warn me." She bit her lip. "So, I believe I can trust your word. And I want your word that you'll protect me if I get you out of here. I know Samantha well. I'll help you track her down and find the Scroll of the Prophecy for your Siren."

She knew that the last scroll was the lifeline to a drowning McQuillen.

"You'll have my protection if you never intended to poison my queen," McQuillen said. "You'll be treated well in Sphinxes as an honored guest. You'll have freedom."

"I'm going to steal a warplane." Bayrose swallowed back her hot tears after she let McQuillen see them sparkling on her lashes. "Do you know how to fly one?"

She would get him a jet without enough fuel.

The escape must be dramatic enough to feel real.

Chapter Thirteen

ATHENS

Ice in her veins, heart in her throat, Lucienne heard Director Pyon order one of his men through the radio, "Revive a guard!" Then there were background noises. "Inject him with the new drugs!" Curses, a repeated pumping sound on a chest, and a loud gasp. Then a team leader demanded answers from a jihadist jailer who had regained consciousness. Amid the chaos, Pyon shouted into his encrypted phone, "Miss Wen, activate the second tracer in Chief McQuillen, now!"

A second tracer. That was Pyon's secret weapon. If Lucienne had known, she'd have demanded he activate it and gone after Kian the next second instead of giving Pyon three days. The director must have threatened Ziyi not to inform her, and lately her friend had been terrified of setting off Lucienne's insanity.

Her people did what they had to do to protect her from harming herself and others. Their good intentions only hurt her more than they could know. Her friends and warriors no longer trusted her. They no longer relied on her. She wondered if they also feared her, especially after she'd put a knife in her own boyfriend's chest.

Self-pity was a mind-killer, a disease, like fear. And she banished it out of her head. Pyon had made the right call. He'd waited until it was absolutely necessary to activate the second tracer. The Sealers had removed the first one, but hadn't expected the second, dormant one in Sphinxes' chief. The new tracer was also one of the Lam Industry's new inventions. Because Pyon hadn't trusted her on this mission, they still had a chance to find their chief.

"Lucia," Bansi Soni called, "Ziyi just called Director Pyon's private line."

"Put it through," Lucienne said.

Ziyi sounded edgy on the speaker. "The chief is in Athens, sir. He's thirty miles from Lucia and her team. Should I inform her?"

"Absolutely not!" Pyon yelled.

"The chief is under fire," the girl said. "The Greeks have blocked every mountain road and waterway in and out of Athens. Obviously they know the chief is in their territory. But I thought the Greeks were our ally."

Dark fury leapt from Lucienne. Just as Schmidt had bragged in the Sealers' temple, the Brotherhood was the governing force behind many countries. Sphinxes had cut only a few branches of the ancient Sealers' tree.

Pyon cursed.

"Director," Ziyi said, "your team might be too late to reach the chief. If Lucia loses him, she'll be more than devastated. She'll never recover. I can get Adam and Thaddeus to lead the men to—"

"Her guards won't lie to her under any circumstance," said Pyon. "They've all sworn an oath to her. If they know, she'll know. So under no circumstances will you involve the Siren and send her into a war zone! Am I clear?"

"Yes, sir," Ziyi said. "But I'm really worried."

"I'm sending Greek agents from other locations. We'll get there in time." Pyon cut off Ziyi and ended the call. His radio buzzed the next second. Lucienne could hear him panting from running. "Set Hornets on course to Athens," he ordered. "Get Chameleon III down now!"

Lucienne turned to her team. "Let's go get our chief."

On the satellite screen, orange flame and black smoke erupted in the sky and extended miles into the desert.

Director Pyon had allowed the Hornet jets to bomb the Sealers terrorist base in Libya before leaving for Athens.

Chapter Fourteen

SNIPERS IN PLAKA

Safe house V7 was in Plaka, the oldest section of Athens.

Lucienne and her warriors hurried on a pebbled, granite road. Most of the streets were closed to automobile traffic. Sunlight shimmered on ivy vines and pink blossoms over the walls along the alleys.

The team was nearly two dozen men and women dressed like tourists, except for the three agents from the Greece op. One of them took the role of tour guide, the second walked at the front of the group, and the third brought up the rear.

The members wore bulletproof vests and carried at least two guns each inside their jackets. Lucienne was placed in the middle. Adam and Thaddeus were on either side of her.

The tour guide had a small flag in his hand and a whistle around his neck. "Plaka is a village within a city," he narrated. His English was perfect with only a slight Greek accent. "This favorite neighborhood is mainly residential with a deep archaeological past." He led the group to push through the crowd in the square. Two street musicians occupied each side of the plaza. A Hungarian played accordion and a Russian the violin.

"Try not to look dangerous," the tour agent whispered. "Look casual and show interest in what I'm saying."

The task force relaxed their muscles, yet their eyes remained sharp.

Soon, the group left the square and the crowd behind, rushing toward the street of clustered shops and cafés. Their façades were a mélange of yellow, red, and dark scarlet.

"Around the east corner," the guide said, "we'll see a painting shop."

That was where safe house V7 was located.

The group kept the same pace as they rounded the corner.

Lucienne could hear the beating of thunder in her chest. She'd have Kian back in a few minutes. But instead of feeling joy, a stream of anxiety flooded her stomach. Her acute senses kicked in. Something didn't add up. Ziyi had said that Kian had been under fire. Even if Greek authorities blocked the news of the most recent gunfire, this street still seemed unnaturally quiet.

A jewelry store occupied the northeast corner in an L-shape. There wasn't a single customer inside. A clerk in a suit behind the counter stared down at the glass cabinet which displayed diamond rings. He looked too stiff for a salesman. Next to the jewelry store was a flower shop. A flower girl wearing an apron stood out front. Her wet gloves had dirt on them. The pretty girl was close to Lucienne's age. She smiled at the tour group, but it somehow felt phony to Lucienne.

Something was off. Or was she being paranoid? Lucienne could no longer trust her gut feelings with the poisoned power in her.

"Wood carvings are Greece's—" The tour guide dropped to the ground. A pool of blood formed under his head, soaking up his tour guide's cap.

The flower girl had disappeared into the shop.

Pain burst from Lucienne's chest.

With her hyperawareness, she'd instinctively dodged, so that the bullet meant for her head from a sniper had eaten into the wall behind her. But the next bullet had found her chest. Many of her men had been hit too, though the impact hadn't pinned them down. Her excellent warriors instantly fired back into the flower shop and some roofs. Flowers, glass, concrete and sprinters flew in the air amid muffled gunfire. Lucienne's team also carried guns with silencers. The plan had been to find their chief and quietly retrieve him.

And they'd entered an ambush.

Two guns appeared in Lucienne's hands—one her standard

Armatix gun and the other from Marloes. She kept it to remember her former captain. Thaddeus and one of her guards shoved her back toward the safer alley. Lucienne shrugged free of them and snarled, "Stop!" She fired at a roof where a sniper hadn't been before. Her bullet and Thaddeus' found the sniper at the same time and dropped him.

Adam, a former sniper himself, located the other one on a sloped roof and gunned him down in two blasts.

Other shops on the streets slammed shut their doors.

Without breaking a sweat, Lucienne swept her Armatix toward the flower shop and shot a Sealer agent in the forehead the moment he poked it above a windowsill.

Covered by his marine friend, Thaddeus threw himself over the counter and into the flower shop, his guns in both hands finding three more targets. One of them—a twenty-something Greek cop—looked shocked at the big Asian man's speed when he tumbled, his machine gun smacking the ground.

Within minutes, the shootout quieted down.

"Clear!" Adam called.

Lucienne stepped into the tattered shop. Nine bodies were scattered amid broken anemone flowers of pink, purple and yellow. The flower girl slumped against a stool that displayed pots of daffodils and bougainvillea, dead, a gun with a long silencer still clutched in her gloved hand.

The civilians in the other shops had been cooperating with the Sealers' agents to make it look like a regular shopping day. How could her enemy know that Lucienne's group wasn't made up of tourists? A thought clicked: they'd been expecting her team. That, and her fine warriors' strides were different from the civilians'. Every member had been handpicked by Kian and Pyon, and most of them were taller than her. Their height was a requirement. Kian wanted her men to be able to shield her.

The march of a group of men and women over six-feet-four would certainly draw attention. They'd all been in such a hurry to get to their chief that they hadn't thought of the impression they'd make walking among regular folks.

Lucienne inserted a hand into her jacket, yanked out the bullet that cut into her vest, and tossed it to the ground.

"Are you hurt, cousin?" Thaddeus asked, concern ringing in his voice.

"Siren?" Adam and the rest of the warriors looked equally worried.

"I'm fine," Lucienne said. "Go get the chief."

Their grim faces mirrored her worst fear: Kian might have been re-captured, or—

Lucienne refused to think the worst.

The scouts sprang forward, their guns thrust in front of them. The rest of the team fell into formation again with Lucienne squarely in the center. Their weapons ready, they raced along the alley. Four of the warriors carried their lost members—a marine and the dead Greek agent.

The scouts secured the painting shop. Lucienne stepped through the door, heart sinking at the sight of bullet-ridden walls and bloody corpses. Two of them were her field agents. One was a shop owner. The other six bodies were strangers, probably the Sealers agents.

A few paintings were trampled on the floor, and some barely hung on the walls in broken frames. A wood-carved, full-sized statue of Athena in battle armor was beheaded by bullets.

Two scouts came down from the upstairs with the same expression of dismay.

A second rescue had failed.

As dread, like cold stone, settled in Lucienne's stomach, a red wave started rolling toward her. *No, no, no! Not now.* She dug her fingernails into her palms and let the pain orient her. *No news is good news. Kian is alive.* She told herself again and again. *So snap out of it!*

She pulled out her encrypted phone and dialed Sphinxes' headquarters.

"Lucia?" Ziyi picked up immediately. "Pyon went berserk when he learned you went for the chief. Bansi Soni is afraid of getting court martialed. He keeps saying he's dead."

"Kian isn't in V7," Lucienne said. "Find him." She put the phone on speaker so her men could listen too.

"Monastiraki flea market." Ziyi's voice came back after a few seconds. "Our local agents are overpowered. No one can come to aid you or the chief."

Many lives had been lost. Lucienne swallowed her grief.

"The flea market isn't far," a surviving Greek agent said. "I know a shortcut."

"Keep your line open, Ziyi," Lucienne said. "I'm going for the chief." And she disconnected her phone.

The team followed the Greek agent through several zigzag turns into different alleys. The sun was overly bright. Vines and blossoms climbed down from packed balconies amid a blend of orange and lemon-colored houses. Shooting broke out somewhere nearby. The fight was in the open now.

The team raced toward the gunfire and wound up in an area of fancy restaurants. The courtyard smelled of coffee, milk pie, smoked pork, and gunpowder. The patrons on the patios rose and looked around in alarm, their coffee and feta cheese and bread forgotten.

A group of Greek policemen emerged, shooting at the group without warning, turning Plaka, the sunniest Greek neighborhood, into a war zone. Lucienne's warriors immediately retaliated. The remaining patrons fled, a few of them caught in the curtain of fire coming mostly from the police.

Lucienne's phone vibrated. She picked it up. Her other hand held her gun tightly.

"Every alley is swarming with hostile troops," Ziyi said in panic. "Both Chief and you are surrounded. You need to hide until Director Pyon's team can get to you. They're still in the air."

Right before Lucienne's team gunned down the last of the police, the Sealers' reinforcements arrived. Shouts, gunfire blasts, and fleeing tourists were everywhere.

Thaddeus yelped in pain and cursed profusely. Blood streamed from his temple.

"Take out the damn snipers, man!" Adam called. He shielded Lucienne as they dashed toward the entry of an Indian restaurant, its protruding doorway providing a natural shelter.

"Thaddeus!" Lucienne called over her shoulder.

"A graze," Thaddeus called back, taking cover.

"Lucia!" Ziyi's voice sounded shaky on the phone.

"Can't talk now." Lucienne shut the phone, waited a second, and moved the phone's black screen out of the alcove, trying to find the snipers' positions.

Adam pulled her back. "I'll take care of the snipers."

Lucienne gave him a glare. "I'm a member of the team."

"And I'm in charge of it and your safety," Adam said. "Please, Siren."

Another horde of Sealers' special forces poured into the street, blocking both ends and cutting off any escape routes. They shouted through speakers in both Greek and English for Lucienne's team to surrender.

They're enjoying the hunt, thought Lucienne. *They believe they're in control with their three-dimensional advantage.*

"Get in the restaurants!" Adam shouted.

Lucienne darted an uncertain glance at her captain. He was planning for the team to use the restaurants as shelter, then to exit through the back door and out of the alley. But the snipers would see their flight, and every street was infested with the Sealer soldiers. Retreating into the restaurants was only buying time. It wouldn't improve their situation.

But it seemed the only option.

The enemy's task force closed in, pushing hard. The exchange of fire increased. Their snipers were picking off Lucienne's men one by one.

Anxiety churned in Lucienne's stomach. Every minute, she would lose more men, and Kian could be lost to her. It was time to summon Forbidden Glory even though she promised Pyon not to use it.

And there was one big problem: Forbidden Glory would bring out the red rage. When she lost control, she might hurt her own team. She could be more dangerous to her men than the enemy's force could ever be.

"Thaddeus!" Lucienne called out, gesturing frantically.

Thaddeus turned to her from the entrance of a café opposite her and Adam. He gave her a nod, understanding what she wanted him to do—he must knock her out cold at the very moment she put down the enemy's force. One mistake could cost the entire team.

Before Thaddeus darted toward Lucienne, a scar-faced marine shouted, pointing at a sniper, "Thaddeus, cover me!" and dashed out of his hideout from behind a table. Metal tore into the thick planks he used to shield his head. The marine turned his machine gun toward one end of the street, then the other. The enemy's force still pushed forward, their gunfire cutting him down. Lucienne's team returned fire, the furious, flying bullets dropping a line of enemy soldiers.

Thaddeus moved, incredibly fast, to a position where he could see the sniper on the roof. One bullet from his gun, and the marksman's gunfire ceased. A shot from the second sniper hit him in the leg. Thaddeus fell with profane curses and immediately rolled behind a boulder.

The remaining sniper dropped another marine, then a Greek agent.

Lucienne flung her hands forward, calling for her power.

"Lucia, wait!" Thaddeus shouted, struggling to rise from behind the boulder on his wounded leg.

The second sniper tumbled from the roof, hitting the sharp fence below with a sickening sound. At the same time, the enemies from both ends of the street dropped in heaps.

Sphinxes' reinforcements had arrived! Lucienne's remaining warriors joined the slaughter, their bullets ripping through the air.

Blood flowed along the granite path.

At one end of the street, Finley appeared with a high-powered machine gun in his hand. Behind him was his team of two dozen men and women in Greek police uniforms.

"Siren." Finley saluted as he marched toward her.

She'd made Kian cast Finley out of Sphinxes for ganging up on Vladimir. How did he find her in Plaka so quickly?

"I came from Tibet," Finley said before she asked.

What had Finley been doing in Tibet? Lucienne immediately narrowed her eyes. Had he gone to finish off Vladimir since the Czech prince was out of Sphinxes' shelter?

"I've sworn not to touch Blazek," said Finley. He dropped his gaze before meeting her icy stare again. "When I heard of chief's capture, I came up with a plan of my own. I intended to exchange Blazek for the chief. I'm sorry, but Blazek would find a way out even if I traded him. Everyone knows the new elder girl has a thing for him."

Lucienne glared harder at Finley. "He fended you off, didn't he?"

"We didn't get to see him," Finley said. "The Lama sent his monk warriors to Lhasa when we landed. They knew I was coming. They knew my plan." He pressed his palms together before his chest in a gesture of respect. "Saint Lama is an oracle. His disciples passed on his message. He said Prince Vladimir would be useless in this crisis, and he told me where to find the chief. He also said you would need urgent assistance."

"The Lama?" Lucienne said, pondering.

"He said I'd find you here," Finley said. "Everything happened exactly as he said. Now we must go toward the archaeological site—Hadrian's Library—to meet the chief."

"Lead the way," Lucienne said.

Sporadic discharge broke out in nearby streets. Finley led the group up an alley of endless stairs that had graffiti on the walls on each side.

Three figures appeared at the top of the stairs.

Lucienne raised her weapon, then immediately lowered it, as did her warriors.

A bloodied Kian McQuillen led two teenage girls down flights of stairs. The girls were Bayrose and Violet.

"Kian!" Joy bursting inside her chest, Lucienne raced up the stairs to him.

Her protector's hard eyes warmed and brightened at the sight of her, but the warmth was gone the next second, replaced by blinding rage. "Who brought the Siren out for a street fight?" Gritting his teeth, he scanned the area for threats. The next he screamed.

He raised his gun, fired, and raced to reach Lucienne, but he was too late.

Lucienne turned her head, hearing the sound of a bullet ripping through the air. Her power responded instantly. She flung her hand forward to deflect it, but a hard body had thrown her out of the path of the bullet. Finley dropped onto the stone stairs, a pool of blood under his head.

"No!" Lucienne cried. Her power would have guaranteed her survival by warding off the bullet. But Finley hadn't known. Neither had Kian or her men. Even if they had known, they'd still have taken the hit for her. They'd have left no chance. How could she blame them for their loyalty?

A handgun was in Lucienne's hand. She joined her warriors and angrily fired several blasts toward a balcony window, where the shot had come from. The window shattered, and the assassin went down.

Lucienne crouched beside Finley. *They keep dying for me, and I can't stop it.*

Finley blinked vacantly. He was still alive. The kill shot hit the side of his head. "The Lama warned me—" he said.

"Shush. Stay with me." Lucienne shrugged off her jacket and pressed it against the bullet hole to stop any further bleeding. "We'll get you out of here." She wished her power could heal him, but it only knew how to kill. "You'll live. You must, soldier!"

"Get the Siren out of here!" Kian ordered the men while staring at Finley. His gaze soon returned to Lucienne to see if she was hurt. Relieved, yet still in grief, he barked at the men, "Now!"

"He's still alive!" Lucienne refused to leave Finley. "Take him to the nearest hospital. When he stabilizes, we transfer him to Sphinxes."

Adam and her wounded cousin half dragged and half carried her away from the fallen Finley. A marine medic took over and tended to him.

Fierce gunfire rose again. The Sealers' forces chased the Sphinxes' chief down here, but then backed off. Five helicopters zoomed in, allowing SWAT on board to open fire at the enemy militias.

Chameleon III, hovering above Plaka, sent rockets amid the remaining Sealers.

Inside Valkyrie, a heavily bandaged Kian McQuillen leaned against the headboard of a make-shift bed in a relatively private section in the rear of the jet. He'd lost weight during his captivity. The enemy's harsh treatment had added more hard lines to his face, yet he remained ruggedly handsome.

Lucienne lounged on a coach beside him.

"I should court martial your men for risking you," he said. "Time to set an example."

"Then you should court martial yourself for doing something so stupid."

"Stupid?" Kian narrowed his eyes. "Look who you're talking to."

"And look who's talking to you."

They glared at each other until Kian shook his head with a resigned look, his hard-edged face softening. But hers hadn't. "Next time you decide to make a useless sacrifice, think twice. Think what kind of danger you put me in. Think what I'll do to get you back."

"I'm sorry for what I put you through, kid," he said.

That was almost the first time he'd ever apologized, so she decided to cut him some slack. "I'm only glad I got you back," she said, blinking back tears. She'd been on the brink of losing him forever. Her gaze fell on his bandaged hand. He had two broken fingers. The medic said that he also had a broken rib.

The Sealers who had tortured Kian would pay for this, Lucienne vowed. Many of his tormentors had died when the Hornet fighters blasted their base to rubble. But Mirrikh Schwartz, the new elder, had survived and chased her chief to their safe house in Athens and gunned down many of her agents. She'd find him. And she'd break him until he could no longer scream.

Kian's rough palm wiped away tears from Lucienne's cheeks. Then he pulled out a silk handkerchief from the inner pocket of his jacket. He'd kept it for her while being held captive. He'd hoped to return to her. That brought another curtain of tears to her eyes. She dabbed them with the handkerchief and sniffed.

"Let's go over again," she said. He'd brought Bayrose, the Sealers' new elder, back with him, and Violet, whom Vladimir had irresponsibly left behind with the Sealers.

"I made a deal with Bayrose Thorn," Kian said. "She was fed up with her life in the Sealers. She wants freedom."

"As the deal went, she helped you break out of a *fortified* military base."

"She stole a warplane, but it didn't have enough fuel. We had to land in Athens."

"And Mirrikh Schwartz and his elite guards followed you all the way to the safe house. That was quite a chase. Yet you fought your way out in one piece, as injured as you were, while protecting two unarmed teenage girls."

"No injuries could stop me," Kian gave her a look. "But we lost some good men."

Lucienne nodded grimly. Her tone softened. "I'm trying to piece everything together from a different angle."

"And to find a logical flaw," Kian sighed. "You don't trust the elder's daughter. You think the whole breakout could be staged."

"You're the one who made the pact with her."

"I made the best out of the situation," he said. "Staged or not, I gave her my word that she'd be well taken care of. Will that be a problem for you?"

Lucienne knew what he meant. One girl was her rival for Ashburn, the other for Vladimir. The irony was that she wasn't really their competition. She couldn't be with either boy completely. "I'm not that petty," she said. "They'll have all the comforts of Sphinxes, but they'll live outside the castle with no access to the restricted areas. They're our honored guests, but they aren't our people."

"That's exactly what Pyon decided," Kian said. "He's still interviewing them in Chameleon III."

"I'll help them settle down."

He regarded her. "Bayrose explained to me that she didn't know Nexus Tear was poisoned."

"But she did know that we killed her father in the war," Lucienne said. *And that I took back Vladimir.* "If I were her, I'd be out for blood."

"But she's not you," Kian said.

"So she's an angel."

Kian shook his head with a smirk. "I thought when you grew older, you'd lose some edge."

"I lost baby fat, not edge."

Kian chuckled, then winced. His rib hadn't mended yet. A surgeon in Sphinxes would do that when they got home.

"No matter what her agenda is," Lucienne said, "she returned you to me. And for that, she's earned her keep in Sphinxes." She made a mental note to do a mind sweep on Bayrose. After all, the girl was the Sealers' speaker who carried the founder's will. And Lucienne was still the most wanted on that man's list.

"I came back empty-handed," Kian said in despair.

"Kian McQuillen," Lucienne said, "you brought my world back by returning alive."

"Not all hope is lost, kid." Kian forced a hopeful smile. "Jekaterina escaped Abaddon 5 with the scroll. We'll find her. Bayrose said she could help us track her down."

Her people refused to accept the hard truth that there was no cure. Her ancient enemy had no idea of the true power of Forbidden Glory, but they knew there was no antidote in heavens or on earth once Blood Tear mixed with aether.

Although she wouldn't go down without a fight, she probably should start making arrangements for her people to carry on when she couldn't. "There's always hope, of course," she said with a smile. "I haven't had a lapse for thirteen days. The poison might have run its course—"

Then the red mist came. It was everywhere all at once and enveloped her. There was no exit. No back door. No place to run. She widened her eyes and opened her mouth. "Kian, I—"

And the red mist invaded her.

Chapter Fifteen

ASHBURN

Retrieving Lucienne's images through other people's memories was like looking at her through a thick glass—it couldn't alleviate Ashburn's thirst for her.

He watched insanity toy with her again and again, her every struggle a brutal bash on him. Until he couldn't take it anymore.

That was when he'd left. He hadn't abandoned her as she believed. How could she think he had the strength to do that? He had to find a cure even though his database flashed with confirmation again and again that there was no antidote anywhere.

Ashburn chose not to trust his incomplete databank and held onto an impossible hope. Lucienne was his destiny. If whatever cosmic force had a plan for them—no matter how terrible it was—it wouldn't let her fade away like this. Weren't they the pair that was supposed to come together to bring humankind to extinction?

Ashburn had come to the one place where he could think clearly, with no sounds, images, or other people's memories bombarding his mind. Only in this sanctuary could he have pure silence. But peace didn't come, not like before. Not when Lucienne wasn't well.

She was asleep now, and not peacefully either. As Ashburn returned to the Rabbit Hole, she was still in his mind, accompanying him, not from others' memories, but his own.

He wandered in this alternate universe that was like outer space, but without stars and cosmic rays. In order to find a cure, he must understand Forbidden Glory and its five fundamental forces—fire, metal, water, aether, and earth. None of them were of this planet.

They were stolen from the outer worlds, and humans were forbidden to have them.

Forbidden Glory gave the Siren race superpower, but no Sirens could harness it, not until Lucienne came into the picture. She tamed it, but then aether became infected.

The poison was made of ancient ingredients that weren't from this world either. What was its origin? The Sealers' family chronicles documented that a female angel gave the first Sealer Blood Tear. Did the record hold any truth? Was the giver a real angel with wings, or a visitor from a higher civilization? Did the visitor teach the earthlings to use fire and calculate the stars' movements, as it was told in mythology? They interfered with the human race and sped up civilization, which was unlawful according to their moral code. Did they end up warring against each other in their world? Humans recorded wars in the heavens and called the rebels the fallen angels.

If fallen angels were real, were there any still walking the earth?

And were the fallen angels the same race as the Exiles? Seraphen had said that the formidable race would cost everyone to return to earth, and that the element of time stopped them from coming back, meaning they had to erase time on earth first. Was that why the Eye of Time forced him to take in TimeDust to make him a second-hand vessel in order to remove time?

Lucienne had laughed unkindly at his speculation. And she'd spat on Seraphen before his demise. "No one can erase time. You're absolutely crazy!"

But Seraphen had insisted that Ashburn and Lucienne's union would change earth forever, and Ashburn hadn't found Seraphen to be wrong in the past. Troubled, he broke into a run to blow off some steam. This infinite realm had no end and no illusion of an end.

All the questions in his mind were like a snake biting its tail. They went in circles without offering answers, partly due to his insufficient database. Would he be able to find all the answers and the antidote for Lucienne once his TimeDust reached full power? He would have to merge with the Eye of Time. Ashburn shivered at the mere thought of being possessed by the ancient entity, but at the same time, he had to put great effort into repressing TimeDust's desperate longing to link to its source.

It had never stopped challenging Ashburn's will, but as long as he had breath, he wouldn't let it overpower him.

As all sorts of dark thoughts flitted through his mind, even in his sanctuary, Ashburn turned to Lucienne's images from his own memories to seek comfort. He loved to watch sunlight fall into her remarkable eyes. She was light to him, the only light amid the massive darkness and noise of the human collective consciousness. Her pink lips were delicious and enticing beyond words. Fantasizing about kissing her full lips, his mind wandered to the one time when he'd almost taken advantage of her.

Even when she was lost to her insanity, he still couldn't resist her.

It wasn't just the Lure, no matter how much he wanted to blame his lack of self-control on that seducing force. Over and over, he'd indulged his own need for her. It didn't matter which Lucienne surfaced—the sane or the insane—she remained his weakness.

Sadly, she laid bare her feelings for him only when touched by insanity. The mad Lucienne chose him. The uninhibited Lucienne was full of passion, drawn to him like a pin to a magnet, but the sane one stubbornly chose Blazek every time. When she returned to her normal self, she turned aloof toward Ashburn. The shift was instant. With her usual mask in place, she was the steely Siren queen, who had no idea how close Ashburn had come to ripping the mask off her face.

Did he prefer the wicked-but-fun Lucienne? If she kept that side, she wouldn't need to carry burdens, grief, and responsibilities. She could be free, and she could be his. Instantly, Ashburn felt sick with himself. How could he wish that for her? Without regaining her sound mind, she'd never be whole. The fear of losing her to Blazek had eventually turned him into someone he truly despised.

Darkness had taken root in him. The old Ashburn wasn't a brooding, calculating selfish jerk. He couldn't fully bring himself to blame the Lure for his lust for Lucienne.

However convenient for him, he couldn't let her stay unhinged. If he didn't find a cure in time—and no one knew how long she had— she'd die. Her insanity was the transitional area that had bought her time, but time was running out.

The idea that he'd live on without her and have her only in memories chilled him to the bone.

He shook off the unbearable image and treaded back toward the invisible elevator. At the sight of a faint, floating glow in the distance amid the void, a panic came over him. How long had he been in here? Time didn't exist in the Rabbit Hole. This realm of infinity was cut off from the real world, from the world that afflicted Lucienne.

He wanted to go back to her world to see her, hear her, feel her, but he also dreaded watching her suffer—and it was all Blazek's fault.

Hatred burned in Ashburn. He hadn't hated anyone like this, not even the King of Nirvana or Prince Felix, who tortured him and made him and his family second-class citizens.

He didn't want this black hate to dwell in him. He knew how hard and far a man could fall when driven by it. Nevertheless, he hated Lucienne's ancient enemies for poisoning her, and he hated that stupid Czech even more. That despicable man caused Lucienne's misery, yet still competed for her affection. His rival would never give up clinging to the girl Ashburn loved.

How could she not see the truth of it? Ashburn thought in dismay. Ironically, she saw the truth only in her insanity. The mad Lucienne loathed the Czech prince, but that didn't give Ashburn much satisfaction. He didn't want intense affection from the insane Lucienne. He wanted her love when she was her complete, unbroken, and undivided self.

Speaking of the devil, what was that no-good prince doing now? Was he scheming to have Lucienne all to himself and trap her deeper in his net of devotion and deception? Ashburn gritted his teeth. He was going to find out. His heart sank at the promise of seeing Lucienne and Blazek together.

He stepped onto the invisible lift and commanded it to take him all the way to the rooftop. As soon as he walked out of the Rabbit Hole, billions of collective memories screamed at him.

Ashburn grabbed his head and stumbled back. He could never get used to this—the horrible sensation when his databank went online. He could feel his facial muscles distort from the onslaught. He immediately wanted to return to the Rabbit Hole, his safe haven, and never come out again. But he stood his ground. Torrents of memories bombarded his mind, like a hurricane battering a lone glass house. When the storm passed, Ashburn harshly executed a command to brush aside memories of the living and the dead. He didn't care about them, any of them. He wanted only Lucienne.

He followed Aida, Kian, Ziyi, and Lucienne's guards' memories. Pain sliced into his head. TimeDust didn't want him focusing on an individual's memories. It didn't want him developing empathy or growing attached to anyone except Lucienne. It was trying to rob him of his humanity. Ashburn withstood the agony and located Lucienne through McQuillen's memories.

She was inside Valkyrie with an injured McQuillen.

"There's always hope, of course." she beamed. "I haven't had a lapse for thirteen days."

Thirteen days? Ashburn's heart sank. He felt the passing of only a few hours inside the Rabbit Hole. He must bear in mind that time flowed differently in the two worlds. He'd be doomed if he loitered in the Rabbit Hole too long and Lucienne's world passed him by, and she'd become but a spark of memory.

Then his heart lightened at her improved condition.

"The poison might have run its course," Lucienne continued, voicing Ashburn's hope, then she stretched her hand toward Kian and stuttered, "Kian, I—"

His chest tightened as red rings formed in her eyes, claiming her.

With a renewed hatred for Blazek, Ashburn picked through the Czech's recent memories. A vindictive smile rose to Ashburn's lips. His opponent hadn't had a good time either.

Blazek had left Sphinxes because he couldn't bear to watch Lucienne miss Ashburn. Gratitude and satisfaction swelled in Ashburn's heart as he realized that the sane Lucienne actually wanted him.

The severe pain in his head from poking into Blazek's memories was worth it.

Wait! What was that devil doing in Samye monastery?

Ashburn narrowed his eyes. Blazek was looking for a cure! Ashburn shook his head in disgust. If there was an antidote in Tibet, Ashburn would have been there before anyone. Fury rose in him. The Czech was wasting time. Shouldn't he stay at Lucienne's side and make himself useful? Then he caught his own logical flaw. Hadn't he wanted his rival to stay away from the girl he desired? He now realized that he loved her enough that a part of him had accepted that she also needed Blazek, at least temporarily.

Ashburn looked deeper into Blazek's memories to collect the evidence of his rival's idiocy and uselessness.

Blazek was in the middle of a ritual that hadn't been practiced for two thousand years. He lay nude on a stone bed covered with thorny vines. Amber-colored herbal water flowed from seven bamboo pipes and filled a pool until it reached him. The stream washed away the blood seeping from his back, and the tiny wounds the thorns created in his flesh sucked the herbal ingredients into his body.

Blazek stared up at the cloudy sky. Ashburn knew this was the only time of day the Czech could come out of his dark room and see light. He was in seclusion for two weeks now, repeating the arduous ritual bath every morning.

The ancient ritual was preparing the mind and body of a healer.

Blazek was turning himself into the antidote.

Chapter Sixteen
RITUAL

Ashburn watched the Czech prince strive to contain his pain, but the muscles on his jaw twitched and twisted. Blazek was playing Lucienne's image in his head—her beaming at him and bantering with him—to expel his agony. Annoyingly, he replayed a romantic fencing scene with Lucienne several months ago, over and over, relishing every detail.

Lucienne parried Blazek. They matched in every way, their sabers crashing in perfect arcs.

"We know each other's weaknesses and strengths too well," he sighed. "We can go on like this forever until one lies down."

"Then you lie down, pretty boy," she purred with a husky voice, gazing at him through her thick lashes. Her rich, brown eyes became expressive, turning all honey and wine, and only for him.

He appeared smitten. Seizing the advantage, she struck. The tip of her saber found an opening in his heart, but before she could claim victory, he'd moved, of course, with his usual, incredible speed. The opening was a feint. In the next heartbeat, he disarmed her, holding her saber in his hand. "The Lam lioness always knows how to take advantage of her opponent's weakness. I fell once, but never twice."

Their faces were inches apart, and she pulled back and punched him. He threw up his hand to cover his eye, stunned. She kicked the saber out of his hand, caught it, and tossed it to the ground with her gloves. She swung her long leg toward him. "But I hoped you'd always fall," she said. "Maybe it's just a silly girl's fantasy."

He turned his palm vertically and blocked her vicious kick. "I'll fall for you a

thousand times, if that's what you want. And I'm still falling for you, but does it
matter to you? You're not here anymore."

"I'm here."

"Your body is here."

"And what isn't?"

"Your heart."

"How can you know where my heart stays, or where it belongs?" Furious, she
tried to slap him.

He caught her wrist, and she tripped him. He dragged her down with him.
She fell on top of him, but he moved his hips to pin her under him. She
maneuvered her hips and legs, countering his moves and fighting to stay on top. At
last, she straddled him after he let her.

Ashburn gritted his teeth. This scene was intolerable! The Czech
distorted the reality to make it fit into his bad taste. Containing his
temper, Ashburn kept riffling through the rest of Blazek's memories.

"I saw how you looked at Ashburn Fury," the Czech prince said, his eyes
spitting sparks of dark fire. *"All I wanted was to strangle the life out of him with*
my bare hands!"

"And I want to snuff out your miserable, useless, harmful life,"
Ashburn shot back, even though his opponent couldn't hear him.

"Ashburn's my asset, just like the Eye of Time. That's all," Lucienne said.

That hurt. Ashburn shut his eyes. Though he knew she hadn't
meant it, hearing it from her mouth, even through Blazek's memories,
still cut him deeply. Ashburn was openly cursing the Czech as he
watched his rival move on top of Lucienne, thick desire filling his
hazel, animal-like eyes.

The Czech felt Lucienne's every curve and savored it.

Blazek gazed into Lucienne's wine-colored eyes that burned with fire and
desire. She wrapped her legs around his thighs. Her fingers moved underneath his
clothes, tracing the hard lines on his firm abdomen and then further down ....

Ashburn spat in fury. The Czech was now mixing reality with
fantasy. He was fantasizing about exploring Lucienne's body. Could
anyone be more despicable than that? If Blazek were in front of him,

Ashburn would surely punch out a tooth before throwing a black lightning bolt at the Czech.

On the thorn bed, Blazek murmured, "I'd rather die than lose you."

And in the Czech's mind, Lucienne thumbed his Z-shaped scar above his left eyebrow. He got it from a forbidden kiss two years ago. Lucienne's lips dropped him from his black horse in the Red Mansion's forest.

Lucienne could kiss no man except Ashburn.

Yet Blazek and Lucienne both challenged fate.

"You're mine, Vladimir Blazek," she said.

"Yours forever," Blazek answered on the thorn bed.

Then Lucienne screamed. Blood tears streamed down her lovely face.

Ashburn had to stumble back, even though it was only a memory in Blazek's mind.

His rival was now using Lucienne's suffering to punish himself and enhance his will to finish the ritual because all he wanted was to return to Lucienne. Physical and emotional pain filled his mind, leaving no room for anything else.

The monastery's bell finally chimed an hour's time.

The seven monks stepped toward the throne bed and chanted. Then they retreated into the shadows, leaving the prince to his own devices.

Blazek struggled off the thorn bed with an anguished yell and threw himself into the pool. He repeatedly gasped for air as he rose from the pink water, finally limping off without a word. He'd be in isolation for the rest of the day.

Through a monk's eyes, Ashburn saw the Czech's bloody back. Fresh wounds lay atop old ones. Blazek was notoriously vain, and now his back was ruined.

Ashburn left Vladimir's world. Watching his rival's ordeal hadn't given him any gratification; instead, it drained him and made him even more sullen. Ashburn shut himself inside the outdoor elevator on the rooftop of the Ghost House and slumped against the cold glass.

He stared ahead at the ring of distant white mountains.

What wouldn't they do for the girl they loved? Would Ashburn go through the same pain for her? Without a doubt. But he couldn't be her healer.

Whenever he touched her, he wanted more of her. The Lure enhanced his darkest lust, and the insane Lucienne was an irresistible seductress. One day it would strip off his self-control. If they slept with each other before they were ready, the consequence would be dire. Seraphen had said that their union would bring the apocalypse. Ashburn didn't know exactly how and why, but his instincts agreed with Seraphen. And Lucienne would never forgive him if he took her virtue in her insanity.

Despite the drawbacks and the luring danger for them both, he'd tried to heal her in the beginning. He'd managed to push back the churning poison in her veins, but her madness always returned. It was an undying leech clinging to her. So unless her condition was severe, he had to stand by and watch her take hit after hit.

Ashburn lifted his gaze from the mountains that encased Nirvana. It was time to gather all the information he could regarding the ancient ritual. His databank opened a window—

The ritual had once made an effective healer five thousand years ago. However, there was no assurance the healing would work on Lucienne. Even if Blazek could dilute the poison in her, he couldn't flush it out completely. Without the ultimate cure, she'd still fade away like the last flame of a burning candle. But Blazek could buy Lucienne time, and that was what Ashburn needed.

If no antidote existed, he was going to create one.

But how?

He returned to the Rabbit Hole and wandered through the vast space like a lost soul before he stumbled onto something and almost fell on his face.

The silhouette of Seraphen's body glowed faintly.

When Lucienne and her warriors had retreated from the Nirvana valley after the battle, Ashburn had brought Seraphen back to the Rabbit Hole, letting this plane be his resting place. Because she owed her life to Ashburn, Lucienne hadn't insisted on taking Seraphen to Sphinxes for an autopsy, despite her scientists' zealous requests.

Seraphen's body didn't decay like a mortal's. Ashburn's eyes darted to the gaping hole in the man's chest, then quickly looked away. The wound reminded Ashburn how he'd helped Lucienne kill his own protector.

If Seraphen were alive, he'd have information on the cure. Ashburn once suspected that Seraphen was the one who gave the ancient poison to the first Sealer, but that Sealer founder insisted a female angel granted him Blood Tear. However, her image was a shrouded memory as soon as it formed in that human's mind.

If only Seraphen were alive—

An idea struck Ashburn like lightning. What if he could bring Seraphen back to life?

Seraphen wasn't exactly human, so resurrection wasn't completely impossible. But if Ashburn succeeded, Seraphen would pose a deadly threat to Lucienne again. His protector had been programmed to kill Lucienne and would never rest until he achieved that goal.

Lucienne was running out of time, and Ashburn was running out of options.

Ashburn sank beside Seraphen.

Chapter Seventeen

THE SHIELD

Lucienne read the *Bible* to Finley.

Sphinxes' team had brought back their dead and wounded from Greece. Finley, a Catholic, had been in a coma since then, hooked up to life-support tubes.

"You're a hero, Finley," Lucienne said, putting the book down on the bedside table. "Sphinxes needs more heroes. Your new mission is to fight on and come back to us." She waited for a minute. There was no reaction from the unconscious soldier.

"We won't give up on you," she squeezed his rough hand, "so you won't be able to give up either. We'll be right here when you wake up." She rose as the nurse Mary came in to check on the patient.

"Lucia," she said, "Chief McQuillen checked out. He hasn't even half recovered. He threatened us when we tried to stop him."

"Assign a medical professional as one of his aides to keep him in line." Lucienne sighed. "Do you think Matthew is up the job? I'll give him a raise and an extra week of vacation days."

"Matt might not take the offer," Mary said.

Lucienne nodded as she headed toward the door. "Chief McQuillen is the worst patient in history, but I'll talk to Matthew."

"Lucia," Mary called after her, "your routine physical check was due two days ago. Dr. Wren—"

"Tell him I'm fine." Lucienne exited.

Mary murmured something about pot calling the kettle black.

Lucienne trekked down the hallway of the hospital in the castle. Her guards trailed after her. Rounding a corner, she headed toward a rehabilitation room where dozens of her wounded marines stayed. A girl's silvery, voice rang distinctly amid rumbles of laughter from the usually quiet room.

Vladimir used to say that Lucienne's laughter was the loveliest sound in the world, but he'd been mistaken.

Lucienne halted in the doorway. Her men had never laughed this heartily in her presence. She considered falling back, not wanting to disturb her soldiers, who were obviously enjoying themselves, but a couple of them had spied her. Their chortle turned to coughing. The marines rose immediately and snapped to attention, despite their injuries.

"At ease," Lucienne said. "I swung by to see how you're all doing."

All of them stood tall and straight and saluted her. Lucienne sighed inwardly and wistfully. She couldn't crack up with her regular soldiers, but she'd never felt such a gap with them. She felt like an intruder in front of her own people.

"I said at ease," she repeated.

The marines murmured their thanks with reverent expressions. Many were new and unaccustomed to the Siren's visits. Lucienne's eyes landed on the two nurses in the room. They were the ones entertaining her soldiers. The lovely laughter must have come from one of them. Lucienne thought she knew all the nurses. Were these two new?

Bayrose lifted her head—she'd just finished changing bandages for a blond-haired soldier—and turned to Lucienne. Violet, Ashburn's redheaded friend from Nirvana, put away a bottle of medicinal alcohol with a bang, not sparing Lucienne a glance.

Both girls looked adorable in white nurse's uniforms. Lucienne caught more than a few admiring glances toward the girls from the men.

Bayrose bowed to Lucienne and greeted her. "Siren."

Having returned to Sphinxes for a week, Lucienne hadn't arranged a meeting with Bayrose and Violet. Her first concern was her own unhinged mental condition. The second was Vladimir and Ashburn. She wasn't sure if the girls had moved on. What was she going to tell them about either man should they ask? Either one could have a life with either girl, but Lucienne had strung both men along. And now they'd both left because of her.

"Call me Lucienne," she told Bayrose. "And you don't need to bow to me. No one does here."

"I want to show my respect," Bayrose said.

Violet, on the other hand, gave Lucienne a scathing glare.

"Are the accommodations here acceptable?" Lucienne asked.

Violet sneered, "Like you care!"

No one but her enemies showed such disrespect toward Lucienne. The soldiers turned unnervingly quiet, and the guards behind Lucienne tensed up.

Bayrose elbowed Violet's waist. "Please, Violet," she whispered. "Don't do this."

"I do care," Lucienne said. "You're Ash's friend, and I promised him to take care of you when you come to Sphinxes. As for Miss Thorn, I'm forever grateful for what she risked for my chief. Making you both comfortable in my home is the least I can do. So do tell me if anything isn't up to your standards, and I'll make an improvement."

"Where is Ash?" asked Violet. "Why can't anyone answer that simple question? Are you hiding him from me?"

Thaddeus growled behind Lucienne, but she held up a hand to stop him from either insulting Violet or advancing on her. "No one knows exactly where Ash is at the moment," she said. "He left Sphinxes three weeks ago. As my honored guest, like you, he's free to come and go."

"Then you must have driven him away," Violet said.

Pain slapped Lucienne in the face. The truth hurts every time, no matter how it's delivered.

"Violet," Bayrose chided her friend again, "please don't be rude. We must be grateful we have such a nice place to stay."

"Your mansion is much nicer," Violet said. "I don't understand why you gave it up to come here!"

"Things have changed," Bayrose said softly. "I was trapped in a gilded cage. Now we have a chance to build a new life. The Siren didn't need to take us in, but she did. Her people are good to us. We should be grateful and earn our keep."

"You've earned your keep—" Lucienne said, then frowned at Violet for overstepping her bounds.

"How can you say that, Bayrose?" Violet demanded. "Hasn't she done enough to you? Have you forgotten how she took your boyfriend and killed your father?"

Bayrose's face dimmed and a hard edge appeared on her soft face. Lucienne sensed a high temper underneath the girl's suppressed feelings. "There are casualties in war," Bayrose said. "My father initiated the conflict, and so he brought this on himself. He also caused great harm to the Siren. I can never repay her for what he did, but I'm also a victim. Thanks to Chief McQuillen and the Siren, I've escaped a doomed life."

The others might not be able to detect the contradiction in Bayrose's words and her undercurrent emotions, but Lucienne had her Siren's power aiding her.

The new elder is too eager to convince me with pretty words. She still didn't buy into the girl's story. She and Bayrose were both raised in political environments. Neither one could afford to be naïve. Bayrose's act of giving up her prestigious life among the Sealers to surrender to her father's enemy was illogical, if not outright ridiculous.

Lucienne dove into Bayrose's mind. She needed to know where her opponent stood while the girl's emotions were still raw. She must know if Bayrose had come to seek revenge instead of shelter.

The first she saw in Bayrose's mind was a shade, almost like a floating shadow. She blinked, unable to decide what it was. But then the girl's good intentions toward Lucienne and Sphinxes were laid out in front of her. There wasn't an ounce of pettiness, jealousy, or malevolence in her.

She's a better person than I. No wonder Vlad had trusted the girl. Emmanuel Thorn had deceived his own daughter and used her to mislead Vladimir.

But—

The elder girl couldn't be such a saint. Lucienne must have read her wrong. She probed deeper into Bayrose's mind. This time the girl's memories and thoughts were like a broken record, and it played pain. As Lucienne listened for more, the record shrieked a broken love song. With a gasp, she retreated from the girl's mind.

A strange, uneasy feeling haunted Lucienne.

Unlike Schmidt, Bayrose had no high-tech helmet to shield her, and Lucienne had pushed her mental net deep into Bayrose's consciousness, but she couldn't find the slightest hint that the elder girl was even angry at her, despite the girl's suffering. It wasn't plausible. It was unreasonable. Hadn't Violet spat out that Lucienne killed Bayrose's father and took her love?

Had the poisoned Forbidden Glory undermined Lucienne's reading ability?

Or had Lucienne become so cynical that she was unable to believe the pure goodness in someone from the enemy's trenches, especially in a girl who was in love with her boyfriend?

The pain she'd read in Bayrose came into a sharp focus. That might explain the shade Lucienne had first glimpsed in the former elder's mind. It was her defense mechanism. The prince hurt Bayrose badly. He'd broken her heart.

It was clear now that Bayrose's true intention was Vladimir. The girl wanted to be near him. Only by rescuing Kian and coming to Sphinxes could she achieve that. Love made people lose otherwise sound minds. Sympathy for the girl welled in Lucienne.

As long as Bayrose didn't come for anyone's blood in Sphinxes, Lucienne would allow her a fair chance to compete for Vladimir's heart, though it would bleed her own heart to see Vlad with another girl. But love, unlike anything, had its own will.

She wondered how Vladimir would react to seeing Bayrose again once he returned. Her heart instantly pounded her rib cage at the prospect of seeing her Czech warrior soon.

"You've earned your keep here, Miss Thorn," Lucienne said. "As I said before, I'm forever in your debt for Chief McQuillen's safe return. I'm glad we won't be enemies. If it's your wish to build a life here, my team and I are more than happy to be of assistance."

"Thank you, Siren," Bayrose said, as tears formed in her lovely brown eyes.

"Bayrose, don't trust that witch," Violet said hotly. "She already bewitched Ash, and she's done the same to your prince. We don't know how many men she's snared in her black spider's web—"

Thaddeus stepped toward Violet, towering over her. "Remember who you're speaking about, you ungrateful little bitch!" he spat. "Another slander against my cousin, and I'll toss you out the window so you can crawl back to the hellhole you came from."

Violet recoiled at the man's menacing stare, seemingly realizing that she couldn't throw a tantrum in Lucienne's realm. In Nirvana, the king's subjects had to tolerate her, for she was the bastard daughter of King Henry, but here she was nobody. She was at the Siren's mercy.

"Thaddeus, let her be," Lucienne said.

"Violet, please apologize to the Siren," Bayrose said.

"She is not my queen," Violet said. "And I do have a backbone."

Violet will never find it in her heart to forgive me, Lucienne realized. *She insists that I stole the only man she's ever loved.* Without Ash, Violet had nothing to cling to. No home. No anchor. Adrift forever. Lucienne felt sorry for the girl, but that was no excuse for bad behavior.

"I let you stay here because of Ash," Lucienne said, "but it's not my obligation to take care of you. If you want to leave, I'll have you shipped back to Nirvana this moment. But while you live on my land, you'll learn basic courtesy. Do you understand?"

Violet remained silent.

"Say you understand," urged Bayrose. "Violet, please! For me."

The girl finally nodded curtly.

There wasn't much Lucienne could do for Violet when it came to Ashburn's feelings. She hoped as time went by that Violet would find the meaning of life for herself other than in Ashburn or any man. She turned her attention back to Bayrose. "Thank you for tending to our brave soldiers."

Lucienne waved at the marines to carry on as she exited. They'd been laughing and joking with Bayrose before Lucienne had invaded their space. She didn't feel wanted, but that was fine. They were her people. She was comforted to see that they were enjoying good company. She was also pleased to see Bayrose fitting in. It was time to let go of her petty grudge against Bayrose for the poison incident.

Then a marine's voice carried out to the hallway where Lucienne and her guards treaded on. "Miss Bayrose, we'd love to have you visit again, but we don't want your friend near us. Anyone who is rude to our Siren isn't welcome here."

Lucienne blinked. A soldier of hers shouldn't take it personally when another teen insulted their Siren.

"You look surprised, cousin," Thaddeus said beside her, "that you're loved by your soldiers."

"I should've tried harder to help her adjust," Lucienne said. "She's Ash's friend."

"If there's anyone who needs help, it's you." Dr. Wren took long strides to catch up with them. "It's time for your physical, Lucia. No more excuses."

Chapter Eighteen

SERAPHEN'S HEAD

Fighting his natural aversion to dead bodies, Ashburn studied Seraphen's corpse.

Seraphen had a complete set of organs, like a human, but he had no blood. The fluid in his body looked like mercury. His heart was charred meat, burnt by the combined powers of Lucienne's Eye of Time and Ashburn's black lightning.

Ashburn stared at the grotesque sight of Seraphen's heart and winced. "Seraphen?" he called as if he could summon the dead. He then immediately felt foolish.

Seraphen's glassy, sightless eyes stared into nothingness.

Ashburn inserted a hand through the hole in Seraphen's chest and touched his heart. It was cold and hard like a rock. He shrank back, quickly removing his hand. For a moment, he didn't know what to do.

What was Seraphen made of? During their brief time together, Seraphen had never revealed his origin, but he'd uttered once, "We're alike, Ashburn Fury."

Ashburn had regarded that statement as a humorless joke. Now he wondered if Seraphen had meant that they were linked. When Ashburn had activated the Eye of Time, he'd also activated Seraphen. Yet the creature had held fear and hatred toward the ancient power, hatred as strong as his own.

Ashburn had never delved into their link when Seraphen had been alive. He'd rejected all things that would bring him closer to the Eye of Time and fulfill his terrible purpose. But if he wanted to save

Lucienne, he must resurrect Seraphen. And to revive Seraphen, he must find and activate the shared link.

He needed to go up to the Ghost House to perform the task. Inside the Rabbit Hole, all connections to the outside world were shut down. Ashburn dragged Seraphen toward the invisible platform under the glowing liquid interface. The man was dead weight, literarily.

As soon as Ashburn pulled Seraphen out of the Rabbit Hole, he gasped again at the onslaught of images and sounds rushing into his mind. He dropped Seraphen to the ground and clutched his head. He gritted his teeth as he forced the flowing consciousness in one direction—backstage. He hadn't the power to deny their existence, but he was the traffic controller in his domain. Still shouting their presence, the collective consciousness reluctantly flushed into the background under Ashburn's harsh commands.

They were a collective humming now, unsatisfied and hungry. Ashburn ignored them. He released his hands from his head after he was calmer. He took another minute to brace himself for TimeDust to frantically record the updates from around the world. The human population came alive in his databank.

A pained laugh escaped him. How ironic! He hoped this world was dead in his mind except for Lucienne. He brushed aside the world's gossip to find new memories that centered on her.

Violet's and another girl's memories popped out. Violet was in Sphinxes, bitter, lonely, and desperate. She missed him terribly. Ashburn turned away from her memories. He could never give her his love. He was no longer the Ashburn she knew. The gap between them had grown light years across. Her devotion was but a burden to him. She used to be his only friend, but now his childhood didn't belong to him. It had merged with the collective consciousness to become a drop in the ocean. When it hit the bottom, no one could hear a splash. As he momentarily reflected on that, even the bile he used to taste on his tongue had faded.

But the collective consciousness couldn't swallow Lucienne. She was never a part of his collection. He'd once felt so frustrated that he couldn't figure her out. Now he was only thankful that he couldn't have her memories. She stood out amid the billions. She was a beacon of light to him, his only remaining tie to humanity. If he couldn't find a cure for her, his light would be gone forever. What would become of him?

The other girl, a newcomer and an enemy to Lucienne, was Bayrose Thorn. What was the new elder doing in Sphinxes? Ashburn sorted through her memories. The girl had taken in the Shadow, which shrouded her present thoughts. Nevertheless, the girl was still a part of his vast collection of human memories. Like Bayrose, many broken people had ruptured memories. Ashburn could barely stand to look at them.

Were Lucienne's memories distorted and broken in her state of insanity? He could never know. It pained him just picturing that reality for her.

Ashburn couldn't pass the Shadow's armor in Bayrose's mind, but he'd seen her past. She'd sought to harm Lucienne, like many others. She was capable. In a short period of time, the girl had gained the love of the men in Sphinxes by serving and tending to injured marines and patients in the medical facility. She didn't bother to conceal her identity as the new elder in the Sealers' rank, but used her former status to her advantage. Her courage and sacrifice became a legend in Sphinxes. As word spread among the soldiers, she turned bigger than life—a Sealers' princess had become one of them and loved them.

When he returned to Sphinxes, Ashburn would shatter her false image. He would expose her lies. But he'd need to talk to Lucienne first. There was more to this girl than met the eye. He looked at the elder girl a little longer, until he was sure that he didn't need to make the trip to Sphinxes right away—Bayrose didn't pose an immediate threat to Lucienne.

His childhood friend was also actively seeking to harm Lucienne. Violet wished her dead, which grieved Ashburn more than her unrequited love. He didn't want to hurt Violet, but he couldn't turn a blind eye to her vicious intentions. If there was any consolation, he knew neither girl could, at the moment, reach Lucienne.

The Siren kept her distance, though she arranged help for the newcomers to slip into their new lives. While Bayrose was working hard on winning Sphinxes' love, Lucienne became reclusive after having another mental lapse.

Through Aida's most recent memories, Ashburn saw the world of red runes—the ones etched on the opal basin that once contained the ancient poison Blood Tear.

Lucienne, wearing a lacy red gown, was painting the runes on her bedroom wall.

"You should rest, my sweet girl," her nanny said.

"Do not interrupt me again," Lucienne snapped, "or I'll throw you out and force you to stay with the guards. You don't like them much, but I can't always watch out for you. I've been trying very hard to be sensitive and not hurt your feelings, and your feelings are the size of the pea and just as easy to crush."

"Sorry," Aida murmured as she slumped onto a chair, turning to glare at the guards in the adjacent sitting room. They tried to be as inconspicuous as possible, knowing their mistress was testy today.

Lucienne turned back to the wall, holding a red pen in the air. "I can't remember half of them." She frowned. "I need to remember them all to decode them. These ancient runes said something about me and death, but they're like whispers in the dark that I can't catch up with."

"Perish the thought." The nanny jumped up from her chair. Lucienne's talk of death pumped fear into the older woman's heart. The nanny was superstitious. She was terrified the prophecy would come true if Lucienne finished the runes. "Now, sweet girl, let me comb your hair and get you ready for bed. It's past midnight."

"No," Lucienne said. "Stop trying to put me into bed. I'm not a little girl anymore. I'm the Siren. I have responsibilities. I must finish this." She tried to add a curved line to a half-finished rune, but stopped in the middle and turned to her nanny with a wild look. "Why is my mind a messy thread? Where's Ash? I think clearer when he's around."

Ashburn's heart leapt. She asked for him first instead of the Czech. In that instant, all he wanted was to go to her, wrap her in his arms, and bury his face in her midnight hair. Her scent was forever intoxicating to him.

"Ash?" the nanny asked, then she got an idea. "We like Ash. Why don't you put down the pen so we can talk about him?"

Lucienne looked at the nanny, then at the unfinished runes crawling over the wall, then at the pen in her hand.

"Don't you like Ash?" the nanny coaxed.

"Ash," Lucienne sighed, tossing the pen onto a nearby desk.

The nanny led Lucienne to a seat before the vanity desk and started combing her mistress' hair. "What do you think of that boy?"

Ashburn held his breath.

"Ash is very good looking," Lucienne said.

"Yes, everyone thinks so," the nanny said as she smoothed a lock of Lucienne's knotted hair.

"Sometimes everyone makes me feel crazy, but he never does," Lucienne said.

"He has a way," the nanny said.

"I miss him, terribly, Aida, but he'll never know. He can't read my mind. Many times I hope he can, so he'll know how my heart aches for him."

And Ashburn's heart ached. It took all his strength to ground himself like an anchor in the seaport and not summon Spike. He hardened his heart by telling himself that this was the insane Lucienne talking. When she was herself again, she'd think only of the Czech prince.

But he still longed to go to her.

Ashburn tore his sight from Lucienne's lovely face and lacy gown and shut down the memory window. If he went to her now, he'd have to watch her die. He'd be useless and helpless. He turned his attention back to Seraphen's corpse.

Amid an ocean of data, Ashburn searched for the link to Seraphen. He'd traced his former protector in his databank before, but hadn't had much luck. Seraphen wasn't part of the collective human consciousness since he wasn't exactly a human. Ashburn summoned the subprogram. It hadn't surfaced in a long while because Ashburn had suppressed it. Whenever it came to him, it urged him to kill Lucienne. It was disturbing to hear that murderous thought echoing in his head as if it were somehow his idea.

Although he'd pushed back the subprogram, Ashburn had also shielded it from TimeDust. The rebel force—as TimeDust called this malware—existed to stall the terrible purpose that TimeDust had set in him.

As soon as he created the virtual wall that blocked TimeDust, the subprogram surfaced like a fish breaking a net of bubbles.

"The Siren's line—" it started.

"This isn't about the Siren race," Ashburn interrupted. "I summoned you for Seraphen. I must bring him back."

"Then he'll continue his mission and remove the Siren."

Ashburn winced. If Seraphen returned, he'd surely hunt down Lucienne. He'd never stop until she was dead. Would Ashburn have the stomach to kill his former protector again? What if the resurrected Seraphen became too powerful for him and Lucienne to handle?

But she was already dying. He couldn't create an antidote without Seraphen's help or the full power from the Eye of Time.

"How do I resurrect Seraphen?" he asked the rebel.

The walls he'd built began to rattle. TimeDust was trying to breach his fortress.

The subprogram vibrated nervously, wanting to flee for self-preservation.

"How do I resurrect Seraphen?" Ashburn asked again urgently as he enhanced his mental fortification. He could resist TimeDust for a few more seconds. He and the subprogram had a very narrow window.

"The angels' tool wants to eradicate me," the subprogram said.

The rebel called TimeDust the angels' tool. Ashburn didn't want to go there. "What should I do to I bring back Seraphen?" he demanded. "Tell me!"

"Lightning—" the subprogram said.

A punishing pain exploded in Ashburn's head, but he sustained it. *I'm no stranger to pain,* he sneered at TimeDust through another channel.

"What lightning?" Ashburn pursued.

One side of the walls cracked.

" . .. link … loophole … head—" the subprogram said.

A knife-hand made of dark lightning moved in through the crack in the wall, reaching for the flickering beam of the subprogram. Ashburn threw his own lightning toward the hand, but it absorbed his bolt.

I'm the source of your power, TimeDust said.

Cursing, Ashburn raised his arm to parry the knife. It cut a deep gash on his flesh.

"Seraphen must end her line." The subprogram disappeared.

The walls crumbled, and TimeDust withdrew in frustration.

The throbbing in Ashburn's head ebbed, but the pain along his left arm remained. He glanced at the black marking on his skin and brushed aside any thoughts of revenge. How could he punish an entity inside him? He sighed. Despite their "love-hate" relationship, hurting one hurt the other. That was why TimeDust wouldn't severely damage him either.

The rebel had mentioned "lightning." An image came. At the battlefield in Nirvana valley, he'd tossed lightning at Seraphen and unmade his protector. *Yes, the lightning.* It could destroy. It could also remake Seraphen.

Ashburn slid his hand through the hole in Seraphen's chest and grasped his charred heart. Breathing out, Ashburn let out his lightning. The dark bolt hit the corpse. At the third strike, Seraphen jerked up, eyes blinking. Ashburn jumped back.

Seraphen stared ahead, his glassy eyes staying sightless.

Had he imagined the blink? Ashburn thought so, until Seraphen's blacked heart turned pale pink.

Ashburn's own heart slammed in his chest.

"Let there be light," God said, and there was light.

The creation story swirled alive in his databank.

Light and lightning revived lives.

Ashburn eagerly struck Seraphen again, but was carefully not to use too much force, in case he fried Seraphen.

Despite the black lightning sizzling from his body, Seraphen didn't respond again.

Something was missing.

After having revealed the first ingredient "lightning," the rebel had spat out, "... link ... loophole ... head," before it'd fled.

Ashburn tapped a finger on his jaw. He hadn't shaved for days. Lucienne's insane version was strict on personal hygiene. No, he mustn't let his mind wander to her and then indulge himself in watching her through others' memories. He could lose hours that way. He must finish what he'd started with Seraphen. But Lucienne ... she'd once tried to kill him because she'd figured out the link between him and Seraphen. She'd found Seraphen's Achilles' heel—if Ashburn died, Seraphen ceased to exist. So Seraphen had fought to preserve Ashburn at all cost.

Their lifelines were linked, which meant that as long as Ashburn lived, Seraphen wasn't really dead. He'd only been deactivated. Ashburn sat back on his heels, gazing at Seraphen's pink heart. He was certain now he could bring back Seraphen. But once he did, he'd face an immediate threat—Seraphen would spring forward to pursue Lucienne and bring about her demise. Seraphen could also summon Spike. If he reached Lucienne before Ashburn did, she'd be dead before Ashburn could create an antidote for her.

Ashburn stared at Seraphen's body before looking away in defeat.

Time flowed by in memories brought by billions of conscious minds. Time was both tangible and abstract to him. And just like any mortal, he couldn't stop it, not even in his memory bank. For Lucienne's sake, he couldn't lose another minute.

How could he solve this dilemma and preserve both Lucienne

and Seraphen? He darted his gaze back to his former protector, desperate for an answer.

And the answer came like the lightning having snapped fingers.

The subprogram had whispered "… head." The link was hidden inside Seraphen's head.

Ashburn pressed his palms against Seraphen's temples, his energy pouring into Seraphen's head searching his old ally's remaining consciousness. He felt a distant, feeble response. Their link was preserved.

Yes, head.

Ashburn knew what to do next. He had no need of Seraphen's heart—all he needed was his head. It would be a cruel, bitter end for Seraphen. What wouldn't he do for the girl he loved? He chose her. Always had. Always would.

"I'm sorry, Seraphen," he murmured and rose to his full height.

A flux of black lightning sparked. Ashburn raised a hand, and the lightning shot out like a dark blade toward Seraphen's neck. In an instant, it severed Seraphen's head from his body. Ashburn grimaced at the gruesome sight of Seraphen's headless body bouncing once, twice, then a third time, before it stilled.

Ashburn shut his eyes for a moment, disgusted with himself. *What have I become because of her?* No, it wasn't her fault. His humanity had been leaking from the pipe because of TimeDust. She was still his light. He just needed to walk through the dark passages to be with her.

Ashburn kneeled beside the head, pressing two fingers against Seraphen's nape where a network of nerves gathered. The invisible link pulsed inside, then extended like an endless spiral staircases.

Ashburn let a stream of dark lighting hike up the stairs.

An electric shock jolted his head, followed by a burning sensation. Ashburn recognized that it wasn't real. It was a sensory deception from TimeDust to prevent him from performing the resurrection. He commanded his dark lightning to keep moving. The virtual stairs seemed infinite, but everything in this world had an end. So did the stairs.

The shock in his mind increased. *You underestimate my increased tolerance for pain,* he snorted at TimeDust, *thanks to you.*

The lightning finally reached the end of the stairs. A connection was made, and the link swirled online.

Ashburn removed his fingers from Seraphen's temples.

One, two, three …, Seraphen's golden-mold eyes flashed open.

Ashburn had been prepared this time, yet he still leapt back from Seraphen's living head.

Seraphen's gaze trained on Ashburn.

"Seraphen?" Ashburn whispered.

Seraphen rolled his eyes slowly to the left, then right, until he spied his discarded body. He returned his stare to Ashburn. "What have you done to me, Ashburn Fury?"

"I had to." Ashburn said defensively, though guilt ate him up from the inside.

"You threw away everything for one girl?" Seraphen said.

"She isn't just any girl."

"If she were, the world would be safe."

"You see? You'll never let go of your obsession for murdering her. That's why I can't bring you back completely. I'll keep only your consciousness alive so you can't hurt her."

"What do you want from me?"

"The antidote to the Blood Tear."

"The ancient poison worked." Seraphen chuckled in delight. "It's taken an eon for the grand design to come to fruition." Without his body, his throaty laughter sounded eerie amid the discarded machinery that littered Ghost House.

"Were you the one who gave the first Sealer the poison?" Ashburn asked through clenched teeth.

Seraphen didn't answer, as if savoring his victory.

"Because of you," Ashburn grated, "she's trapped in insanity."

"She won't last long."

"Tell me the cure."

"Are you as mad as her?" Seraphen said. "I accept that you don't have it in you to end her. But now the circumstance has done you a favor. Let her fade away. Let the world be safe."

"I can access your memories if you refuse to tell me the truth," Ashburn said.

"You've modified the pathway in me, I see," Seraphen said. "I'm impressed by your increasing abilities. But even you can't change my original program. I'm still set to exterminate the Siren's line. You'll only create conflict in me, which will cause me to malfunction."

"Let me worry about that!"

"Blood Tear has no evident antidote."

"Then I'll create one for her!"

Seraphen tried to cock his head, only to realize he could no longer conduct that simple act. "You're tempting fate."

Ashburn narrowed his eyes. "It's funny you mentioned fate. The force that forged the Eye of Time—you called them the Exiles—picked a pair: Lucienne and me. So if there's fate, by cosmic design or conspiracy, she won't expire easily." He studied Seraphen's expression and knew that he'd hit a nerve. Seraphen didn't have a human's ability to lie.

"You always twisted my words," Seraphen sighed. "And now you're getting better at it."

Ashburn lifted his protector's head, eyes boring into Seraphen's golden orbs. "Where did you acquire Blood Tear in the first place?" he demanded.

"I had nothing to do with the poison."

"Then who?" Ashburn recalled the shroud memories. The first Sealer had called the giver an angel. And the angel had come in a vaguely female form.

"Someone older than me. I wonder who it could be. Will you let me know when you find out?"

An "angel" had bestowed the first Siren with the Forbidden Glory. Another "angel" then had helped the first Sealer steal one of the elements from the Glory and handed him Blood Tear, intending to compromise the power of Forbidden Glory. Were the two "angels" from opposite sides of the same race, or were they different species? And what was the role of the ancient humans in the angels' war, if there had been such a war?

"I can't help you save your dear girl," Seraphen said with satisfaction. "Even if I had knowledge of the cure, most of it was lost. As you know, some of my memories were corrupted, some were broken, and some were—simply gone."

"I won't listen to your excuses. You'll assist me in creating a cure."

"That's beyond my ability," Seraphen said, but one of his eyes winked.

"You can't lie." Ashburn didn't miss a beat. "But you skipped the truth. What is it?"

"You have to get to the bottom of it while you can still walk away."

"What is it?" Ashburn raised his voice.

"Your prophetic dreams tell you the answer you've been seeking."

Ashburn swallowed. Night terrors had visited him every night after he'd first broken contact with the Eye of Time in Hell Gate and then escaped the eternal land of nothingness where time was dead. Then, a week later, all dreams had stopped. There was no room for them once billions of collective consciousness paraded and buzzed in his mind like numerous bees. Until lately, after Lucienne had been poisoned, his nightmares had returned.

He'd tried to dismiss the recurring dreams of horror the way he bashed back dark thoughts, but they always came back, dancing around in his skull.

"You can't tell if they are fantasies or reality when you dream them," Seraphen said, "but often savor that one erotic dream."

Ashburn blushed.

Between the nightmare sequences, Lucienne always came to finish what they'd started on the rooftop of Ghost House. She was atop him in her flimsy, half-white, half-red gown. There was no inhibition and no consequences. Their lust burned brighter and fiercer than any flame.

Their skin, having hungered for each other for so long, pressed against each other without a barrier. Their limbs entangled; their joining together in flesh made Ashburn feel truly alive for the first time in his entire existence.

Then their inextinguishable passion sired supernatural fire. It spread to all corners of the earth, until the land became parched, the oceans ablaze in unending flames. It was a terrifying yet spectacular sight. There were no survivors except them. Their union brought an inferno to earth.

The post-apocalyptic world was still raw when Ashburn woke up, soaked in cold sweat. *No, it's impossible.* Their union couldn't be that cursed. Their coming together couldn't have that kind of destructive power.

Then, on other nights, he had been granted a choice in his dream.

At the end of their heated passion, he found his hands forming a noose around Lucienne's elegant neck. Her lovely eyes met his, trusting him, then accusing him, then pleading for her life. Still, he kept throttling her. Until he heard the sickening creak of her windpipe. Until she no longer thrashed her shapely legs.

The light in her eyes dulled, and the light in him went out completely.

But the world lived. The collective consciousness cheered at their continued existence, at the cost of Ashburn's dead soul.

That dream offered him this: he could have her once and still save the world, if he killed her afterwards. And that damned dream sickened him more than anything could.

"How do you know about those nightmares?" Ashburn demanded.

"We're more linked than you know. Your vision—"

"They aren't visions!" Ashburn shouted. "They're awful dreams caused by my anxiety."

"Lie to yourself if you want, but you know as clearly as I that those were prophetic dreams. The future of the world is in your hands, Ashburn Fury. The question is: what will you choose?"

"You call that a choice?" Ashburn's nostrils flared in anger. "Who put that sick, sadistic game in my head?"

"Prophecy. Fate. Destiny," Seraphen said. "They exist and entwine, yet no one knows which force is behind them. They favor some humans but detest others. I'm not without sympathy for your situation, but I have to remind you—the game is on."

"I refuse to play. How's that?"

"You're already playing," Seraphen said. "You brought me back to save Lucienne Lam, the last Siren."

"Yeah, I'll save her, and that's it. I won't pursue her. I won't touch her after she gets well, if having her is that damned costly."

"Now you're excellent at deceiving yourself. Do you think the Siren being poisoned is spur-of-the-moment revenge? It was planned eons ago. I tried to neutralize their game by playing mine."

"Right, yours was more direct," Ashburn snorted in fury. "The petty Sealers used poison, and you attempted to punch a hole in her chest."

"The Sealers are pawns in this game too. Who gave them the poison in the first place? As you said, the Exiles picked a pair to erase time. The Siren won't expire easily. She hangs in there stubbornly, doesn't she? She's waiting—the force is waiting for you to save her. So, yes, my intention was different than the Exiles. I wanted to end the game, but they've resumed it by forcing your hands. I now see their agenda more clearly. If you don't trust me, then test my theory. Try to end her life, and see if some force will stop you."

"Thanks for your brilliant suggestion," Ashburn grated. "Kian and the rest of Sphinxes will skin me alive first."

"You can handle the mortals," Seraphen said lazily. "Now look at the stream of the events. You fought to stay away from her in the beginning. You knew the time bomb was in you, and she was the detonator. You vowed that you wouldn't go down the path with her to destroy the world. Have you forgotten your vow?"

Tracking down the memory lane, Ashburn looked tormented and ashamed. Then his fury resumed. "I was doing fine by avoiding her until you came along and messed everything up. You almost killed her, so I had to stop you. It wasn't them but you who pushed my hands. You set the wheel spinning in the wrong direction in the first place."

Seraphen gave him a pitiful look.

Ashburn looked away from Seraphen. Would he have stayed away from her if Seraphen hadn't been so zealous to kill Lucienne? When she'd decided to leave him alone on Ghost House's rooftop, he'd failed to let her go. Instead, he'd followed her to Sphinxes. "I choose to go with you because I can't bear not to see you," he'd told her. "I'm going to let my feelings run their course, so my desire won't drive me mad. I hope it wears off if I don't fight it so hard."

His feelings for her had never worn off. They amplified.

"Fine. Blame me," Seraphen said. "But look at you. You've fallen only deeper and harder. If you had let me kill her at the time—"

Ashburn wanted to punch the head, but instead grabbed Seraphen's short hair and twisted it hard.

"I can't feel pain," Seraphen said. "If you want to punish me or inflict pain, you should connect my head to my body."

"So you can keep scheming and pursuing Lucienne's demise? Not a chance."

"If I hadn't interfered, you wouldn't have had a chance to stand here right now. She'd have let the Eye of Time take you. Have you forgotten the excruciating pain that was like a thousand needles stabbing at your brain when she set the entity on you? Your screaming is still fresh in my memory if you need to extricate it as a reminder."

"Give it up," Ashburn said, "You can't put a wedge between Lucienne and me. No one can. We've put the past far behind us."

"Sure, you both did. She hasn't used the Eye of Time on you after you *killed* me and saved her. But look at what happened then."

Lucienne had had to find an alternative to move forward. She'd ended up being poisoned.

"The Exiles won't allow you two to stall their plan," Seraphen said leisurely, as if none of the consequences had anything to do with him anymore, and he was just a bystander watching with certain interest. "Her being poisoned set the wheel in motion again. It brought you here. It brought me back. The game never ends until you two play your parts. Until you dance to its tune."

"That's crap!"

"Is it?"

A dark thought hovered in Ashburn's mind. The first two scrolls had led Lucienne to the Eye of Time, and thus to him. The third predicted her poisoning. The rest of the inscriptions spreading over the three scrolls remained undecipherable.

Who had written the scrolls? Anger kept building up in Ashburn. Who had planned all this that led to Lucienne's and his suffering?

"They want you to heal her," Seraphen said. "You must go against your primal need to protect her. The antidote is almost impossible to come by, so ease your guilt. You tried. You can't help her. Let her rest with her ancestors, and the earth will enjoy peace in another millennium."

"What's the world to me if she's gone?" Ashburn hissed. "I'll never find peace."

"After she's gone, your bond to her will automatically sever. You'll feel differently. You'll feel liberated. I'm speaking from experience. Nihum—"

Ashburn felt a hot iron ramming into his heart. He could not tolerate Lucienne's end as the price for their severed bond. "Stop hoping for her death," he grated. "I won't accept either outcome from my dreams." His voice was bitter, determined. "I won't have a union with her. The terrible purpose in me won't come to pass, and the world will be safe. But I won't allow the poison to waste her either. I'll tear the world apart to find the ingredients for the antidote. And no one—not you, not me, not any force in heavens, earth, or hell—can stop me from keeping her alive."

"You're full of enthusiasm to go down the path of destruction for one girl."

"No more idle talk," Ashburn said. "We've wasted enough time. Tell me all you know about the antidote."

Seraphen shut his eyes.

"You said the antidote is *almost* impossible to come by."

"You're a hopeless fool, Ashburn Fury." Seraphen opened his eyes and let out a low, vicious laugh. "Fine, I'll tell you, if only to save you the trouble of forcefully entering my head."

"That's logical."

"You'll acquire an antidote only by becoming the thing you hate the most."

A cold shiver of fear raised the hair on the back of his neck. Ashburn immediately knew the answer, the truth he'd dreaded the most. He hooked his mind to the link he shared with Seraphen. He must make sure the head didn't hide anything.

A severe headache pounded his skull, but he sustained it as he traced Seraphen's memories.

"You'll need to merge with the Eye of Time," Seraphen said. "When it completes TimeDust in you, it'll become you in flesh with full power. It will heal Lucienne Lam, but you'll be no more. You'll become a vessel, a slave to its will, and you'll never break free. It's a fate worse than death."

Ashburn left Seraphen's mind and found himself crumpled on a pile of shining machine junk. Blood drained from his face. He could imagine that he must look like a corpse. "There must be another way." He finally found his voice.

Loophole. The word jumped at him. The subprogram had also uttered, "… loophole."

"There is no other way, Ashburn Fury," Seraphen said. "You came to me, hoping I'd tell you otherwise, but I cannot lie. The world isn't an easy place, and everything has a price. So, who are you going to pick: you or her?"

Ashburn remained silent.

"On the grand scale, it isn't just you or her. It's you and the entire world or her. Now you can see which side should be sinking."

"She's doomed," he said, entirely defeated. "And so am I."

Ashburn turned his mind back to the world. His databank vividly recorded the current memories of the living. He didn't care for any of them except one girl—the one girl he couldn't have. He summoned Spike. It formed in front of him, humming in light. He'd return to her and spend her last moment with her, and then face the nightmare of the world alone.

Then, suddenly, a speck of light pulsed amid the billions of memories. It didn't belong to the collective consciousness. Where had the radiant light come from? It brightened even more with glowing letters, and then the letters came together and spelled: *Jekaterina.*

She was calling him.

Ashburn inhaled deeply.

She knew who he was and what he was. As she removed a portion of her veil, he stared into her like gazing into the sun.

He felt lightheaded, but his heart filled with new hope.

Ashburn answered the call.

Chapter Nineteen

JEKATERINA

Sphinxes' castle, both modern and medieval, stood lit like daylight, and light dwelled in every glass of champagne. Laughter and chatting streamed in the grand hall and the court. Officers wore their grey and blue uniforms, and ladies donned their fancy evening dresses.

Lucienne wore a white gown with her hair half-pinned up in a diamond headdress. She walked among the crowd, greeting her people. Wherever she passed, she heard whispers.

"They say you're like a fairy queen," Thaddeus said beside her.

"My hearing is quite good," she said. "Not that I don't appreciate compliments." She wished, for her people's sake, that she would wear white forever.

Thaddeus looked happy. "Everyone's having fun, cousin."

Not everyone. Not her guards. Lucienne could feel tension rolling off them. Posted at every corner of the hall, they watched her, carrying her burden. Kian had briefed them to make sure there would be no incident on this special night. Thaddeus was the only guard assigned to her side for the whole evening. He didn't forget to flash a flirtatious grin at pretty ladies here and there, but he stayed alert. At the first sign of a lapse, he'd put her out quietly and bring her out of the castle, just as they'd practiced. She was also prepared not to fight back. She wouldn't allow her condition to get in the way of her people's celebration.

Lucienne strolled toward a group of high-ranking officers in the center of the room. Bayrose laughed her silvery laugh among them, obviously in her element. The girl wore a sunglow-colored gown, the most fashionable style in Paris. Her amber earrings matched her dress and highlighted her soft lips. Her brown hair curled around her nape and made her look lovely with an innocent appeal. A year younger than Lucienne, the teen had an air of confidence, even though she had no official status in Sphinxes.

She's a natural, Lucienne thought, *and still carries the privilege and prestige of a Sealers elder.* She knew that her officers and soldiers loved the idea of a former enemy princess joining them and serving them. Who didn't love it when such a modern fantasy became reality? And so they welcomed the beautiful, young girl with open arms.

Lucienne's concern for her guest adapting to a new life in Sphinxes eased. Bayrose was raised in a political environment and knew how to adjust to life in any court.

At Lucienne's approach, her officers immediately snapped to attention and saluted her.

"At ease, gentlemen," she said. "There's no rank tonight."

They didn't relax. They showed her reverence, but they also appeared to be intimated by her. *It seems I do have a rough reputation,* she thought drily. Her officers were more comfortable around girls like Bayrose when they were off-duty.

"A great party, Siren," Bayrose said.

"Thanks." Lucienne smiled. "This is actually the first dinner party I've hosted in Sphinxes."

"To celebrate Chief McQuillen's safe return," an officer explained to Bayrose.

Interesting, Lucienne thought. Even though the men were quite taken by the Sealers princess, they still regarded her as an outsider.

"And in honor of the services of the men and women of Sphinxes," said Lucienne. She scanned the officers' faces. "Do you know Miss Thorn helped our chief escape the enemy militants?"

"Every man in Sphinxes has heard," a stocky naval officer said keenly. "The soldiers even made a song about Miss Thorn's bravery."

Bayrose blushed.

"We owe her a lifetime debt," Lucienne said, "especially me." She nodded at Bayrose and her officers before leaving the group alone. "You all enjoy the evening."

Ziyi's hilarious laughter burst forth from the next group a few feet away. *Another popular girl,* Lucienne thought. Every soul in Sphinxes knew Ziyi was one of Lucienne's favorite people, even when the girl constantly reminded and threatened others, "You better listen and obey me. Do you know how important I *am* to the Siren? We go way back!"

Lucienne darted a glance at the Chinese beauty in her tight qipao and stilettos flirting with some officers to full measure and enjoying being at the center of the party. Right now Ziyi bragged about being the architect behind this grand party.

The girl never knew the concept of modesty, and she put on a great show to compete with Bayrose in popularity. Lucienne shook her head fondly and decided not to take the spotlight from Ziyi. She glided toward Violet, who cowered in a corner in a short-sleeved black dress more suitable for a funeral.

No one approached the sulking redhead. Words had spread that the teen was disrespectful toward their Siren, which made Violet an outcast. Bayrose was busy building her new social life and completely forgot her friend at the moment.

Lucienne sat down on a bench beside Violet, ignoring her hostile stare. "Hi, Violet," she greeted, sympathy rising in her. Everything about this Nirvana girl was a discord in Sphinxes' symphony. Violet was a girl without a home or a nation. The girl could never have the man she loved. And this girl was Lucienne's new responsibility.

"What do you want?" Violet asked. Her forest green eyes didn't veil her resentment.

"I want to see if I can do something for you," Lucienne said. She'd assigned a tutor to help the girl adapt in Sphinxes after Violet's last outburst.

"Return Ash to me."

"I hope I can," Lucienne said, "but Ash isn't some commodity I can return. He doesn't belong to me."

"He belonged to me, until you took him."

The girl was as hung up on possession as a seven-year-old. It was going to be a hard task to convince her that Ashburn wasn't anyone's property. "He might have belonged to you at one time," Lucienne said softly, "but things have changed. People change. It's natural that people grow apart."

"Ash and I would never have grown apart if you hadn't come to our world."

"Ash was already a different person when he returned to Nirvana," Lucienne said, "free from his wheelchair." From the forlorn look in Violet's eyes, Lucienne knew she'd struck a chord.

"I know I can never compete with you."

"We're not competing," Lucienne said. "Ash cares about you very much. You're like his family."

"I'm not his sister!"

"Then convince him."

"While you're between us, I can never convince him."

"You're not listening, Violet." Lucienne held on to her patience. "It's not I who stand between you two."

"It is *you*," Violet insisted. "I saw the way he looked at you. He never looked at me that way."

"Then, no matter what you do, and no matter what I do, he'll never be yours. Not the way you want. You need to let him go. I can help you. You can make a new life here and have new friends."

"I'll never let him go!" Violet screamed. "I'll never want a life with another man!"

Heads turned toward them. Thaddeus glowered at the redheaded girl.

Lucienne rose. Her intervention had failed. There was nothing more she could do for Violet. She only hoped time would help the girl move on. Then she sighed. Time hadn't helped her move on from Ash and Vlad. From across the room near the terrace, she met Kian's concerned gaze.

He was conversing with the director of Sphinxes' Intelligence

Division, but he kept her in his field of sight. *Why can't he just lighten up and have fun for once?* Lucienne thought in exasperation. The party was mainly for him. If he stayed as tense as a bowstring at all times, one day he'd break. The Sealers had broken his nose, fingers, and a rib to prove he wasn't a man of steel. Oh God, they'd almost beheaded him, her protector and rock. She'd almost lost him.

"Excuse me," Lucienne said to Violet. Then she asked Thaddeus, "Cousin, will you bring Violet cherry ice cream? She likes it." She moved across the room toward Kian, the hem of her white skirt flowing along the marble floor.

The crowd parted for her.

Pyon, who also wore a sharp blue-and-gray uniform, nodded at her when she joined them. "Siren, you look good."

Lucienne grinned at him. "I'm not wearing red. That's what you meant."

"We're working on it so that you'll never need to wear it if you don't want to," Pyon said.

Lucienne fondly placed her hand on his arm. The men held more hope for her than she did for herself.

"Issue with the new girls?" Kian regarded her, the warmth toward her softening the edge in his hard sapphire eyes.

"Nothing I can't handle," she said. "I think we should give them more access to Sphinxes' facilities."

"Too soon," Pyon said. "I know you're eager to make them feel at home, but we have strict security protocols."

"You and Kian trust no one, do you?" asked Lucienne.

"That's not true, Siren," Pyon protested. "We trust you. We just need to watch out for your soft spots."

"You mean blind spots?" Lucienne asked.

"Those too," said Pyon. "But we'll cover them for you, as always."

"Don't roll your eyes, Lucia," Kian said. "That's not queenly."

Pyon roared with laughter.

"I can't win with you two ganging up on me." Lucienne shook her head. "Relax for a day, will you? Have a shot of whiskey." She lifted a glass of white wine from the tray as a cute waiter passed by them.

Kian frowned at her.

"I'll be eighteen in a few months," Lucienne said defiantly. "Today is a special occasion. You're back, so everyone is allowed a few drinks."

Pyon looked worried. "A few?"

Kian's frown deepened. "You can have one-third of a glass. You know your condition."

Thaddeus came forward after serving Violet ice cream. "Should I remove her glass?" he asked Kian keenly. Lucienne glared at her cousin until he backed down. Then, on a second thought, she handed the wine glass to Thaddeus. They were right. She shouldn't take chances. Alcohol might stir the toxin coursing in her blood.

Then she jolted as thunder cracked outside. A cluster of fireworks hit the high sky. The crowd cheered and flowed to balconies and down to the courtyard to watch the blossoms in the night sky.

Lucienne followed Kian and Pyon to their private terrace. Blazing lights from Sphinxes' fleets—where the fireworks launched—brightened the dark ocean and outlined the orchid trees on land.

Lucienne was in high spirits as well, though they couldn't fill the gaping hole in her heart. Vladimir and Ashburn should have been there to celebrate this night with her.

Then her heart leapt into her throat.

Ash! She sensed him. The nearer he was, the stronger their bond. When he'd been far away, their bond had thinned to a thread, but had always been there. Only when he disappeared into the Rabbit Hole had a void replaced the connection. When that happened, it sometimes felt that she didn't have a heartbeat.

Electricity cracked the air. She knew Ash felt her too. She threw a hand to her chest. Oh, how her heart pounded in joy and ached in anticipation.

"What's wrong, Lucia?" Kian asked in alarm at her wild look. And immediately, he, Pyon, and Thaddeus drew their weapons and scanned the celebrating crowd.

A column of light beamed down from the sky amid the backdrop of the fireworks.

Kian shielded Lucienne before Thaddeus had a chance to step in front of her. The guards rushed toward them from all directions, weapons thrust before them.

"It's Ashburn!" Lucienne shouted. "Fall back!"

Spike landed on the terrace with Ashburn riding it like a Norse god.

The men put away their guns with a curse. They could never get used to his dramatic entrances. Ashburn stepped off Spike, his silver eyes fixed only on Lucienne, his undisguised desire and tenderness making her cheeks flame.

Her throat closed, but she managed a whisper, "Ash," and impatiently extricated herself from the wall of flesh surrounding her and scrambled toward him.

Ashburn moved toward her in one long stride, his Adam's apple bobbing up and down. In an instant, they were in each other's arms. He embraced her, his face buried in her hair to inhale her familiar scent. And he whispered her name as if she was his lifeline.

How primrose was his touch. His male musk and body heat were equally intoxicating. Her body sang back. It wasn't just the Lure pulling them together like two magnets, though it created a fairy-like dreamland, separating them from all those around them. They wanted each other more than anything at that moment and had no room for the rest of the world.

His hard body pressed against hers, and hers melted into his.

Someone coughed politely. Kian? Maybe Pyon?

A slice of sense cracked into her skull. How long had she and Ash locked like this? She almost forgot how dangerously enticing the Lure was. If she kept giving in to its whim, she'd mate with Ashburn right here, right now. Her face flaming furiously, Lucienne twisted herself away from Ashburn, calling on whatever willpower she still possessed.

The punishing pain from the Lure that exploded inside her had never been so welcoming. Lucienne needed the pain to gain her dignity. She stepped a little further from Ashburn, and with a wince, looked up at him. "You're back, Ash."

He'd lost weight, though he was still masculine. His silver hair flowed in the breeze. His marble white face was perfectly symmetrical, and his blue silver eyes drew her in again. He was still the most striking man she'd ever seen.

"I never really left, Lucia," he said. "And I brought someone."

Until then, Lucienne had not noticed a distinguished gorgeous woman standing behind him. Her breath immediately caught in her throat.

The woman was of indeterminate age. Her thick brown hair, sprinkled with strawberry blond, pooled around her elegant shoulders. Her eyes were stars in the deep night sky, bright yet ancient, full of mystery and the dangerous unknown—and they gazed back at Lucienne intensely.

Pyon pointed his gun right at the woman. "A Sealers elder!" he warned. "She wears an elder's ring."

Lucienne finally breathed out in order to inhale. The woman was Jekaterina, her mother.

Redness came like the wind. Ashburn's hands on her shoulders tightened. "Stay with me!" she heard him saying.

No, you'll not take me, Lucienne hissed and then begged. *Not now.* But it still came. How could one fight the wind? As she put a hand in front of her, desperate and helpless to fend it off, a pulse of energy poured into her, coursing in her, until the red wind passed through her. Through the reflection in Ashburn's eyes, Lucienne saw the red rings in her eyes fade. He'd aided her with his power. He'd pushed back the assault of her insanity.

Lucienne stared into his eyes in amazement and gratitude. He reluctantly removed his hands from her shoulders as the danger passed. Lucienne turned to Jekaterina. There was a strange sadness and understanding in the woman's eyes. Had her mother actually understood what had just transpired?

"Hello, Lucienne," Jekaterina said, her voice silky. She paid no attention to the half-dozen guns pointed at her head.

"Jekaterina," Lucienne breathed, "why are you here?"

"You should have informed me before bringing her here, boy," Kian growled at Ashburn, but Lucienne knew how delighted he was that Ashburn had delivered him Jekaterina.

"Sorry." Ashburn shrugged. "I don't have a phone."

"That's not an excuse! You can—" Kian stopped himself. Lucienne knew he wouldn't want to spill out Ashburn's power in front of everyone—especially Jekaterina.

"Don't give him grief, McQuillen," Jekaterina said in her soft, enticing voice. "It was my arrangement. I do not come as an enemy. I come so you won't throw yourself into a dungeon again to look for me. I come for my daughter."

"Take her to the interrogation room," Kian ordered.

"No," Lucienne said, "bring her to the house." She swept a gaze at Pyon and the guards. "She isn't armed. There's no need to point that many guns at her."

A subtle smile touched Jekaterina's lips.

"Siren, we don't know—" Pyon said.

"This woman won't harm me," Lucienne said firmly. "Even if she tries, I can easily handle her. You can tag along, Director Pyon, if you aren't sure."

Kian led the group toward the grand hall's side exit reserved for Lucienne. The guards escorted the Russian woman at the front. Lucienne was placed in the center of the rank and file, Ashburn in step with her.

Across the hall, a redhead sprang toward them.

The guards moved, ready to take her down, but Ashburn pushed forward. "Let her pass, please."

Violet flung herself into Ashburn's arms, and he embraced her.

"Ash!" Violet cried. "Ash, you knew I was here and you came for me!"

"It's good to see you too, Violet," Ashburn said. "I'm glad you settled down here." He darted a glance in Lucienne's direction, and she forced a smile.

Lucienne wasn't smiling inside as she fought to snuff out her jealousy. *Ash isn't mine.* She'd told everyone and showed Ash himself that they wouldn't be together. Then why was she so possessive about him? *I'm a horrible person.* Yet she was pleased to see Ashburn pry himself from Violet's clinging grasp.

"I need to take care of something first," he told the redhead. "I'll see you tomorrow. Now go ahead and watch the fireworks with your friend."

"I don't care about fireworks—" Violet protested.

Kian frowned at the teen drama and ordered the guards, "Let's get moving!"

Bayrose stood several yards away from them, staring at Jekaterina, eyes wide and mouth agape. Lucienne bit back a forceful swear. She should have taken greater precautions not to expose Jekaterina like this, but she was a bit overwhelmed to see her estranged mother for the first time in her life.

Bayrose stepped toward the group, face paling, eyes flashing in fear and worry.

A guard blocked her, but Bayrose shoved him. The guard grabbed her arm. "You can't pass, Miss Thorn."

"Let me go, you barbarian!" Bayrose kicked the guard in the calf—she'd never behaved like that since arriving in Sphinxes. "You can't take away my mother!"

Mother? Lucienne felt cold air rushing toward her.

The guard stopped short and turned to look at Jekaterina, then at Lucienne. Bayrose took the chance to break free and spring toward Jekaterina. "Mom?" she asked. "What are you doing here? You shouldn't be here!"

Mom again? Lucienne narrowed her eyes.

"I came for your sister, Rose," Jekaterina said. "She needs my care."

"My sister?" Bayrose darted a perplexed glance from Jekaterina to Lucienne. "I have no sister."

Lucienne stared back at Bayrose, her face a mask of stone.

"Not here," Kian snarled, gesturing for the men to move.

The guards blocked Bayrose and drove back Violet. The girls screamed murder as they struggled to follow.

My mother, a power-hungry whore, bred a Siren and a Sealers elder.

An array of fireworks erupted into the sky, then brought down the red storm.

Ashburn rushed toward Lucienne, but he was too late. The storm hit her in the face before she could raise a hand to defend herself. "Kia—" She sent a warning toward Kian and Thaddeus, her voice whimpering in her throat.

"Don't touch her!" she heard Ashburn's warning. "I'm here now. I'll take her home." He held her in his arms protectively and possessively.

Lucienne blinked. Chaos swirled around her.

Ashburn lifted her as if she weighed nothing. He put her on Spike, then swung his leg over and rode behind her. "Ash!" she cheered. She liked his strong thighs against her legs. She twisted her torso to look up at him, inhaling his clean, masculine scent. "Let's ride to the sunset!" she cried with excitement, only to realize it was night. "To the moon!" she amended it, stretching her hand toward the sky.

None of her guards stepped forward to stop her from flying away with Ashburn. They didn't even protest. Last time she'd gone off with Ashburn, they'd acted like they were having a collective heart attack. Now they just kept quiet and looked grim. Even Kian didn't try to be a buzz killer—his specialty. The men had learned not to get in her way. *Super! A girl's gotta have fun sometimes.*

Spike flew her and Ash toward the open balcony.

"Ash! Wait!" Lucienne heard a girl cry out. She turned to see the redhead wriggling to break free of the guards. Ashburn, however, didn't stop. He didn't even look back at the pretty teen.

Lucienne flashed a triumphant grin at the girl. "Ash is mine," she declared and wrapped her arms around his waist as he flew her out of the grand hall toward the sky.

Fireworks exploded like a thousand little stars.

"Ooo, fireworks!" she called.

Now the blossoms in the sky were beneath her. Lucienne looked down and caught sight of her white gown. Had she lost her mind? Why had she worn a boring white to such a grand party? It was unforgivable negligence on Aida's part. She shouldn't rely on her nanny anymore. Aida was getting old and forgetful. She must immediately relieve Aida of her service. But where would Aida go? Lucienne felt pity for the aging nanny.

"Ash," she called, "we need to go to my house first. I must change my outfit."

"That's where we're going," he said.

Ash was so considerate, so unlike the other one—Prince Vladimir? Now she thought of him … where was he? She hadn't seen him for a while. They said that he'd gone to Tibet. Was he going to be a monk? It might be good for him. That boy needed some discipline—the lustful looks he used to send her way often made her shiver. Maybe she shouldn't be too hard on him. She could be delicious and irresistible. Of course, she couldn't blame herself for that either. Lucienne smirked to herself.

Spike skimmed over a jungle of red leaves and landed on the rooftop of the mansion. Ashburn stepped off and offered her a hand, but she hopped off with the look of I'm-an-independent-girl. His gray eyes didn't move from her, but this time, Lucienne didn't see his "hot for her" but rather an ocean of sadness and resignation.

Lucienne didn't like those negative emotions. They dragged her down. After she changed to her red gown, she'd cheer him up. She sprang toward the stairs. The bulletproof glass door slid aside, recognizing her heat signature.

"Are you coming, Ash?" She looked at him invitingly over her shoulder.

"I'm coming," he said, a twirl of unfamiliar emotion flitting across his face. "I won't leave you again."

She flashed him a feral smile. "Guess I'll have to live with that." After she had her red dress, she'd show him what good fun she could be, and he'd never let her go.

They were in luck that no one was in the mansion. It had been too crowded lately. Good thing she and Ash had ditched the guards at the castle.

Lucienne entered her bedroom and headed straight for her wardrobe without closing the door. She didn't mind Ash seeing her undressing, but blushed at the naughty thought of him watching her.

Ashburn stopped at the door. "I'll be in the kitchen. I'm going to brew coffee."

"At this hour?" she asked, peeking at him through her thick lashes.

"I'm trying to stay awake."

She narrowed her eyes. "Do I bore you?"

"No," he said, "you can never bore me even if you try, but I haven't slept much lately."

She regarded him. He had faint bluish circles under the hollow of his eyes. He was telling her the truth, but he also hid something from her. An amused light danced in her eyes as she saw through what it was. He was worried he couldn't resist the temptation if she revealed her nude body to him.

"Why didn't you sleep?"

"I had many things on my mind."

"Was I on your mind too?" she asked in a honeyed, throaty voice.

"All the time."

That was nice. He hadn't enough sleep because he was thinking of her. All the time! She'd let him go now to make coffee. Once she changed into her red gown, she'd reward him beyond his wildest dream. "Don't be too long," she purred.

The wardrobe door slid open at her approach. Inside the closet was a huge collection of dresses, sweaters, pants, and jackets, all in different shades of red.

What should she wear? Her gaze fell on a gown with a low neckline that would show half of her breasts. Ash seemed nervous around her this time. It was best to let him get used to her first, so she should avoid being provocative. Shrugging off her white gown, Lucienne selected a simple red tank top. It outlined her shape. She was just a non-threatening teenage girl now.

She found a miniskirt to go with the top. Before she put it on, she heard voices. It had to be Ash. He just couldn't stay away from her. She put aside the skirt with a smirk. She wanted to see his expression when he saw her in her cherry-colored panties. The tank top covered half of it, which made her look more suggestively sexy.

She waited, but didn't see Ash coming. The voices came from the open library. Was Ash talking to someone? Who dared stall him? Annoyed, Lucienne pricked her ears to hear more. Ever since she had all the elements of Forbidden Glory, she had super hearing.

"It poses a plight for you to have a mad queen while you're forming a nation." It was the voice of the Russian woman—her mother, who vanished for seventeen years, only to pop up unannounced and uninvited.

But who was the mad queen Jekaterina had referred to?

"How did you know we were going to make Lucienne Lam the queen?" Pyon demanded. "You were locked in Abaddon 5. Who is your informant in Sphinxes?"

Fury leapt from Lucienne. They were calling her a mad queen now? No wonder she often spied grief in her guards' eyes, and tonight in Ash's. She'd heard the rumors and laughed at them, but it was no laughing matter now. Something ran deep. She needed to get to the bottom of this conspiracy.

She quieted her racing heart and listened on. In her anger, she'd missed a few exchanges of the conspirators' words.

"I don't need informants. I knew about her insanity before it happened. It was written on the last scroll an eon ago."

The library sank into awful silence as if everyone was trying to digest the significance of what Jekaterina had revealed. Or perhaps they were trying to tell if the woman had lied.

Of course it was a lie!

"Where's the scroll?" Kian asked.

"I'll share it only with Lucienne," Jekaterina said. "I need to see her now."

"She isn't in condition to receive a visitor," said Kian.

"I'm not a visitor," the woman said. "I'm her mother. I need to see her in that condition so I can decide how to help her."

Her deranged condition, she meant? Lucienne narrowed her eyes to slits. How dare they slander her! Then a cold shiver spiked up her spine. She'd just found out their scheme by pure luck. They must be the ones who had planted the rumors. They meant to lock her up in an asylum and take Sphinxes from her. Was Kian in this thick plot too? Her heart contracted at the notion. What about Ash? He hadn't returned. Was he with them? A sheen of cold sweat trickled down her back.

"Never open your heart, especially to those closest and dearest to you. They're the ones who will bleed you dry if you let your guard down for half a heartbeat." Her grandfather, the former Siren, had never been so right.

"You abandoned her at her birth," Kian scoffed. "Now all of a sudden you show up, and we should just trust your good intentions toward Lucienne, Elder Jekaterina? Or is it Elder Samantha?"

Lucienne couldn't argue with Kian. That was the first thing he'd said so far that made sense.

"All I've done is make sure Lucienne is where she is," said Jekaterina.

"Where she is?" Kian spat. "She's tormented by madness right now."

Not that again! Rage clouded Lucienne's vision. Why was her chief so hell bent on branding her a mental health risk?

"I needed to make sure she became the Siren she was born to be," Jekaterina said. "Her insanity is but a setback."

Lucienne sneered. She knew their strategy: they must defame her before taking her down. "The Sealers must destroy your legitimacy first before they kill you," the Czech prince had once told her. But why would her people work with the Sealers? Had her people forgotten how the Sealers were founded? The secret society's sole purpose was to put her inside a coffin and seal it!

Lucienne pulled off her tank top. She needed to look queenly—not a mad monarch, but a reasonable, formidable leader ready to confront traitors and schemers. In her red gown, she moved out of the bedroom in a blur, descended the spiral stairs, and stormed into the open library.

Everyone stopped short, obviously not expecting her. Lucienne let a cold smile linger on her lips. She knew she looked fabulous from their stunned looks. They named her the mad queen, but she was giving them the Red Queen.

The men's awed expressions shifted to sorrow seconds later, as if her classic, regal appearance only made everything worse. A chilly realization hit her. They really thought she was a lunatic. She wheeled around to Kian, peeking into his sapphire eyes. Though they warmed at the sight of her, they couldn't hide tremendous sadness and exhaustion.

Oh, God, Kian thinks I'm mad, as well. Lucienne drew a cold breath. Who had turned her people against her? Her hard gaze fixed on the woman in the center. Jekaterina! The Sealers elder had first named her the mad queen. Her own mother had come to finish the job that her biological father, Jimmy Lam, had failed to do—destroy her.

How could her men not see through this?

It took a moment, but Lucienne put the pieces together.

Jekaterina wasn't just an unmatchable beauty with a mesmerizing voice. She had powers. Lucienne could sense the elder's supernatural abilities loud and clear. Her people had fallen under the spell of her mother.

First things first: she must expose the elder's lies before her warriors.

Jekaterina gazed back at Lucienne. Emotions swirled in her rich brown eyes. But they were all lies.

"You want to see me in this condition, Jekaterina?" Lucienne asked. "I'm here now. Go on. Keep telling them I'm a maniac. Don't let me stop you from poisoning my men's minds."

Everyone inhaled sharply. Kian's eyes went wild with alarm.

"When are you planning to lock up the mad queen?" Lucienne surveyed her men. "Picked out a specific date yet?"

They averted their eyes. No one could hold a glare that spat fire. Instead, they turned to Kian. Lucienne nodded. Right. The ringleader of the coup. It was sad. So sad. Her chief had all the power one could ask for in Sphinxes. Yet he wanted more.

"Lucia, you got it all wrong," Kian said.

"Do I?" Lucienne asked. "Wrong again? Wrong about you?" She pushed back the tears prickling her eyelids. "I trusted you with my soul, Kian McQuillen," her voice croaked. "I was so blind that I couldn't see that power corrupting you."

Something immediately broke in Kian's eyes. "You can always trust me," he said. "You know I'd give you my life in a heartbeat."

"I'm not sure anymore," Lucienne said. "Aren't you all gathering here in *my* house to stage a coup? You're about to chain me in the dungeon. You'll make a mental case out of me. Aren't you already making my guards the orderlies? You do not plan to let me see sunlight again. Ever heard of the man in the iron mask? L'Homme au Masque de Fer. Are you going to make a mask for me too?"

The men looked appalled and horrified.

"Brilliant strategy," she nodded, "but I caught you. Now who's really brilliant?"

"Lucienne," Jekaterina said, "you're not well. I've come to your aid. I bring you only protection. It's time for you to know the truth."

"You've spun lies into truth since you came," Lucienne said. "You deceived my men. They're brave warriors. They fight well on the battlefield, but not against vile snares laid out by a master manipulator like you. Your former sweetheart failed to annihilate me. You'll fail too, and miserably." And she forced herself into Jekaterina's mind.

Almost instantly, Jekaterina's face distorted in pain.

Lucienne blinked. Her biological mother could feel her mind invasion, and it had caused the woman a tremendous pain. How? Others couldn't even feel her mental touch. She withdrew and staggered back in shock. She shouldn't be so inhumane as to inflict pain on her mother.

Another blink. No, the woman had given up her rights as her mother the moment she'd deserted Lucienne, and even more so when she'd returned to malign her daughter. The agony in Jekaterina's mind was a ruse to stop Lucienne from seeing the truth.

But Lucienne had seen the truth—Jekaterina was lethal. Lucienne's mistake with Schmidt caused the death of Captain Marloes. She wouldn't make the same mistake again. She wouldn't allow this woman who wore her mother's face to take everything from her. She wouldn't lose another warrior on her watch.

"Lucia," Chief McQuillen called, putting his hand on her elbow to try to usher her off the stage quietly. "I'll explain everything to you tomorrow. You look exhausted. Go rest."

Lucienne pulled her arm free. "How dare you manhandle me, McQuillen!" she shouted. Forbidden Glory stirred in her, resonating with her rage. "You're working with this woman who has the very intention of replacing me!" She swept her stare at the rest of the men with contempt. "I trusted all of you. I put my life in your hands. What have I done wrong to deserve such treachery?"

"Calm down, Siren," Pyon said. "There isn't a single cell in us that will betray you. You have our absolute loyalty, no matter what state you are—"

"There you go again. My state of insanity, you say?" Lucienne asked. "Not a national treasure anymore, but a national risk? I'll deal with you later, Director." She turned to Kian. "They're our people, yet you want to make them yours alone. I'd give you everything if you just asked, yet you led them astray. You conspired with my enemies." She heard a sob in her throat as she summoned her power.

The five fundamental forces were fire, water, earth, aether, and metal. Lucienne extracted fire and aether and let liquid fire twirl around her fingers. She removed her gaze from her fire to the men, who looked amazed and disquieted. "Has anyone ever seen a marvel like this?" she asked softly.

Forbidden Glory urged her to act, and she raised a hand toward Kian. "Time for justice."

"Lucia," Kian said. He was calm, but his complexion had never been paler. "Don't blame yourself after this. Sphinxes and your people will always need you. Stay strong."

How could the warmth and sadness in his sapphire eyes be deeper than the night sky when he knew she was going to burn him alive?

Lucienne's elite guards, Kian's aides, and Pyon all moved, not to stop her but to form a wall of flesh to guard Kian. They collectively wore expressions of dismay and despair. They'd seen the demonstration of her power. They knew no one could stop her.

"How loyal!" she exclaimed. "You were good men once, but all of you have removed your loyalty from me. So if you want to become a pile of ashes with your chief, that's fine with me."

"Leave!" Kian shoved the men away. "I'm her target. Let her deal with me alone."

The men refused to move.

"I'll court martial you!" Kian yelled.

"No one's going anywhere." Lucienne gave a harsh laugh. "I'm the Siren. I give orders here." She let the liquid fire leap high from her fingers. "One moment you were all traitors; now you act like heroes." She fixed her gaze on her chief. "Truth is, I don't really want to end you, Kian McQuillen, though I should crack you like a bad egg. I decide to give you a chance to repent. I'll give you all a chance to turn away from your evil ways." She turned to Jekaterina. "As for you, Jekaterina, you don't get the chance they're getting."

Her mother widened her eyes but stood still, awaiting her fate.

"No, Lucienne!" Kian roared. "It'll destroy you." He darted toward the Russian woman to shield her.

Too late! Lucienne's mouth curled up in a sardonic smile. She called forth the elements of water and air. Their combined force formed a cloud of gale force wind, throwing Kian and the men back several feet, away from Jekaterina.

"I can love you, my daughter," Jekaterina said. "You're much more than I expected."

"And that will be your last lie," said Lucienne.

Stop this madness, Lucienne Lam! Stop! A small voice that resembled hers pounded in her head. The word madness enraged Lucienne more than anything. She rejected the pleading and let her fire roam free.

"No! Lucia!" a cry arose. Then, in a blur, Ashburn lunged in front of Jekaterina, shielding her. His hair was still dripping with water. He must have rushed out from taking a shower. And she'd been wondering where he was.

A stream of fire hit his chest, knocking him down.

Writhing on the ground, Ashburn became a human torch.

Then the rings of redness receded from Lucienne's eyes.

Lucienne threw herself at Ashburn in an attempt to shield him from her own fire, and screamed.

Chapter Twenty

THE THIRD SCROLL

Lucienne had locked herself in her bedroom for three days now, watching the red maple trees wither. She could barely face herself, let alone others.

The image of her fire engulfing Ash was still imprinted on her mind. Anyone else who had caught that fire would have been incinerated. Ash had put up a shield—his black lightning—to diffuse the flame, and she'd sent the water element to aid him just in time.

Even with his regenerating ability, he still had light burns over much of his body. Her Forbidden Glory had proved to be too powerful, even for Ashburn.

Just then, as if called, he landed Spike on the balcony and entered her room.

"Hello," he said and lounged beside her on a couch.

"Hello." She forced a smile. "Does it still hurt?" she asked, her eyes examining his face.

His usual marble-white face was pink, the aftereffect of the burn.

"It looks worse than it feels," he said, touching her face as she suppressed a shiver of pleasure. She shouldn't be feeling good. She deserved to be miserable. No words or punishments could rectify her horrific act.

She'd antagonized Kian and accused the man who loved her above everything of being a traitor. How could she be so monstrous? Her insanity had aggregated, making her see the world with a distorted perspective. A psychotic disorder and paranoia were now her constant companions. Some outside malevolence force was no longer the most dangerous thing to her people—she was.

Ashburn's hand left her face reluctantly. She didn't want it to go. It would be really nice if he could hold her, but she wouldn't ask, not while she had a firm grasp on reality.

"How are you holding up?" he asked.

She sighed. The color of his eyes turned gray. She knew he knew it too—she wasn't getting better. "How's Jekaterina?" she asked, changing the subject. If Ashburn hadn't stepped in front of Jekaterina, she'd have reduced her own mother to ashes. But Jekaterina hadn't walked away without a scratch. Sparks from Lucienne's liquid fire had singed her hair.

"She's at the lab, studying the scroll," he said.

Her mother had been put under tight surveillance. No way could that woman disappear into thin air again. Kian had made sure of that. From what Lucienne heard, Jekaterina didn't seem to mind the treatment. "You can chain me in a dungeon," the woman had said, "as long as I can do my work and visit my daughters when I want."

Did Jekaterina truly want to save her, or did she have another agenda?

"The last scroll?" Lucienne asked.

"Jekaterina insisted that she'd show it only to you," Ashburn said. "Somehow, she always gets her way." He gave her a look. "You don't trust her."

"I don't know her."

"She wants a chance to get to know you, and to let you know her."

Lucienne gave a non-committal shrug. She'd longed for a mother when she was a little girl in the Red Mansion surrounded by enemies. But now that her mother had come, she was terrified of knowing her. "How did you find her?" she asked. "You said her memories weren't in your collections."

"She removed the veil. She called me."

"Remove the veil?"

"An electronic veil. I believe she has some kind of superpower, like you and me, but I can't find out anything about hers. She's more than a mystery."

"If your game theory is true, you think she might be one of the players?"

"Yes."

"All the more reason to keep an eye on her."

"You can't imagine how many eyes are on her. She's no better than a prisoner here."

"You sounded sympathetic."

"I felt kinship with her. I can't explain it." He placed Lucienne's hands into his. "At least she came forward to help you when I couldn't save you. Lucia, I'm sorry."

Lucienne stayed very still, afraid that if she moved, Ash would withdraw his hands. "You cannot and should not take on that responsibility."

"I chose not to save you," he said, shame and agony twirling in his eyes.

Lucienne felt her heart skip a beat. Ashburn knew of a cure, but couldn't give it to her. The torment in his eyes had told her this much. Deep inside, she always knew he was her only bet. If he didn't see any hope, then there was no hope for her. It was only a matter of time before she completely gave in to the ancient poison. She was the last Siren. The line terminated with her.

"Then there must be a good reason," she said softly, withdrawing her hands from his. The heat between them was getting too strong, and she had to make a countermove before the temptation became too great. The Lure responded by shoving a sharp pain into her stomach, displeased at the broken connection.

"You must hate me," he said, misunderstanding the removal of her hands from him. "I chose me and the world over you." A storm of sorrow and self-loathing darkened his ice-blue eyes to gunmetal gray.

He'd once chosen her above himself and the world when

Seraphen had tried to ram his fist into her heart in Nirvana. "I can never hate you, Ash." She comforted him. "You fight for me as hard as anyone. You've done enough for me. Thank you."

"Never enough," he said. "Seraphen told me it'd be the end of me if I cure you."

"But I killed Seraphen."

"I resurrected him."

Lucienne's throat tightened. Seraphen had terrorized her more than anyone. She wasn't afraid of the creature coming to finish her, but rather her people. She regretted that she'd let Ashburn keep Seraphen's body. Every one of her missteps had a dire consequence. Must she put her people in harm's way even after she was gone?

"Why would you do such a thing?" she grated. "You don't need to bring him back to finish me. You know I won't last long."

He looked like she stabbed a knife in his guts and twisted it. "Lucia," he said, eyes filling with pain. "He won't pose a threat to you. I resurrected only his head. He's the only one with the knowledge to the cure."

"The knowledge is unnecessary," she said. She didn't want to sound bitter, but she heard the bile in her voice. She shouldn't be so selfish. She should allow him to choose himself over her. If their situations were reversed, wouldn't she do the same? "I'm sorry, Ash. You're doing the right thing. Just don't let anyone else know." If Kian and her men knew that Ashburn had a possible antidote, they'd do everything in their power to make Ash deliver it, even if it cost him his life.

"You and I will go to the bitter end together," he said.

A realization hit her. He returned to spend her last moments with her. But she didn't understand what he'd meant by 'together.' Was he going to—? She didn't want anyone to go to the bitter end with her. She wanted them to keep going and live well. "Don't say such a silly thing," she chided him. "We'll enjoy what we have. Let's not talk about the cure."

"Lucia," he said, wringing his hands together to keep himself from touching her. His knuckles turned white.

She needed him as much as he needed her, but she didn't encourage him. She couldn't win a fight against herself and the Lure at the same time. Her willpower was but thin paper, and she needed her dignity more than ever while still possessing her sanity.

Ashburn let out his angst in a deep breath and dropped his head in his hands. Then he stirred and raised his head. "Kian's coming."

"He comes every day," Lucienne said drily. She was too ashamed to face her protector.

"He won't leave this time if you don't open the door. He thinks he's given you enough space and now's the time to get over your childish behavior."

Lucienne narrowed her eyes. "Childish? That's what he thinks of me?"

Ashburn sighed. "I should not read other people's thoughts to you. I'd better get going. I'll check on you later." He rose to his feet and jogged toward the balcony.

She watched him get on Spike like a knight. The machine beamed in light. In a second, Ash was gone.

Lucienne opened the door before Kian's knuckles touched it.

Two guards stood on each side of the door, saluting Kian and her.

"Lucia?" Kian looked both surprised and relieved that she was to receive him.

"Since you won't go away if I don't answer the door," she said, "I'd better save us both some trouble."

Kian nodded. "That's the smart thing to do."

"Not so childish?"

Kian blinked, then realized, "I hate it when that boy gets into my head. The least he can do is zip his mouth! Doesn't he know how to respect people's privacy?"

"Like he has a choice?"

Kian followed her into her suite and shut the door behind them. "How are you feeling, kid?" he asked as he settled himself on a chair beside her in the sitting room.

She wanted to dig a hole for herself, but she looked straight at him. "Kian, I—"

"Don't apologize," he said. "We're long past that—ever since you bit me as an infant. That was a hard bite. You didn't apologize then."

Lucienne grinned. "I bit Jed too, twice, on the nose."

"No one had ever bitten him," he said. "The great Siren was greatly humiliated and was forever wary of you."

"I miss Grandpa. He wasn't a monster like others said he was."

"Neither are you."

Tears came. "I almost killed you, Kian."

"Almost, but not quite," he said. "You couldn't do it, no matter how convinced you were that I betrayed you, and you value loyalty more than anything. Didn't you give me a chance to repent in spite of your terrible rage?"

She'd demanded that he and the men repent. She'd told him that she could crack him like a bad egg. Lucienne buried her face in her hands as she recalled her outrageous words.

"You couldn't truly hurt me or the men, so you found an excuse not to punish me. You took it out on Jekaterina instead. The Lucienne Lam I know wouldn't hesitate to execute justice, but even when you were convinced I was your mortal enemy, you couldn't kick my butt."

She raised her head, deciding not to be a whining baby. In her last moments, she should be the Siren she was born to be. "No one wants to kick your rock butt. It'd hurt my nice boots. Not worth it."

"True." He smiled. "Jekaterina is working with the decoding team. She believes the prophecies will point us toward a cure."

Even if Jekaterina could decipher the inscriptions, runes, and symbols in time, she'd realize her effort was futile. "We're wasting time seeking a cure," Lucienne said. "We should focus on Sphinxes and its future. It's time for us to be realistic. I want you and the men to be prepared. When I'm gone—"

"No more of that kind of talk!" Kian cut in, dark fire leaping in his sapphire eyes. "I'm not giving up hope, and neither should you!"

"Fine," she said. "Whatever—you say."

"I hate it when you say whatever!" he yelled at her. "You won't go down. You won't lie down! You'll fight as a true warrior, and I won't let the end take you. Not while I'm here."

She sighed. "How can we fight our mortality? We aren't gods. I need you to embrace—"

"I'll embrace the day you get well."

"Fine, I'll fight as hard as I can." She rested her head against his shoulder. She was so tired, but his strength held her up.

They sat there quietly for a while, watching the wind ruffle the crimson leaves outside the window. Lucienne traced back to the days in the Red Mansion. He'd trained her. He'd surrounded her with an ocean of warmth and strong protective walls amid the coldness and her relentless enemies. He was her true family, but she'd never told him that she loved him. She needed to say it now, or she might never get the chance.

"I love you, Kian," she said.

"That's all right, kid," he said, his big, firm hand squeezing her shoulder gently. "Your mother needs to see you. You can't hide here forever."

"I wish I could."

"And Bayrose—now your half-sister—keeps asking about you. She's keen to see you too."

She lifted her head from Kian's shoulder. "But I'm not sure—"

"Give them a shot, will you?"

After Kian left, Lucienne stepped out of her room. The guards looked happy at her appearance. After breakfast, Adam drove her to the castle. There was no need for her to hide anymore. The whole of Sphinxes now knew she was inflicted by madness.

Her cousin and another guard joined her. They usually joked with her, especially Thaddeus. Now everyone remained quiet. They were treading carefully, afraid of setting her off.

"I'm not that terrible, am I?" she asked, then admitted with a groan. "I *am*."

"No, Siren, you aren't terrible," Adam said. "You're terrifying."

Lucienne opened her mouth, but then shut it. Thaddeus roared with laughter, and the other guards joined in.

"Well, that settles it," said Lucienne.

"But we'll still follow you until—" Adam immediately put on a brake.

Lucienne knew he was about to say "the end" only to realize the word "end" was like a curse to his mistress.

"Follow you to Eterne," Thaddeus picked it up. "That is your call, and our duty is to deliver you there in one piece—and maybe hitch a ride ourselves."

Lucienne felt tears brimming in her eyes. Eterne—she'd never get there. She and her family had once dreamed of the glory. When she'd obtained the Eye of Time a year ago, she'd believed anything was possible. She'd believed Eterne was within arm's reach.

After she was gone, who would carry the torch and lead her people to Eterne? Who would harbinger the first quantum evolution of the human race?

"Hitch a ride? It might be too much for you," she said. "Now let's go harass our civilian scientists."

Which, of course, was a ruse. She really wanted to see Jekaterina.

Stopping in front of the research laboratory, Lucienne pressed her palm on the scanner. Adam pushed the door open wide and entered first. Even in their most secure home base, the guards followed protocols. She strode in after her captain.

The two guards assigned to watch Jekaterina saluted Lucienne. They were selected from her team, and everyone knew no one could corrupt Lucienne's guards.

The decoding team was taking notes from Jekaterina. It was a surprise for Lucienne to see these learned men and women—some of whom could read part of the dead languages—humble themselves before her mother.

Dr. Alexander Kubrick, a symbologist and mathematician, debated Dr. Susan Cross, a cryptographer. Bansi Soni, the programmer, ignored the dispute and typed frantically and loudly on his keyboard.

A copy of the first scroll with ancient inscriptions and symbols lay on a large desk. The original was inside Lucienne's secret chamber. The first scroll predicted the coming of the Eye of Time, while the second revealed the lost city. Lucienne had found both.

The three scrolls formed a complete circle with a full code. Jekaterina had told Kian that the code was the key to purging the ancient poison and liberating her daughter from the infliction of insanity.

Jekaterina was drawing unfamiliar inscriptions and runes on the board. Lucienne realized they were from the third scroll. The woman didn't trust anyone. Did Jekaterina really want to help her, or had she come here for something else? Lucienne couldn't read her mother's intent.

Bansi Soni stopped typing and looked up from his screen. "Lucia," he said, "they make me work so hard. I get only four hours of sleep every night."

Lucienne regarded him coolly. "I also hear you take a two-hour nap during lunch and spend an extra hour playing computer games."

"I designed the games, but who told you?" Bansi Soni looked around, trying to find someone to glare at.

"Shouldn't you use your play hours to build a platform for us, Bansi, at this critical time?" Jekaterina cut in, her voice soft, silvery, and assertive.

Dr. Kubrick, Dr. Cross, and the researchers turned to Lucienne, greeting her before making their own demands and complaining about one another.

Unlike her warriors, these civilian scientists still viewed her as a teenage girl who could be easily swayed, even though she was their boss.

"Enough," Jekaterina said, and they immediately hushed.

This woman had taken control of Lucienne's most opinionated

team within a week.

"I've been waiting for you, Lucienne," Jekaterina said in the now quiet lab.

Lucienne met her gaze, but gave no hint of emotion. She was glad that Jekaterina didn't call her Lucia. Only friends and family called her that. "Here I am," she said flatly.

Jekaterina gestured for Lucienne to follow her, as if she were the host. Lucienne raised an eyebrow, but went along anyway. The guards fell in around them. The woman led them toward the east wing of the castle.

After climbing step after step, they stopped before a door at the top of the tower. Jekaterina chose to be Ashburn's neighbor, but Ash had moved into Lucienne's mansion.

As Jekaterina strode into her dwelling, Adam and another guard followed her in.

"I did not invite you," Jekaterina said. "Wait outside."

The guards hesitated, but didn't obey her.

"For heaven's sake, I won't harm my own daughter," Jekaterina said, turning to Lucienne. "We need privacy."

Lucienne gestured for the guards to wait outside.

"After I do a sweep," Adam said.

"Seriously?" Jekaterina said.

Lucienne gave a small shrug. She was tired of fighting them over the precautions, so now she just let them finish their procedures until they were happy. "They'll ask me to shoot them if I stop them from doing their jobs."

"Shoot them," Jekaterina said. "They need to know who's in charge."

"Then we start with you, Jekaterina," Lucienne said coldly.

The guards sent Lucienne a grateful glance before going in to examine the room. Before they came out, one guard looked down from the window to estimate the harm if the Russian woman threw their Siren through it.

Adam gave Lucienne a nod, and Lucienne stepped into the room and closed the door behind her.

Jekaterina's temporary place was simple as a nun's—a single bed, a desk, and a chest. She didn't offer Lucienne a chair, and Lucienne didn't intend to get that relaxed. A small smile appeared on Jekaterina's face. "You've grown up to be a beautiful young woman. You've exceeded all my expectations, daughter."

Lucienne was having a hard time thinking this woman was actually her mother. The youthful, gorgeous Jekaterina looked more like her older sister. "I hope you didn't come to pick up what was left seventeen years ago," she said, keeping her face bored. "If you do, you'll be very disappointed. All I need from you is the knowledge on the scrolls. I assume that's why we're alone."

Jekaterina sighed. "Aren't you curious why I left when you were born?"

"No," Lucienne said. "You said you came with the gift of the third scroll. Where is it?"

"I'm the gift. I'm the last scroll."

Lucienne narrowed her eyes. "You're wasting my time."

"I have all the time in the world, daughter, but I don't waste it because you don't have time." Jekaterina pulled the amethyst-colored sweater over her head, then started unbuttoning her black silk shirt.

Lucienne could see her mother's fashionable black bra underneath.

Classic, she thought. Did Jekaterina hide the scroll in her cleavage? Legend had it that the third piece was on a dinosaur bone. Let's see how this woman hid a big bone between her breasts.

Jekaterina tossed her shirt on the bed. Lucienne didn't see anything in Jekaterina's bra, only that her mother had a perfect body—not the body of a woman who had given birth to two daughters, but the radiant body of a nineteen year old.

Jekaterina's hands went behind her back, working on the hook of her bra. It came loose.

What game was she playing? Lucienne had no interest in watching anyone perform a strip tease, and definitely not her own mother. Yet she didn't object, but looked on with cold clarity.

As Lucienne remained untouched, Jekaterina, however, turned around, her back to her daughter, and removed her bra. Lucienne stared at her mother's smooth, creamy back. "What is this nonsense?"

"Watch." Jekaterina breathed in deeply, and her shoulders rose and fell.

In front of Lucienne's eyes, ancient inscriptions and runes became visible on Jekaterina's back, glowing faintly. Lucienne widened her eyes. "How?" she whispered, coming closer to Jekaterina to inspect the blazing symbols. "May I?" she asked.

"Go ahead, daughter."

Lucienne touched the runes on her mother's skin. They weren't inked or engraved. They came from beneath her skin. At her touch, the inscriptions and runes fluctuated like waves. Some dimmed and some brightened. She gasped. Before she could mark out the ancient runes again, they disappeared without a trace. Jekaterina's bare back was blank.

"My ancestors said the third scroll was etched on a dinosaur bone," Lucienne whispered.

"Not anymore." Jekaterina put her shirt back on and turned to face Lucienne.

"How?" Lucienne asked. "How did you become the conductor of the scroll?"

"You don't need to know how, my daughter," Jekaterina said, suppressing a shiver as if she was sparing Lucienne from the horror. "It was difficult, but I succeeded. I became the scroll for you, so no one could use it to harm you again."

The Sealers had already poisoned her.

"For seventeen years, I stayed with the Sealers to get this scroll, so I could protect you."

"Protect me?" Lucienne was suddenly furious. "My enemies have hit their target—me. I have the slimmest hope of recovery. You knew about their plan to poison me, yet you didn't whisper a thing. And now you come to my door claiming you want to help me. What's your real agenda, Jekaterina?"

"The prophecy foretold you being poisoned. It was meant to happen," Jekaterina said. "Who am I to interfere with the grand design?"

"The grand design?" Lucienne stared at Jekaterina incredulously. "You let me be poisoned for the greater good?"

"You can't see the whole picture yet. In order for the world to move forward, for the wheel to be set in motion again, you'll have to suffer just a little longer, my daughter."

"Don't call me daughter."

Jekaterina's expression saddened. "I never intended this fate for you, but you're chosen. Like the hero in a story, you don't get to choose your own path."

"So you and your Sealers comrades decided to choose it for me— insanity before death?"

"Your death won't come while I'm here," Jekaterina said. "I've made progress in decoding the prophecies. I'll acquire the final code, which is the key to your survival and the future of Earth."

Lucienne couldn't tell if this woman was telling the truth or as mad as she, but she knew about the grand design Ash had told her. Jekaterina was almost echoing Ash's words. Only Ash feared that future, while Jekaterina looked forward to it.

"Who are you really?" Lucienne demanded. "Who sent you? You won't get out of here, so there's no use denying it. You're not an ordinary woman. First, you manipulated the genes and produced the first female Siren in an eon. And second—"

"Let's not go that far," Jekaterina said. "In time you'll know everything, but now I have work to do. You're welcome to join me on deciphering the scrolls." She opened the door, gesturing for her daughter to depart. "Shall we?"

Chapter Twenty-One

POISON OF LOVE

Lucienne hadn't visited Jekaterina since joining her on deciphering the ancient inscriptions on the scrolls a week ago. Today she lingered in the twilight zone. She couldn't stand wearing white or red. Aida finally found her a grey-silver flowery dress as a compromise.

Lucienne paced from her bedroom to the sitting room, where the guards waited. They were watchful, which irritated her even more. She couldn't decide if she was mentally sound—only that she felt as if she were being suspended upside down in the air.

She wanted to scream, but that wouldn't help either. In frustration, she retired to her room.

Real. Not real. Real. She glanced at a bundle of fresh yellow roses in a wooden vase on the white vanity table. *Who bought me roses?* She sauntered toward it, tore a pedal off, and sniffed it, wishing its scent brought back a memory.

It almost did. A colorful image flashed by, but before her mind could grasp it, it was gone. A flicker of light sank under the surface of her consciousness. She needed to figure out something, but what was it?

She heard talk from the sitting room. Thaddeus stood with Bayrose. Her half-sister had come to visit. Or had she been loitering around for a while now? Kian believed being around her family would do her good. Lucienne didn't object, though she also didn't show any keenness. Her paternal family had spurned her, and she wasn't exactly optimistic about her maternal relatives.

"It's getting worse," Bayrose whispered, "isn't it?"

Now her cousin and her younger sister were confiding in each other?

"I can hear you." Lucienne shot back. "What's getting worse?"

Bayrose left Thaddeus and approached Lucienne. She wore a lemon-colored skirt and looked lovely. "Lucia," she said, "why don't you sit down? You're making everyone nervous."

"Then don't watch," Lucienne said.

"Sit down, Lucia," Bayrose said. "Let me fix your hair. You liked the braids I did for you last time."

That sounded like a good idea, but something wasn't quite right. Something to do with Bayrose. Did she still blame her half-sister subconsciously, even though she thought she'd forgiven Bayrose? Her sister hadn't meant to hurt her. Bayrose and Vlad had both been tricked.

Lucienne forced herself to concentrate, and for a second, her senses sharpened. Bayrose's presence was affecting her. She felt a force from her sister, as if Bayrose possessed a will that could bend hers. In the past few days, Bayrose had made her do things she hadn't wanted to do and say things she hadn't wanted to say. Did Bayrose have the power of persuasion? She'd been watching her sister interact with others. The guards often accommodated Bayrose, but Aida and Ash had dismissed Bayrose easily. Maybe her younger sister had a way only with her?

A second later, Lucienne lost her focus. *I'm being paranoid again, even when I'm not in the grip of insanity.* She sank onto the chair before the vanity.

"It would be nice if you had a mirror in here," Bayrose said, standing behind Lucienne and combing her long, midnight hair.

"Kian removed it," Lucienne said.

"Why?" asked Bayrose.

"Because of an accident."

"What accident?" Bayrose asked.

After she'd smashed the mirror with her bare hand in a rage, Kian had taken away all things sharp in her room. But why did she succumb to Kian? It appeared that everyone could run her life, and that she, their Siren to whom they pledged their undying fealty, had the least say on everything.

When had it become like this? Right, her mental illness. They were doing everything they could to protect her. She should be grateful, but why wasn't she? Why couldn't she think straight? It was like a shadow clouded her mind.

"I don't want to talk about it," Lucienne said.

"But I want to know," Bayrose said. "I want to know everything about you."

Tell her. Tell your sister all your secrets. Lucienne felt the spur, but a stronger part of her told her to resist: *Do not let anyone have power over you.* After a torn moment, she accepted the second voice. She was the Siren. She was born to rule. She wouldn't allow anyone to dominate her. Yet, rejecting her younger sister's small, innocent request made her feel ashamed.

Then, for a second, clarity opened a crack in her mind. She needed to divert her sister from focusing on her. "Tell me something about Jekaterina," she said.

"What do you want to know?" asked Bayrose.

"Was she ... always being there for you when you grew up?"

"Mmm hmm."

Her mother abandoned one daughter, yet raised the other.

"So you two are close."

"Kind of."

"What do you mean 'kind of'? You're either close or you're not," Lucienne said, then caught herself. Had Bayrose detected the hidden bitterness in her voice?

Bayrose halted the comb in the air. "Mother is an enigma," she said. "She's not the conventional mother type."

"I can see that."

"Yet I want her approval more than anything," Bayrose said with uncertainty, "Am I too immature?"

Though abandoned by Jekaterina, Lucienne found herself secretly wanting her mother to be proud of her too. But whenever she realized that, she went on the offensive and challenged Jekaterina instead. She figured she wasn't any more mature than her sister. "Jekaterina is overbearing," she concluded.

Bayrose's lovely laughter was light as a feather. "Mother was frustrated that she couldn't order you around. It's refreshing to see you confront her. No one has really defied her before."

"Don't let her run your life," Lucienne advised.

"I'll try," Bayrose said. "I got used to obeying Mom. It's hard to break the habit." She started to braid Lucienne's hair into plaits. "I'm glad we can talk about this. I can't believe that I have a sister, and it's *you*, the famous Siren."

"I know I'm not what you expected," Lucienne said. "I'm not the kind of sister who's on anyone's favorite list." Her half-brother had called her "the abomination," and more than half her family from her father's side had once launched a war to dethrone her.

"I'm happy with you as my sister," Bayrose said.

"Oh, thank you," Lucienne said in surprise.

"You're welcome."

Then they both stopped. This sister talk was awkward.

"By the way—" Bayrose hesitated for a noticeable second, then said casually, "your cousin said Prince Vladimir would return in a couple days."

Lucienne's heart pounded. Vlad was coming home. She'd thought he'd fled her. She'd thought his feelings for her had changed. In her insanity, she had been unforgivably malevolent to him. Yet he was coming back to her.

And her half-sister hadn't gotten over him. How was Lucienne going to untangle this thread? It had been messy before Bayrose and Violet entered the frame.

"Vlad should be returning anytime now." Lucienne tried to keep her voice even.

Just then, a stir rose from the sitting room.

Lucienne turned her head in the direction of the commotion. A lock of her hair caught in the ivory comb in Bayrose's hand. She ignored the tug of pain and fixed her gaze on the figure in a trench coat at the door.

Vladimir stormed in, bringing in the scent of snow and wind and herbs. Two guards moved toward him, but neither stopped him.

"Vlad!" Bayrose dropped the comb and sprang toward him.

Vladimir stopped in his tracks, his hazel eyes narrowing on her. Before she could throw herself into his arms, his hand shot out, grabbing the girl's throat. "What are you doing here?" His voice was cold, and his stare colder.

Bayrose gagged. Tears of pain streamed down her face.

Lucienne was at their side in a second. "Vlad, let her go."

Vladimir turned to Lucienne, the cold, hard look in his eyes shifting to tenderness. And in their depth was heartbreak and yearning. "Lucia," he said in a husky voice. "You have no idea how treacherous this viper is."

"What you call a viper happens to be my sister," Lucienne said. "Now let her go before you choke her!"

Vladimir snickered. "Sister? You believe her crap?"

"Bayrose is my half-sister," Lucienne said. "DNA tests can't lie. My mother is here too."

Just then, Kian strode in. He must have heard the report of Vladimir's arrival before the Czech prince had landed. "Let Lucienne's sister go, Blazek," he ordered.

Under Lucienne's glare, Vladimir finally released Bayrose and shoved the girl aside. "I don't care if she's your sister," he said. "She can't be trusted."

Bayrose caught her breath. "I'm sorry, Prince Vladimir," she said in a mist of tears. "I never meant to deceive you. My late father played me as well."

Vladimir turned to Lucienne, his hungry gaze roaming over her face as if he wanted to make sure every line was the same as in his memory.

One of Kian's aides stepped over to Bayrose and directed her to the couch in the sitting room. Kian and the rest of the men drew back to give her and Vladimir some privacy.

Lucienne's gaze didn't leave Vladimir. His wheat-colored hair was cropped short. He looked leaner. His once square jaw was angular now, which gave him a harder look. His hazel eyes moldered to golden fire, burning brightly for her. Her disapproval of his rough demeanor toward Bayrose vanished. All was forgiven. Her joy at his returning overpowered all the heartache and disappointment since he'd left.

"Vlad," she whispered and smiled.

With one long stride, he eliminated the distance between them and crushed her against his chest. She read the message—he'd never let her go. Never again! And she didn't want him to.

He must have come to see her as soon as he'd gotten off the jet. His new scent of snow and herb confused her for a second, but his usual aroma of wild river and sunlight anchored her. She needed to hold onto something familiar. She leaned her face against his unshaven jaw as he nuzzled against her hair, as if needing to reconcile her scent with the one he'd remembered.

She pulled herself a few inches away from him just to look up at him, to see if he was real. "You're truly here, Vlad," she said in amazement and ache. "You're here."

"I'm here," he confirmed, then over her fluttered look, added, "I won't leave again."

A shadow shoved into Lucienne like an invisible knife. It was the same force she'd felt before, but now she was at her rawest moment in Vladimir's arms. While she had no shield up, the shadow oozed into her brain like slime.

"Can't resist me, can you?" Lucienne heard herself purr.

Wait. Had she just said that? *No, no, no. Don't lose it.* Lucienne hissed at the shadow and shoved it out of her head, but its slime clung to her mind. Lucienne gritted her teeth and tried to peel it from her brain tissues. She must give Vlad a few good hours before she lost it. He'd just come back.

Her will and the shadow played seesaw, and she was up and down, struggling to regain her balance.

"I can never resist you, láska," Vladimir said. "You never need to doubt that."

She felt her cheeks go up in flames. Did he realize that she'd started saying the dumbest things? But he didn't seem to care. He gazed at her as if she was all he had in the world. How could she get the message through to him? Warn him of her borderline state? The malevolent shadow aggravated, in a strange desperation to pin her down. It wasn't from her poison. It was an alien element. She was sure of it. If Ash were here, he would give her aid to cast out the foreign element. Where was he?

But if Ash were here, how could she handle her feelings toward both of them at Vlad's return?

Vladimir brushed a kiss on top of her hair. Lucienne clung to his trench coat and pulled him closer. She desperately needed his strength. *Get out!* she commanded the shadow in her mind. Vladimir tightened his arms around the small of her back, sensing her need. She felt his need for her was even greater. How could she give herself to him while she engaged in a heated battle with the alien thing? She dug her fingernails into his arm. The natural pull between them, different from the bond her and Ash shared, enhanced and pushed through.

Her old love stood right here in front of her. No, he was still her love. And his blazing, forever love for her shot through her, shining so brilliantly. Suddenly, the slime was gone from her head.

Lucienne wiped the sweat off her hairline with the back of her hand and tilted her head to gaze up at him. "You look exhausted. When was the last time you slept?"

"Not in a while," he admitted. "I like to sleep on my own bed."

He'd once mentioned that he'd give everything just to share a bed with her. In order to break her Siren's curse and be with her, he'd gone deep into the enemy's heart to retrieve Nexus Tear. "When you have the last element," he'd said, "we'll have a shot at being with each other completely. I'll finally get to sleep with you—if you want, too."

He must have seen the glint of desire in her eyes. A smoldering desire immediately roamed across his darkened hazel eyes. He seemed to have a hard time reining it in.

Lucienne's pulse quickened. Her lips parted involuntarily. Her blood flowed hot. Too much heat. More than she could handle. Then the redness hit, so fast, before she could register it.

Red was passion, and passion was inside her like fire. She was burning. But she felt good.

A whimper from the sitting room pulled them from the moment. Lucienne turned her head. Bayrose stared back at her with undisguised enmity.

"Ooo, someone is jealous." Lucienne winked at Bayrose and moved closer to Vladimir to press against him. She enjoyed having her half-sister watch. "Vlad," she now purred loudly, and smirked at her sister's sizzling anger, "where have you been? I was looking for you all over! I missed you terribly. Didn't you know?"

The whispers from the sitting room dropped to a hush. The guards rose to their feet. Kian was on the move in a second. Lucienne threw her head back and giggled. She had such an effect on men.

Vladimir looked alarmed. "Láska?"

The Czech word for love. She was his love. She knew.

The prince darted a glance at her dress. That reminded her. She'd been so distracted by his possessive lust that she forgot to check what she was wearing. The gray on her looked so dull. "Wardrobe malfunction," she said with a groan. "It happened again. Aida! Aida is getting old and forgetful. You'll have to forgive her, but don't you worry, Prince Vlad. I'll go change. I know you love me wearing red."

A storm moved into his eyes, sweeping away the ravenous desire in them. In the wake of the storm came an ocean of grief that could break anyone's heart. What saddened him so? Lucienne didn't need any more sorrow. Lately, she'd seen it over and over—in Kian, in the guards, in almost everyone! She must host another party to cheer them up. That fireworks dinner party hadn't gone well. Next time she'd make sure her mother didn't crash her party. She wouldn't allow wicked sorrow to drag her people down.

"This silver dress is perfect," Vladimir said urgently, his warm breath on her earlobe. As she was distracted by his breath and scent, he wrapped an arm around her shoulder and led her to sit on the sofa in the corner. And he made her turn away from the window and the forest of red maples beyond.

"I must show you what perfection is," she said, protesting in his arms. As soon as she had her fabulous red dress, he'd see. With her red dress, she always felt prettier, cleverer, and more in control.

He held her hands to prevent her from leaving. He was so possessive even without seeing her in a red dress. If she put on the high slit gown, he'd never let her out of his sight. Lucienne tried to retrieve her hands. Instead of letting her go, he shouted at the guards in the sitting room, "Everyone out. Now!"

Kian stood between the bedroom and sitting room, watching her warily. He regarded Vladimir for a second, and the prince gave him a curt nod. Kian gestured to the guards, and they filed out.

"I'll stay." Bayrose approached Lucienne. "I'm her sister."

"I don't give a damn who you are," Vladimir said. "Get out."

"Lucia, you want me to stay with you, don't you?" Bayrose asked. "We're family."

"If you want to stay, then stay," Lucienne said with a shrug and turned to Vladimir with a giggle. "Bayrose is family and she likes to watch."

Vladimir gave Bayrose an angry stare before looking upon Lucienne with all the gentleness in the world. "I haven't seen you for so long, miláček," he said. "Would you deny me a small wish to be alone with you for a few minutes?"

Lucienne gave him a sultry look. "Since you put it that way—" She turned to Kian and Bayrose and said with a flutter of eyelashes, "Prince Vlad needs some alone time with me. I'm his sweetheart. You two gotta go."

Biting her lip hard, Bayrose turned and exited. A guard pulled the door closed behind her.

"I stay." Kian strode toward them and sat on a chair across from her and Vladimir, without invitation.

Lucienne widened her eyes, surprised that Vladimir didn't protest, but then she nodded an understanding. "I don't want to fight Kian, either. Last time we fought, I almost killed him. So I'm being careful now. I don't want to do anything that I'll regret later. But be warned. Chief McQuillen is notoriously overprotective. He'll frisk you before he lets you be alone with me. If you're carrying any weapon, now would be a good time to hand it over to him. He won't have a problem with you if you just cooperate."

The outside door flung open. Lucienne took a peek. Ashburn charged in.

"Ash!" Lucienne rose and cheered.

Vladimir got to his feet too, frowning. "Can't he just be gone for once?"

"Like hell I'll let you do that without my presence," Ashburn said.

"Do what?" Lucienne asked, scanning the faces of the three men. "Ooo, mystery!" Her eyes sparkled. She spent her whole life trying to unveil one mystery after another.

Vladimir stood facing her, putting her face in his palms and gazing deep into her eyes. "We're going to do something together."

"A game?" she asked eagerly.

"Láska." Vladimir leaned forward and pressed his forehead against hers. "Remember, I'll never harm you."

So the game had started? A thrill ran through her, even though she didn't know the rules of the game. But who cared about rules? "Harm me?" she laughed. "Worry about yourself."

She looked up through her thick lashes and darted a glance at her other companions. Ashburn tensed, and Kian looked torn between hope, desperation, and apprehension. They both seemed ready to jump on the Czech prince if he cheated, like good judges in the ring.

She stood for several more seconds before losing patience. Was this how the game was played—she and Vladimir stood with their foreheads against each other and saw who moved first? She thought the prince would reintroduce some new excitements after his long absence. Disappointment seeped into Lucienne, but she was in a predicament. If she moved first, they would declare she lost. And she didn't like losing. She needed to come up with a quick excuse to end this dumb contest.

Scent of herb and snow.

Hmm. Vlad had developed a new aroma. Was that why she liked him better this time? She vaguely remembered they had some issues of late. He'd wronged her, but she couldn't keep track of what that was. She hadn't been blameless either. At times, she'd been dismissive, even cruel, toward him.

Let bygones be bygones.

A trail of cool air whiffed into where her third eye leaned against Vladimir's.

What was that? She tried to pull away, but Vladimir held her face tightly between his rough palms. "Shush, Láska," he whispered. "It's fine. I love you. I'll never hurt you again." His voice sounded affectionate yet broken.

Had he broken her heart before, or had she broken his?

Scent of herb and snow.

Her Czech prince had changed. The sunshine boy now had cool air in him. It was welcoming; especially when her body started growing uncomfortably warm.

Fire, like a sentient being, dwelled in her. She was drawn to its dangerous beauty. In the scorched wildness, it beckoned her near. And she did. At its center was the deepest darkness, same as the black hole at the core of the galaxy.

Fire burned her skin. Its orange spark singed the streaks of her midnight hair. She was the moth. But she shouldn't be. The Siren was never born to be the moth. But the unnatural fire was irresistible. Lucienne kept inching toward it—until the cold air came. It solidified into walls of ice and cut off the dark fire's reach for her.

Her body and mind started cooling.

Clearness and lightness returned.

Blink.

She was home. In her bedroom.

Vladimir's forehead was still glued to hers. His breath was cool and ragged on her face. And he was trembling.

She immediately knew what he'd done.

She pressed her hands against his chest and pushed, breaking their connection.

Vladimir stumbled and swayed. Ashburn and Kian each grabbed one of his arms before he fell on his knees. "It worked." Her Czech warrior grinned at her in comfort and triumph. His face was ashen. A sheen of blood appeared along his hairline.

He'd absorbed part of her poison.

"How could you do this to me and yourself, Vlad?" Lucienne asked. She'd never felt worse, even though her body was feeling cleaner and lighter.

His eyes turned dark and wild. The poison kicked in him, bringing the madness.

Her hand shaking, Lucienne placed her palm against his face. "You should never have done this. This poison isn't for you to bear."

He didn't hear her, though her touch did something to him. He struggled against Kian and Ashburn, wanting to pull her into his arms to protect her, but his strength failed him.

Lucienne turned to Kian and Ashburn. "Are you all in on this?" she asked coldly.

"We need to buy you time, Lucia," Ashburn said.

"At his expense?" she asked, tears burning in her eyes. "Do you all think I'm that heartless? If I am, I don't deserve to be healed."

"Lucia, sit down please," Kian said. He let Vladimir lean on him alone, then nodded for Ashburn to calm her down. Kian's free hand pulled out a phone and dialed a line. He barked an order into the receiving end.

Lucienne shrugged off Ashburn's hand on her arm.

Duncan, who had escorted Vladimir back from Tibet, sprang into the room with Thaddeus. They each supported Vladimir by a shoulder and helped him out of the room.

Lucienne followed. "Where are you taking him?"

"His room," Kian said. "He needs rest."

Ashburn blocked Lucienne before she got to the door. "I'm sorry, Lucia," he said. "While he's like this, he'll need to be alone."

She glared at him. For the first time, she was mad at him more than anyone else. "Stay out of my way."

Ashburn didn't flinch at her fury. "He'll be fine, but he needs a few hours to recover. Your presence won't do him good."

My presence doesn't do anyone good. Lucienne sank into a chair near the door. "By saving me, you're turning me into a monster."

"You'll never be a monster," Ashburn said. "You always come back."

"Stop talking to me, Ashburn," she said and turned to Kian. "Promise me you won't let Vladimir try that again, and I'll forgive you. You know I can't stop him when I'm in another zone, but you can."

"I can't," Kian said. "We'll do what we have to do. And when he wants to heal you, no one can stop him. You know that too."

"This is cruel," she said. "And he just came back to me."

"No crueler than you stopping us from helping you," Kian said. "If you take hope away from us, you take everything away from us."

Lucienne closed her eyes. The cursed Siren's line. She'd cursed everyone who cared for her. If Vladimir had never met her in Desert Cymbidium and hadn't fallen for her, his life wouldn't be like this—little joy and endless suffering.

But if she hadn't crossed paths with him, would she have been poisoned? Didn't the same truth apply to Ash? The three of them were like forces of nature colliding against one another, but even disaster and ruin couldn't tear them apart.

Their love only burned brighter, yet neither of them had a future with her.

The poison of the Siren's love.

With Vlad's absence, Ash's presence grew stronger. The Lure was calling her relentlessly.

Lucienne flashed open her eyes. Ash watched her intently, waiting for her to call him to her and forgive him. She could read his silent message: he'd be at her side, comforting her. He'd have her in his arms and make her forget about her heartache and guilt and Vladimir, even for just a second.

Her need for him was as great as his, but she resisted it, despite her body catching fire at his calling, at his scent.

The poison of my love.

Chapter Twenty-Two

BEACH AND BOYS

Lucienne ran in her white tank and capri leggings, her sneakers hitting the sand rapidly. The waves were high, the sun was bright, and she was tired. She kept running, no longer caring about the ridiculous sight of a squad of soldiers racing after her. She needed to get in shape. The poison had aggravated. It didn't just cause her to slip into insanity; it often wormed its way into her lucid states. She felt wearier as days passed, as if being dragged under water by a chain, the iron grapnel at its end getting heavier every day.

Someone raced past her guards. A second later, Vladimir fell into step beside her, running with her. "Hey, sweetheart," he said between breaths.

He'd slept for two days after he'd taken a portion of her poison into himself. She'd visited him several times and stayed with him while he remained unconscious.

Color had returned to his face, yet he still had faint shadows under his hazel eyes. She wanted to brush them away. Lucienne slowed her pace and asked, "Shouldn't you stay in and drink Aida's black chicken soup?"

Vladimir wrinkled his nose. "Your nanny is crazy. I googled the recipe. Black chicken soup is for women, particularly those who have just given birth."

Lucienne could barely hold back her smirk before her expression faded to something serious. "You looked worse than a woman after labor when you took in Blood Tear."

"I thought we'd gotten over that."

"We'll never get over it," she said. "You'll never try it again."

"Have you forgotten I was the one who poisoned you?"

Lucienne stopped, facing him in fury. "After all this time, how could you still think—"

"Of all the people I could hurt," he interrupted her, "I hurt the only one I love? I'd rather cut my hands off than hurt you. Let me do this for you, láska, and I won't feel like I'm living in hell every second of the day."

"Don't you know the poison will eventually take your life?"

"The ritual says the poison will dissipate through my meditation and digestion. I'll be fine."

"That's not true. I talked to the Lama when you were out cold."

"That Khampa needs to learn to shut his big mouth sometimes," Vladimir said.

"Respect the man of god," Lucienne said. "He said eventually you'll be lost in the land of insanity and never return. The poison will reach its limit."

"I won't let it reach my limit. I'll be careful."

"Why is it so goddamn hard for you, Kian, and all the boneheads, to accept the fact that there's no cure?"

"The cure is out there," Vladimir said stubbornly. "We just need to buy you more time. And that's exactly what I'm doing—buying you time."

Even though he diluted the poison in her for the moment, it always came back. Nothing could quench the fire of the poison that pumped through her blood.

But Kian, Vladimir, and the men wouldn't listen. They refused to face the reality that one day her fight would be over. She must find a way—even using manipulation, lies, and threats—to stop their unnecessary sacrifice.

"You should not trust the Lama," she said. "We stole their Holy Sentinel of Tibet. Surely they hold a grudge against us, but since we're too powerful for them to take the scroll back, they're using you to get me." She was opening his old wound—the Sealers had used him to get her and succeeded—so he'd voluntarily quit. She watched pain fill his eyes, but she spurred on. "This healing thing seems to work in the beginning, but it's a sugarcoated weapon."

"I didn't go through the ritual to become a weapon to hurt you."

"Of course you meant well. That's how the monks could manipulate you. They took advantage of your desperation to save me. Didn't we hear them confess before they chased us into the chasm? They exist to purge evil in the world, and they believe I'm the Darkness."

"Their perception of you has changed," Vladimir said. "You now have their absolute allegiance. Someone reached them before I did and convinced them that you'd bring light to the world. So they revealed the secrets of the ancient healing. 'So the Light in the world will be preserved.' Those were the Lama's words."

"Who was that someone?"

"I overheard their whispers about a female of rare beauty, intelligence, and indeterminate age."

Did Jekaterina visit the monks before she came here? Lucienne mused.

"And they said she was one of the old goddesses who still walks among us," Vladimir added.

"Everyone can tell how absurd and ignorant that sounds, but you—a skilled, modern warrior and a well-educated member of the royal family—still listen to their nonsense and try to kill yourself inch by inch?"

"I'm not killing myself. How many times do I have to tell you that?"

"Lucia." Thaddeus stepped forward and passed her a phone. "It's Bayrose. She said it's urgent."

Vladimir glowered, "What does she want?"

"Bayrose, I'm in the middle of running," Lucienne talked into the phone. "What do you need?" She listened for a few seconds. "I'll get back ... soon ... How soon? How do I know?" She sighed at more of Bayrose's questions and demands. "Fine, I'll make it in five, or seven minutes ... I'm not doing rocket science. It's a long way from my house." She hung up and turned to the guards. "Guys, the running day's over. They want us back."

"What is it?" Vladimir asked.

"Jekaterina's coming," she said. "She has a breakthrough."

"Why didn't Jekaterina call you directly?" Vladimir asked.

"This isn't one of Bayrose's schemes to cut short our time together," she said. "Dating me, you're also dating my whole family, even though my family is always a mess. Try to be nice to Bayrose."

"Lucia," Vladimir said in a measured tone, "my instinct says you shouldn't trust this side of your family either."

"Her other side of the family—those who have sworn their fealty to her—have proved to be loyal and worthy," Thaddeus said.

Lucienne waved her cousin back into the rank of the guards. "If you ever had a good instinct, Blazek," she said softly, "you'd have run away from me the first time you laid eyes on me."

"The first time I laid eyes upon you, I wanted you. And now I want you more than ever. Nothing—not even fate—can stand in my way."

Lucienne blushed. "Look what your instinct got you into."

"It found me a home, with you," he said.

Chapter Twenty-Three
SISTER IN LOVE

Two people weren't thrilled at the sight of Lucienne and Vladimir walking toward the mansion hand in hand: Ashburn Fury and Bayrose Thorn.

Through her binoculars, Bayrose watched them from the rooftop of Lucienne's mansion. The pair was cozy with each other. *For the moment.* Bayrose bit her lip and tasted blood.

She'd waited for Prince Vladimir to emerge from his room this morning, but when did, he had brushed past her and hurried out of the front door to pursue Lucienne.

Jealousy was the bitterest flavor.

How could he choose her mad sister over her? She was no less than Lucienne. Unknown to the world, she was actually the new Sealer founder, equal to the Siren. Even though she was in the shadows, for the time being, she could be more powerful than her sister. One day the world would know.

It must be guilt and pity that drove Vladimir to Lucienne.

Bayrose wasn't a total cold stone toward her half-sister. She'd been walking on the thin ice when she'd first come to Sphinxes. She'd tried to befriend everyone and volunteered in the medical facility to build up her reputation. How she hated the sight of blood and gore! She'd broken into a profuse sweat when she'd detected the Siren's mind-probing ability. The Shadow in her had deflected Lucienne's attempts. Bayrose had to constantly remind herself never to let her shield down. The Siren, though a wounded tigress, was still deadly and menacing.

Before Bayrose could enact her next plan, a rare opportunity knocked on her window. As soon as she'd gotten over the shock of learning the Siren was her half-sister, she'd actively pursued a relationship with Lucienne—a shortcut to the heart of Sphinxes.

Lucienne welcomed her. Bayrose was now a regular visitor to Lucienne's house with access to her food, library, and her room. That led Bayrose to discover another weakness she could exploit— Lucienne's concealed, yet deep longing for a close family tie.

She'd studied the Sirens race and their history as a child, a requirement for the heir to the Sealers founder. Her half-sister had been surrounded by enemies in the Red Mansion in her childhood. Lucienne was merciless toward her enemies, but extremely loyal to her friends. Bayrose knew well how to feed her sister's need for family acceptance, and soon she'd wrap the Siren around her little finger.

She'd been amused when Lucienne had asked about their mother in a disguised careless tone. It nagged the Siren that their mother abandoned her, but raised Bayrose. Her sister's hidden bitterness and jealousy greatly satisfied her. She would never tell Lucienne the true nature of her relationship with their mother.

Jekaterina had no understanding of motherhood. Mom didn't seem to possess human emotions, yet everyone sought her approval. Father had been one of the most brutal and controlling men she'd ever met, but he'd been a puppy in front of mother. Bayrose knew he'd always feared her.

Had Jekaterina had her agents poison her firstborn? If Daddy had ordered the hit, Mom sure hadn't stopped it. Bayrose felt cold air slither up her spine. But Mom had come to find a cure for Lucienne, and she'd been working in the lab day and night to save her elder daughter.

Bayrose was out of her depth at the games Mother was playing. She was the founder now, but was Mom still the real power behind the throne, even when in Sphinxes? She knew that Mom's followers were absolutely loyal to her, and they were many and powerful.

It was ironic that the Siren and the Sealers had come together. But when the day called for Bayrose to take over Sphinxes, the Siren would be no more. The Sealers would be the only force that led the world.

She wouldn't allow herself to feel sorry for her sister, though sometimes it was hard for her to see Lucienne's suffering. She would not care for Lucienne. The Siren stood in her way to greatness. The blood feud of an eon couldn't be erased by their shared DNA. The commission to wipe out the Sirens' line had been imprinted in her blood at birth, just like her father and all the Sealers founders before them.

For Bayrose, it was even more personal and urgent. Only with Lucienne gone could Prince Vladimir come back to her and belong to her. She refused to live in the Siren's shadow, and the Sealers would not settle for being a shadow power.

Why has it taken them so long? Bayrose again trained her binoculars on Lucienne and Vladimir along the beach. The Siren threw her head back, laughing. Bayrose's stomach churned. The prince must have cracked a joke. He used to tell jokes to Bayrose only. He used to make her laugh all the time. Now his teasing and flirting were for Lucienne alone.

The sight of him still made Bayrose's blood sing. She couldn't help it. No one had ever made her feel this way. First love was first love, and nothing could replace that.

Bayrose had called her mother, requesting she come to the mansion when Vladimir had gone after Lucienne. Then Bayrose had summoned Lucienne to break up her beach time with the prince.

Wait, what was happening? Lucienne shoved Vladimir away. Were they fighting? Bayrose yearned to hear their conversation. Lucienne yanked her tank top over her head. Underneath, she wore a lacy, white bra. She gave Vladimir a sultry look before her hands went to unhook her bra. The guards immediately averted their gazes. Lucienne twirled the string of her bra with a finger, then flung it at Vladimir's face.

Bayrose widened her eyes, only to realize that Lucienne was having another episode. The Siren's reputation was spinning down the drain faster every time she lapsed! The gloating light in Bayrose's eyes faded quickly when she saw that instead of turning his face away like the guards to preserve Lucienne's virtue, Vladimir openly stared at Lucienne's full, perky breasts, looking awed.

Vladimir's throat rose and fell. Lucienne giggled. Bayrose wanted to ram her fist into her shameless sister's face. How dare that girl show her nakedness to Vlad? And why couldn't he see how cheap she was? *You won't laugh long, Sis*, Bayrose vowed. *Your end is coming. I'll make sure it comes sooner.*

His hand holding Lucienne's bra, Vladimir jogged toward the Siren. Bayrose's heart contracted. What was he doing? Was he going to touch her? *Oh, no!*

With another giggle, Lucienne sprang toward the ocean and charged the waves. Vladimir dove into the water after her, and then half of the guards jumped in as well. Vladimir was an excellent swimmer. He could keep Lucienne safe, though Bayrose hoped her sister drowned. If drowning wasn't possible, then let a shark be lurking in the ocean, hungry for the Siren's sweet flesh.

Instead of the shark, a beam of light dropped from the sky.

Ashburn sat on a lighted, translucent motorcycle.

Lucienne waved at Ashburn, then surfed on the wave, trying to impress him. The machine landed beside her, half under the water, where Ashburn lifted Lucienne from the wave and sat her in front of him on the machine.

Vladimir was shouting angrily at his rival.

Ashburn snatched a white robe from his lap and put it around Lucienne, covering her bare torso. The Siren twisted her body to look up at Ashburn, obviously flirting with him. She'd totally forgotten about her former flame, Prince Vladimir.

It's your wakeup call, Bayrose shouted inwardly at the prince. *She's nothing but a slut!*

The machine took off, carrying Ashburn and Lucienne toward the mansion. Bayrose felt smoke pour from her nostrils. The Siren forever had tons of rescuers. Was it so hard for her to die quietly and exit the world in dignity?

In an instant, Ashburn and Lucienne reached the mansion. They went straight for Lucienne's bedroom balcony. Bayrose tossed aside her binoculars, lifted her long skirt, and rushed down the stairs.

A guard stationed outside Lucienne's door let Bayrose enter. All of Sphinxes knew Bayrose rescued their chief, and she was the Siren's long-lost sister.

Ashburn got off his ride and turned to Lucienne, who kept playing damsel in distress. She clasped her hands behind the neck of her knight in shining armor as he scooped her up. They were so wrapped up in each other that neither paid Bayrose any attention.

Through a side window, Bayrose looked out at the beach. Vladimir raced toward the mansion as if his tail were on fire. The guards ran behind him.

As Ashburn and Lucienne held onto each other, Bayrose prayed they kept at it until Vladimir's arrival. She wanted him to see with his own eyes that the Siren was nothing but a whore.

"As you can see, Ash," Lucienne purred. "I've been naughty."

"You're not yourself," Ashburn said.

"True. I don't know what came over me," Lucienne said. "It doesn't make a good impression to swim naked in front of everyone, especially my guards. Do you think they'll get over it?"

"You might get over it, but I doubt they'll ever forget that image," Ashburn said grimly, as if his own virtue had been compromised.

"What about you, Ash? You saw me too."

"It'll be hard to forget," Ashburn admitted as he brushed Lucienne's wet hair from her face. "But I see you differently."

"Do explain." Lucienne flashed Ashburn a seductive beam, which made Bayrose sick to her stomach.

"I see you not as the powerful Siren, but a kind girl I fell for," said Ashburn.

Lucienne raised one eyebrow. Bayrose hated to admit that her sister resembled Mom. She, however, took after Dad. But she shouldn't complain. Daddy had been a handsome man.

"Under your hard shell, you're more compassionate than anyone," Ashburn continued, "but your humanity has a certain complexity to it."

"That's not the compliment I was looking for." Lucienne pouted.

"You should focus on my irresistible feminine side and fall for me harder."

Bayrose wanted to puke.

But Ashburn said, "I fall for you every day, deeper than the day before."

Bayrose now felt a little crazy hearing men constantly profess their love for her sister.

"That's nice. Thank you," Lucienne said, resting her cheek against Ashburn's jaw. "Now I'm going to tell you something I haven't told a soul."

"What is it?" Ashburn asked softly.

They were so engrossed with each other that neither of them registered Bayrose's existence, as if she was a piece of furniture. Though their neglect of her worked to her benefit, Bayrose really wanted to scream at them to force them to notice her. But she stayed motionless, her heart pounding at what Lucienne was going to reveal.

"I've had this doomed feeling," Lucienne said. "Lots of times I'm terrified when you aren't around." She clung to him. "Will you save me, Ash?"

Ashburn's silver blue eyes turned storm gray, as if he couldn't bear to hear her say that. "Not this time, Lucia," he almost sobbed. "I can't save you."

For the first time, Ashburn's raw brokenness got to Bayrose, making her feel sorry and awkward for intruding on his intimate moment with Lucienne, but it was too late for her to withdraw. All she could do was stay as quiet as possible.

Lucienne and Ashburn fit perfectly. Why couldn't Vladimir see that and let go of her? The Siren discarded the Czech prince as easily as a trash bag whenever Ashburn appeared, yet Vladimir flew toward her like a moth. She would burn him worse than she'd done. Bayrose needed to rescue her prince and make him see that she was the real deal—that she was better for him than Lucienne could ever be.

The door flung open. Bayrose let out a pent-up breath. Vladimir had finally arrived. He would see Lucienne for what she truly was—a tramp and a cheater.

But it was Aida who came into the room, holding a tray of drinks and snacks.

Lucienne inserted her elegant hand into Ashburn's silver hair. "I was playing with you." She giggled. "I'm perfectly fine." She twirled her fingers around a lock of his hair. "But I got you, didn't I?"

"Sweet girl." Aida handed Lucienne a glass of almond milk, breaking the lovers' embrace.

Ashburn jabbed a hand into his hair where Lucienne's hand had been previously. He flushed under Aida's glare. The old nanny's sharp gaze didn't linger on him. It trained on Bayrose, questioning her presence and intention. There was no trust or affection in the nanny's eyes.

The nanny pulled Lucienne's robe tighter to cover the Siren completely. The pink on Ashburn's usually pale face went deeper. "Young man," Aida scolded, "you should know better than let her be like this. She could catch a cold."

Murmuring an apology, Ashburn glanced around the room, and for the first time noticed there were more people in this room than he realized. As his gaze fell on her, Bayrose couldn't help but rub the bridge of her nose anxiously.

Violet had told her about Ashburn, and in Sphinxes, everyone seemed to stay out of his way. She'd heard whispers about his powers. Some said that Ashburn could read anyone's memories except for the Siren's. Could Ashburn read hers while she was sheltered by the Shadow? Hadn't it been created to fend off superpowers like his and Lucienne's?

She'd been treading carefully around Ashburn. This man could be her most dangerous foe or her powerful ally. As she met his gaze, she had to admit he was a perfect specimen in every way. And no man wore a black T-shirt and a pair of washed-out jeans better than him. He always held a cold control and distant demeanor if it didn't involve Lucienne. Bayrose never wanted a perfect man. She preferred a flawed man. A hotheaded and red-blooded man, like Vladimir.

Ashburn's gaze skimmed over Bayrose and returned to Lucienne, and the remoteness in his ice-blue eyes melted to intense possessiveness in a second.

"I won't catch cold," Lucienne defiantly told her nanny, evidently unhappy that the older woman's entrance pulled her away from the hot boy's warm chest. "You gotta stop treating me like a little girl. I'm seventeen!"

"You'll always be my little girl, even when you're fifty," Aida said.

"Stop it, Aida," Lucienne said with a frown. "I won't be that old. Ever."

Aida's face paled, then she spat three times on the floor. Bayrose knew the gesture was to nullify a curse or bad omen in some Asian cultures. Lucienne's health was a touchy subject in Sphinxes. The whole nation-to-be was afraid of their queen bee's untimely demise.

"Nonsense," the nanny said. "You'll live long and be happy. I'll see to it that your fiftieth birthday is the grandest!"

Ashburn looked away to hide the tremendous pain in his eyes.

Bayrose knew if it hadn't been for Ashburn, Lucienne would have died from Blood Tear—but he was only stalling death.

She should rest her worries, especially after she'd heard his confession to Lucienne that he couldn't cure her. There was absolutely no cure. As the next in line to Lucienne, she would have Sphinxes, and Vladimir would be hers eventually. However, beneath her glee, unwanted sorrow also churned up—she'd just started to get to know her sister, and she'd lose her soon.

Bayrose shoved away the pitiful, depressing feeling.

As long as Lucienne existed, Bayrose would never have what she wanted.

Aida picked up the empty glass from Lucienne's hand and said, "Let's get you to the bath and change into clean clothes."

Lucienne looked down and frowned at her white robe. "I'm going to put on a red dress."

"I like anything on you," said Ashburn. "You don't need a red dress."

Lucienne grinned.

"Let's go now, Lucia," Aida said. "You don't want to smell like seaweed in front of the gentlemen."

Lucienne cast Ashburn an apologetic glance. "How embarrassing." Then she turned to her nanny with an order. "Bring me the one that shows my whole back. Ash will like it."

At Lucienne's words, desire immediately appeared in Ashburn's eyes, overlapping his sorrow. He must have been picturing how Lucienne looked half nude. Bayrose shook her head at him and at all men. Most of the time they just didn't think with their brains.

Vladimir stormed into the room just as Lucienne followed her nanny toward the bathroom. When the Siren passed Bayrose, she noticed her younger sister. "Bay—rose! You're here, quiet as a mouse. Look, Vlad is here too. Don't kill each other while I'm gone." She winked at Vladimir before entering the bathroom.

It took Bayrose's great control not to grab Lucienne's hair, drag her down, and kick her in the gut. Taking in a deep breath, she put on a lovely smile and wheeled around to Vladimir. "Hi, Prince Vladimir. Have you been running? Good exercise."

He gave her a glare, then rudely ignored her as if she wasn't worth his effort. He fixed his hostile look on Ashburn, and the Fury boy glared back.

No one engaged Bayrose, so she found a chair in the corner and sat down. On the coffee table was a novel. She picked it up and feigned to read. In her sixteen years, she'd always been the center of the universe, until she'd come to the enemy's domain. In her sister's realm, she felt more like an outsider than she had anywhere else.

From the corner of her eye, Bayrose saw Ashburn and Vladimir pretending that the other didn't exist. They stayed as far away as possible from one another, but chose to be close to the bathroom, waiting for Lucienne to emerge.

You can't blame me for hating you, Sis. A nutcase you are, but you still have two gorgeous guys competing for you. Bayrose glued her eyes to the page, as if it were telling the most intriguing story. Then she blushed. Did Lucienne read this erotic werewolf romance and lay it out in the open in her insane state? Bayrose flipped the book to the opening page and read Ziyi's signature of ownership. Her sister's best friend must have forgotten to take the book with her. That girl never bothered being discreet or proper. As Bayrose put down the book and pushed it away to distance herself from it, she jumped in her seat.

Vladimir kicked a chair near him to issue another challenge when Ashburn sat down. Ashburn, however, leaned back on his sofa lazily, as if the Czech prince were beneath him, his arms folded across his broad chest.

Vladimir sneered with full disdain, then slumped on the chair he had just abused.

"Aida won't appreciate it if you wet Lucienne's chair," Ashburn said. "It's expensive furniture."

"I can afford it more than you, farm boy," Vladimir said, then looked at the chair and his wet shirt and pants. He darted a glance at the bathroom door, as if calculating how long it would take Lucienne to finish her shower. He waited for a few more seconds, then rose to his feet. "Next time you try to snatch her, let me know first. Even a farmer has to learn manners. Sneaking up on people is more than rude—it's creepy."

"How could I have warned you when you obviously failed to control the situation?" asked Ashburn.

Vladimir's face reddened. "I had it under control. She was just having a little fun. And you spoiled it."

"She was half-naked, going after that high wave," Ashburn said. "You call that a little fun?"

"I'm an outstanding swimmer," Vladimir said. "I was going to bring her back."

"Are you sure?" Ashburn said. "Last time I checked, you had a lousy track record."

The Fury boy hit the Czech prince on his open wound. Vladimir's face turned purple in rage, but he restrained himself from attacking Ashburn, even as his opponent's goading look said "bring it on." He gave Ashburn a hateful look for good measure, then sent Bayrose one too before storming out of the room.

"I should not have reminded that idiot of his wet clothes," Ashburn murmured to himself. "I should just let Aida yell at him, and Lucia will stay away from his salty, wet smell."

Bayrose laughed.

Ashburn gave her a look, as if forgetting he and Vladimir had an audience.

"Well said, Ash." Bayrose broke the ice. Ashburn was like deep space in the far universe that no one had explored. No one except Lucienne. Could Bayrose's feminine wiles work on him like they did on so many others? Her heart pounded at the uncertainty, and panic seeped into her mind. What if the Shadow couldn't shield her from him? What if he'd known her plan for vengeance before she'd taken in the Shadow?

But if he'd read her past memories, he'd have told Lucienne and Kian. And McQuillen would for sure have thrown her into the dungeon. But no one in Sphinxes had come for her. Even if exposed, she would insist that she no longer wanted blood after knowing the Siren was her sister. They'd believe her. After all, she was Lucienne's only sibling.

And Bayrose had planned her exit long before she'd come to Sphinxes.

Ashburn gave her a small nod, which Bayrose considered as a good sign, but she was still stuck. She didn't know what to say to him or how to spark his interest. "You won the first round against Blazek," she said, stumbling along. "Everyone knows he excels at riling up people, but he failed to leave an impression on you."

"He isn't worth me raising a finger," Ashburn said, then rose and headed back to the balcony, as if she wasn't worth him raising a finger either. He was on his lighted machine in a second, and then he was gone.

Bayrose tossed the erotic romance book under the coffee table. A shade of loneliness chilled her spirit. She was in a foreign land amid her enemy. How long could she keep this up—tense all the time and faking her way through every situation? She sank deep into the sofa, elbows on her knees and head dropped into her hands. She had no one to talk to. Mirrikh, her ally and devotee since childhood, was at the other end of the world, and she couldn't risk contacting any of her supporters outside Sphinxes.

"You know, I even hate the weather here," Bayrose murmured to herself. She'd often talked to her imaginary friend as a child. "In the morning it's sunlit, at noon gray clouds gather, and late afternoon, mostly a downpour. Evening isn't so insufferable, but it only makes me think of home. I don't know when I'll ever go home."

"VOLATILE," a voice answered her.

Bayrose almost jumped to the ceiling. It wasn't her imaginary friend's voice she'd pictured as a little girl. This voice was real and soul-deep, and it came from inside her. Was it the Shadow? According to her ancestors' documentation, the Shadow was sentient. But no one had had an encounter with it because no one had risked taking it in. Not until Bayrose.

"Who's talking to me?" Bayrose demanded in a low voice, her heart pounding in her ears.

"Security is tight," the voice said. "Our enemy wired this fortified island with cameras and electric fences. A satellite keeps its eye on the land at all times. By human standard, Sphinxes' underground defense system is top notch. It won't be easy for your army to breach it."

"How do you know all this?" Bayrose whispered, drawing in a sharp breath. This intel was useful. She'd been studying Sphinxes' defense system. As her status here changed, she could go to almost any place on the island, except for the most classified labs.

"I see things beyond human eyes," the voice answered.

It *was* the Shadow. It could communicate with its host.

Bayrose finally had a true companion amid her enemies.

The bathroom door opened, and Bayrose expected to see her nutcase sister in a tacky red gown, but Lucienne stepped out in a simple white dress with weary eyes. She had the bleak look more often in her normal state. Even so, the Siren still looked regal and graceful, though Bayrose hated to admit it.

Lucienne let out a sigh, seeing Bayrose was the only one in the room. "I've developed a hobby of humiliating myself."

"I saw you going topless too from the rooftop," Bayrose said, not wanting to spare her sister's dignity.

"And once again, I made a complete fool of myself in front of Ash."

Bayrose nodded. "You were lucky Prince Vladimir didn't see that."

"I hurt him, didn't I? I hurt him every day. He shouldn't have come back."

"Maybe you haven't hurt him badly enough, because he's still hung up on you," Bayrose said. Luckily, the Shadow helped hide her viciousness.

"I don't know what to do anymore."

"Sit down," Bayrose said. "Let me blow dry your hair, and we can talk more about it."

"I don't really want to talk about it," Lucienne said, though she sat down before the vanity.

Bayrose knew Lucienne liked her combing her hair. It'd become their way of bonding. She unwound the towel from Lucienne's elegant head and swept it over her midnight hair as if wiping a floor. Then she pressed it against her sister's temples and massaged them. If she squashed them hard enough, could she crush the Siren's skull?

"I should not be troubled by men," Lucienne said.

"You have feelings for them both. Even an idiot can see that. The question *is*: which one will you pick? Everyone in Sphinxes is on Team Ash."

"Let's not go there," Lucienne said. Bayrose could feel her sister's shoulders stiffening.

"I was only trying to help, Lucia."

"Sorry I snapped at you," the Siren said. "I didn't have such contradictory emotions when I was younger."

"The rite of passage to womanhood, Sister."

"It isn't fun." The Siren heaved a deep sigh. "And not to mention all the duties and expectations. I've been thinking of stepping down from a position of power."

Bayrose held her breath. "And?"

"I told Kian that I was no longer fit to lead, but he wouldn't hear of it."

"Your chief is afraid of losing his power if he doesn't have you in his lot."

"Don't ever say that if you want to stay my sister," Lucienne said. "Kian is never power-hungry. If I resign, he'll only gain more power."

"Sorry. All I'm saying is that he puts you above the whole nation. Everyone is talking about Sphinxes being a new country, but—"

"An individual's interest should not rise above all."

"Exactly," Bayrose said. "Why don't you go around him? Tell your generals of your decision to step down. Free from the burdens and trifles of reality, your health will surely improve."

"I doubt I'll have much success in persuading my officers either."

"Have you tried? I'm confident that you can make them see reason. I'll go with you if you need a backup. As your only sister, I'll always support you. Wait! What if you tell the generals you've found a successor? Someone who will carry your torch, your burden, and your legacy? And you can just focus on getting well."

Aida came out of the bathroom. "No one will succeed the one and only Siren!" She snatched the towel from Bayrose with force. "Let me take care of Lucia."

Bayrose stepped aside with a sweet, docile smile, her heart slamming in her rib cage. She didn't expect the nanny to eavesdrop on her private conversation with her lunatic half-sister. "Of course, Aida," she said. *Old hag, wait until the day I dispose of you.*

"Be nice, Aida," Lucienne said. "Bayrose has been great to me. She's particularly patient with me when my madness overcomes me."

Instantly, Bayrose felt an inner power tugging in her, as if responding to Lucienne's words. Could it be? Could the Shadow subdue the mad Siren? She noticed a very interesting phenomenon—Lucienne was more prone to listen to her and even obey her when she was her insane self. Bayrose felt lightheaded and thrilled at the discovery.

"Where's Jekaterina?" Lucienne asked Bayrose. "You said she was coming."

"She's always late, but she's on her way here."

"Then shouldn't you call me after she arrives rather than drag me away from my morning run an hour ago? I'd prefer she wait for me instead of the other way around."

"Don't be petty, Lucia," Bayrose chided. "When will you ever get over this grudge against Mother?"

"She didn't abandon you," Lucienne said.

"I did not abandon you, Lucienne." Jekaterina strolled in. "I told you I left you to protect you."

What did Mother mean by that? Hadn't Mom chosen her over her sister? It hurt to hear that Mom had left Lucienne, but stayed with Bayrose as a way to protect her elder daughter. Who could be more powerful than Mom to rob her of her firstborn?

With the Shadow in her, Bayrose knew her mother didn't tell the whole truth.

Mom was concealing something. Something big. But what?

Chapter Twenty-Four

HERITAGE

Why hadn't her guards announced Jekaterina's arrival? How had that woman gotten past them? Lucienne frowned. But could she really blame her guards? She'd visited the lab a handful of times when her mother worked. She noted that when Jekaterina spoke, people obeyed, more eagerly than they did her. Even Kian let Jekaterina have her way, though he insisted on putting her under tight surveillance. Jekaterina had bossed Lucienne around as well, and even she, the Siren, had almost fallen under Jekaterina's authoritative spell once or twice.

"Sure," Lucienne said to her mother, "you didn't leave me in the care of the man who sold me and then poisoned me. Your protection program didn't suck, and your heart was in the right place. So here I am, half mad and half dead. You're the mother of the year."

Bayrose gasped. Evidently, her younger sister had never challenged their mother. But Lucienne wouldn't indulge Jekaterina's every whim.

"I do not measure motherhood by human standards," Jekaterina said coolly. "Nor do I measure my love that way. You're where you're meant to be. All I've done is make sure of that."

Lucienne laughed bitterly. "I'm where I'm meant to be? I'm a mad Siren. I harm my people. And you made sure of that?" Her voice turned icy. "Choose your words carefully, woman. If my men think you were behind the scheme to poison me, they'll take you out in a heartbeat. Even I can't stop them."

"It won't be as easy to bring me down as you think," Jekaterina said softly, "so there's no need to threaten me. You're as strong as I expected you to be. What can't kill you only makes you stronger. As I said, I came here to guarantee your survival. I won't accept failure. You're the true Siren in an eon. You're one of a kind, my daughter."

The pride in Jekaterina's tone sent chills through Lucienne. She talked as if Lucienne had been a successful experiment of hers. But the woman had produced the first female Siren.

"Very encouraging," Lucienne said. "Now I see where my madness comes from."

"At least you admit our connection," Jekaterina said, a faint smile appearing on her lips.

Lucienne stared at Jekaterina's smile, again stunned by her mother's beauty. A thought flitted by her mind. Jekaterina's physique was as perfect as Ashburn's. She brushed aside an uneasy thought— her mother had reached out to Ash first. She could see the tie between them. And Ashburn had admitted that he felt a kinship with Jekaterina. What if she wasn't the firstborn, but Ash was? He was a year older than her, and she was a year older than Bayrose. She hadn't known she had a sister until two weeks ago. Blood called to blood. Was that why she and Ash were so drawn to each other? And if Ashburn was her brother …. A nauseas feeling impaled her.

"We're not as connected as you think," Lucienne said icily. "And you can't tell the difference between sarcasm and a compliment, can you?"

"More than you know," Jekaterina said. "But let's not waste time on empty words. This isn't why you summoned me."

"I didn't summon you," said Lucienne.

Jekaterina darted a glance at Bayrose, who appeared uncomfortable.

"Mother," Bayrose said, "you haven't had time for me since your arrival, so I took an initial step and arranged this family reunion."

Jekaterina's eyes suddenly sharpened like a dagger, turning the rich color of fiery amber. Lucienne saw that her half-sister couldn't help but shrivel under Jekaterina's gaze. Their mother's eyes returned to brown a second later. Lucienne almost thought she had imagined it.

Her maternal family wasn't any less predatory than her fraternal one. Lucienne rose and held her sister's shoulder, but Bayrose didn't relax. Lucienne gave Jekaterina a defiant look, more than ready to slap back any unkind words from her mother's mouth.

Jekaterina's eyes softened, no longer piercing. She heaved a sigh. "Rose," she said, "you haven't excelled at manipulation since you were a child, so don't start now."

Had Bayrose called her to drag her away from Vladimir on the beach? Lucienne's arm left her sister's shoulder.

"Reality is but a perception," Jekaterina continued. "You'll not be your sister's shadow if you choose not to be. You'll become *shadow* only if you stay weak."

Bayrose's face paled like the dead. It took great effort for her not to tremble. That was the strongest emotion Lucienne had seen from her younger sister. She wanted to hold Bayrose again to support her, but her instinct told her not to. Why did Jekaterina keep using the word *shadow*? Lucienne thought of the shadow in her mind the other day when Bayrose had been near. Was there a connection? *No, I'm being paranoid again.*

"I'm sorry, Mom, if I disappointed you," Bayrose said, as if she wanted to be invisible.

Jekaterina never showered much sunshine on her younger daughter. A sudden realization hit Lucienne. Her sister hadn't lived a fairytale life with their mother. For the first time, Lucienne felt a kinship toward Bayrose. "Bayrose is not my shadow," she said, "and she'll never be anyone's. She's building a life here. Is it that hard to encourage your own daughter?"

"Bayrose isn't the one who needs to be encouraged," Jekaterina said. "You are." She sat on a chair facing her two daughters, an unmistakable look of ancient exhaustion in her eyes. Lucienne's heart softened a notch. Despite Jekaterina's failings as a mother, she'd been working day and night in the lab to find a cure for her daughter.

"Anyway, I was planning to visit," Jekaterina said. "I made progress."

Lucienne held her breath.

"I believe you're no stranger to ancient technology beyond human perception," Jekaterina said, her gaze fixing on her oldest daughter. "Modern humans call one type of science quantum mechanics. Ancient humans called it the oldest magic—knowledge from heavens. Same face, different names."

"Like yours?" Lucienne blurted out.

"One day you'll get over your animosity toward me," Jekaterina said.

For a second, Lucienne saw a terrible loneliness and weariness in her mother's eyes, and she was suddenly ashamed for being spiteful. "Maybe," she said in a low voice, "I can try."

Jekaterina gave her a forgiving look. "Ashburn's Spike is fueled by old magic as well as quantum mechanics. The line often blurs. Spike's power source is just like Χρόνος—the Eye of Time."

Lucienne's heart stuttered. How did her mother know about the Eye of Time? Jekaterina, however, kept her mask in place. Lucienne glanced at Bayrose through the corners of her eyes. Did Bayrose know about the ancient entity? Did all Sealers elders know about Ash and the Eye of Time? Anxiety rained on her like acid. Sphinxes wasn't powerful enough yet to fend off all nations if they all came to her door to take what she held in secret.

"My team cracked part of the code last night," Jekaterina said. "The code points to Χρόνος and—" She stopped and turned to her younger daughter.

Bayrose widened her eyes like a child caught stealing. She cleared her throat and forced a certain boldness into her voice. "You never told me about Χρόνος—the Eye of Time. What is it, Mother?"

"It's not your burden, Bayrose," Jekaterina said.

Bayrose's eyes darkened. "I'm not a child. I'm only a year younger than Lucia."

"Then stop acting like a child," Jekaterina said. "I need to talk with Lucienne alone, if you're kind enough to excuse us."

Bayrose looked like she'd been slapped and was about to stomp her feet to protest, but under the weight of Jekaterina's gaze, she recoiled. She turned to Lucienne, visibly hoping her sister would stand up to their mother again. With the same mask her mother had, Lucienne watched a sour Bayrose exit.

"Sane and insane," Jekaterina's voice reduced to a hush, "are both parts of you. Blood Tear only triggered what was already in you when you were made Siren. We all have demons and angels inside us. Your most inner part can only come out freely, disguised as your insane self. It must manifest itself at some point when your dormant gene is awakening."

"I don't think so," Lucienne snorted. "You don't know me."

"I know more than you think," Jekaterina said. "Now, I must prepare you."

Prepare my ass! "Sane or not," Lucienne said bitterly, "I'm running out of time. I won't hang in there for long. You can prepare for my funeral, but Kian won't let you have a hand in it. You haven't earned it."

"You'll survive. I'll make sure of that. I didn't go through this much hardship to just give up on you. I already have part of the code. It'll purge the poison in you, but we'll need Ashburn's assistance."

Ash held the key to the antidote, but he wouldn't and couldn't give it to her. Lucienne had a sinking feeling that Ash and Jekaterina were speaking of the same cure. "What is the part of code?" she asked.

"It's you and Ash."

Light sliced through the recesses of Lucienne's mind. Ash had mentioned the cosmic conspiracy a few times—some force was trying to bring him and her together to remake the world. Seraphen had said that when the two of them came together, they'd cause the extinction of the human race. But what exactly had the creature meant by coming together? Copulation? Or did it require she and Ash merge their powers? She had Forbidden Glory, and Ash had TimeDust.

An ill omen rose with her suspicions. A chill Lucienne hadn't known slithered up her spine. The woman could manipulate her genes and had birthed the first female Siren in an eon. The way Jekaterina talked about the Eye of Time suggested she'd been acquainted with it long before Ash had come into the picture. Ash had admitted that he couldn't penetrate any part of Jekaterina's memories without her letting him in, and she'd flipped only a corner of the veil for him to get a glimpse. Who could have that kind of power on earth?

"Who are you really?" Lucienne demanded.

"I'm your mother, and a mother thinks best for her daughter and her race."

Lucienne narrowed her eyes. Her race? For a split moment, her mind wandered to the female image on the pillar of the Rabbit Hole. She darted a glance at Jekaterina's ears to see if they were pointed ears, but her mother's long, flowing hair covered them. It couldn't be. Mother's hair was brown with strands of strawberry blond instead of silver. But she could wear a wig. *No, stop this.* Lucienne couldn't be so important that she stood in the pivotal position of a "cosmic conspiracy." She was being paranoid again, even when she possessed the coldest clarity at the moment. The poison had grown more aggressive.

But her mother had referred to humankind with such contempt, as if she wasn't one of the "inferior race." Was she? *Stop it.* It was even more disturbing that Jekaterina had used a singular when she'd said "a mother thinks best for her daughter." Was it a slip of the tongue, or did Jekaterina make another choice when it came to her and Bayrose? It was obvious that this time she'd chosen Lucienne.

What kind of mother was that?

Supposing the cosmic conspiracy was true, Lucienne—even being poisoned—had greater use to Jekaterina. She—not her sister—had been picked to mate with the specimen Ashburn Fury.

Facing Jekaterina, Lucienne felt out of depth.

"I can't lie, Lucienne. It's not in my nature." Jekaterina rose to her feet. "It's up to you whether you can trust me." Compassion and understanding softened Jekaterina' features, but the motherly tenderness didn't last long. "I need to go back to the lab. Time can't be wasted." She headed toward the door, her gait more graceful than any human. "I'll have the full code for you."

"Wait," Lucienne called out.

Her mother turned to her at the door with an arched brow.

She did resemble her mother. Lucienne stifled a sigh. "I have one more question—and don't lie to me."

"I won't lie, daughter."

"I must know Ashburn's heritage," Lucienne said. "Is he—my brother?" Her heart beat so hard that she was certain it would explode, depending on Jekaterina's answer.

Chapter Twenty-Five

THE EYE OF TIME

Lucienne felt the poison burning in her bones. She couldn't hold it for much longer for Jekaterina to obtain the full code.

She'd thought the i-Ching oracle that had spoken on the night of her Siren's coronation hinted at her chance of survival. *"Nine years after the Siren has set things in motion, she'll face two boys tied to her irrevocably. One will offer life disguised as death; the other will lead to death with great love."*

Both Vladimir and Ashburn were tied to her now, and neither could tear himself away from her. She was the wrecked ship with two willing passengers aboard.

One will offer life disguised as death—maybe the poison wouldn't lead her to death, because it was only disguised as death? And death is but a passage in life?

The other will lead to death with great love—Vladimir gave her Blood Tear because of his great love for her. So was his love meant to lead to her death?

No, she'd misinterpreted the oracle.

If the first boy was Vlad, then the other could only be Ash.

Her head spun at the riddles.

Kian had pressed the i-Ching master to tell him which boys. Knowing him, he would have hunted them down and taken them out before they neared her to guarantee her safety. Dr. Hsi had refused to oblige him. The i-Ching master had added, "What she chooses will decide how the world turns."

Based on that, she'd believed she had a chance to survive the venom in her body. Fate offered her an option—choose life or death. One boy or the other.

However, what if *"The other will lead to death with great love"* meant Ashburn's death, if he decided to sacrifice himself to save her? She'd rather perish than have him take her place.

And Ash and she weren't blood related. When she had asked Jekaterina if Ash was her brother, Jekaterina had given her a withering look.

Lucienne dragged her sluggish body toward her secret chamber. She needed to see the Eye of Time after being apart from it for so long. When she'd attained it, she'd thought she could climb its ladders to the stars and find all the riches in the universe. And now, powers, ambitions, and dreams were but dust when she faced her own frail, failing mortality.

Her guards trailed after her.

"No need to babysit me," she told them. "I'm only going to my cellar."

"But Miss Lam—" Adam protested.

Lucienne raised a hand to stop him. "If you follow me, I'll shoot you."

The guards stopped. She knew there was ice in her eyes. No one was allowed to enter her secret chamber. She'd made only one exception with Ashburn when they struck a bargain. Her guards didn't like her going in there, but it was her only haven for alone time. "I'll be fine, Captain," she said. "I won't stay long."

If she stayed longer than an hour, the guards would fetch Ashburn. Actually, he'd come without the guards calling him—he had their memories.

Lucienne pressed her palm against the scanner and stepped through the door.

Light flooded the temperature-controlled chamber.

Lucienne treaded past the artifacts in the glass cabinets, stopping when she reached the stone table in the center. The Eye of Time waited, locked inside the black crystal box.

She hadn't neared it for the longest time. She used to wear it around her neck at all times.

It knew her deepest, darkest desire. It'd whispered to her when resting between her breasts, promising her arcane knowledge and immense powers, all from the other world she'd been seeking. All she ever needed to do was let it link to Ashburn and make him its prey. She'd almost fallen under its spell and set it on Ash on several occasions, but her will hadn't been that weak. Still, she wasn't fond of constantly battling her own desire, so she'd taken it off her neck and locked it away.

Opening the box, Lucienne pulled out the platinum necklace. Her fingers caressed the gold locket at the end of the chain. Her heart leaping, she pushed the pin. The pendant slowly opened, revealing an intricately designed holder that contained a half-white, half-black, and translucent liquid—Twilight Water, the only ancient object that could bind the Eye of Time.

The Eye of Time stared back at Lucienne. *Siren, you are not well,* it whispered.

It knew at the first sight of me, Lucienne thought.

Ashburn Fury can save you.

"Sure," Lucienne said. "After I let you go after him."

Only when he merges with me can the cure be produced.

Lucienne's breath hitched and her heartbeat thudded in her chest.

That was the reason Ashburn wouldn't cure her. He'd rather die than let the ancient entity possess him.

He is too selfish not to save you, the Eye said, *but we can make him see reason.*

In fact, she was the selfish one. She was menacing. She promised she'd never harm him, but she'd never really abandoned the dark idea of setting the Eye of Time on him. One day, she would succumb to her desire. She could even find an excuse for herself now—half of the time she wasn't of sound mind. How could anyone blame the actions of a mad girl? With the code Jekaterina cracked, and through the link between Ash and the Eye of Time, she'd open the portal to Eterne—the quantum plane where an ultimate power gave birth to all powers. The poison would lose its claim on her in the realm of the gods and immortals.

"But you're his nightmare," Lucienne said. "If he melds with you, he won't be the same."

Not true. He will be a more advanced species with infinite intelligence and immortality.

"It's Ash's decision to make. You might not be familiar with the concept of human free will."

It is your decision to make when it is your life on the line, said the Eye. *If you cannot persuade him to discard his ungrounded fear, let me convince him.*

The former Siren once had high hopes that Lucienne would be among the greatest women and men in history. Such leaders never went soft when required to sacrifice a few for the survival of the many. But she'd turned her back on the Siren race. She'd backpedaled. She'd let her feelings for Ash cloud her vision and her honor system hinder her moves. She could have remade history in one leap, but instead, she'd set the clock backwards. All for Ashburn Fury. And because of her weakness, she was suffering the consequences—a relentless poison coursing in her body. Soon, she'd pay with her life and her legacy.

Lucienne gasped. No, this wasn't her thinking. It was the Eye of Time whispering in her head.

"You really think you can manipulate me that easily?"

I do not lie, Siren. You know more clearly than anyone that you were born to reach the home of the gods. Have you not found me?

Lucienne breathed out. "How does Ashburn heal me after I let you have him?"

Once TimeDust is complete, it can purge the venom in your Forbidden Glory. You will be powerful beyond any human's wildest dream. When Ashburn becomes who he is destined to be, you do not need to seek the portal to Eterne. Eterne will come to you.

"But the scrolls say we need the full code to open the portal," Lucienne said. "Who's lying, you or the prophecy?"

The Eye paused for a second. *No human has interpreted the prophecy accurately.*

"Then tell me your version."

In time you will know.

It sounded just like Jekaterina. "If you want me to free you," Lucienne said, "you'll be honest with me. At least give me something."

The code is you and Ashburn.

A flash of memory.

Ashburn had once opened his mind and showed her his first encounter with the Eye of Time. It had persuaded him to activate it, but Ashburn hadn't known how. It had explained, "You need to use the code."

"What code? I don't have any code," Ashburn had said.

"You are the code," the Eye of Time had replied. *"It is encrypted in your DNA."*

So both she and Ash were the code? A cold shiver shook her as if she'd just found out she was being strung up by a puppet master. She would be no one's puppet.

"Jekaterina said the same about the code." Lucienne tested the Eye.

Your mother is always right.

"Who's she to you?"

The Eye of Time was silent.

A cold smile tugged at the corner of Lucienne's lips. It indeed had a long history with Jekaterina. "Who is Jekaterina?" she asked.

Your mother, it said.

"I rephrase. What is Jekaterina?"

A thousand names and faces, it said unwillingly.

"What does that mean?"

A thousand names and faces.

"What's her real name?"

Real is unreal, it said. *I can say no more. Your mother is not our target—Ashburn Fury is. We need him to heal you. We need you to survive.*

"Who are 'we'?"

You and I and he, it said. *You are the seed implanted an eon ago. I will assist you to bring back Eterne. Soon you will have no more burdens. You must fulfill your obligations. When destiny is satisfied, you will be all powerful. No secrets of the universe will be hidden from you.*

Thrills and chills travelled in her veins all at once. Her every predatory instinct had kicked in, telling her what to do next.

Her shaking fingers clenched on the locket's pins. One push, and she'd change her future, as the Eye of Time promised, and Ashburn would pay only a little price.

The Eye of Time gazed back at her, its color turning dark red with ravenous hunger.

Yes, she'd walk into the realm of the gods. She'd live.

But Ash—

The Ash she loved would be no more.

With a sob, Lucienne slammed shut the locket, dropped it in the crystal box, and fled the room.

Chapter Twenty-Six

GIRL SCORNED

Mom knows the Shadow is in me, Bayrose thought in a cold sweat. How could Mom know? What would she do? Would she choose one daughter over the other? Even now, Mom was actively seeking a cure for her firstborn. In no time, she might just succeed.

Bayrose must stop her mother before that happened. But how could she beat her powerful mother? And who was Mom really? Jekaterina, Samantha, or someone else?

Bayrose brushed aside her sense of dread being exposed and turned to observe her half-sister.

In a red dress, Lucienne sat on the floor of the white mansion's sitting room, playing with a toy train. Eyebrows drawing together, Lucienne struggled to figure out how to make the electronic train run while holding a Barbie doll in her hand.

Had Lucienne's intelligence dropped to that of a child, or had another personality popped up? The Siren never had a normal childhood. Maybe insanity had her overcompensating and reliving a lost childhood?

Now and then, Bayrose caught a strange glint in her sister's eyes, as if the sane Lucienne was kicking and screaming to make a comeback. The Siren's mental state had become more unstable and unpredictable. She would be the most sought-after patient in the psychiatric world. If it were up to Bayrose, she'd lock up Lucienne in an asylum, where the mad Siren truly belonged.

Prince Vladimir, however, didn't seem repulsed by Lucienne's lunacy. He leaned against the frame of the door, watching her dotingly. He looked exhausted, yet the tenderness for her in his hazel eyes made Bayrose want to claw at Lucienne's face. She hoped Lucienne looked like a hag with messy hair, grayish skin, and saliva drooling from the corner of her mouth. To her displeasure, a mad Lucienne took meticulous care of her appearance. Bayrose hated to admit that the Siren actually radiated wild sexiness in her insane state.

Vladimir jogged toward Lucienne.

The door flew open and Ashburn moved in like a flash, blocking Vladimir before he reached her. "Not today," Ashburn said. "She's doing fine. Let her be."

"Who appointed you head of the household?" asked Vladimir, ready to shove away his rival.

"You were spent healing her last night," said Ashburn. "It's stupid to exhaust yourself."

"When has my wellbeing become your business?" Vladimir grated.

"I am not concerned about you or your health," Ashburn said coldly. "I'm thinking of her benefit. If you don't preserve yourself, then you're of no use to her when she really needs the healing. When the next big wave hits."

Vladimir gave Ashburn a disgusted stare, then returned to lean on the doorframe. Ashburn sat on a chair, distant from everyone, watching Lucienne wearily.

Had Vladimir and Ashburn just put their differences aside for Lucienne? Bayrose had heard that they'd almost killed each other on several occasions. She'd studied, observed, and learned more about Ashburn at close range. His eyes were forever ice-blue until they trained on Lucienne, and then their color immediately shifted to light silver, glowing with longing. But whenever he saw Vladimir and Lucienne together, his eyes were gunmetal gray, and their shade kept darkening.

Maybe Bayrose could find comfort from Ashburn and give him hers? He was evidently hurting from an unrequited love, just like her. He was born off base, as Prince Vladimir constantly called him farm boy, but this farm boy was no less than any prince. The two of them were the opposite forces of nature: one burned like fire, the other had the strength of ice.

If Bayrose could get Ashburn to desire her, it would revive Vladimir's feelings for her. *Men are competitive animals. They don't value easy prey.* She fell for Vladimir too fast and too far. Holding that thought, Bayrose sauntered toward Ashburn and slid onto a chair near him. He gave her a brief glance before turning back to Lucienne.

Lucienne combed the doll's light auburn hair with her fingers, then put the Barbie on top of the train. How could both men—the hottest, most powerful men—be interested in this mental case? Bayrose shook her head in dismay. They were temporarily blind, and she needed to help them see a much better alternative in front of them.

"Hi, Ash," Bayrose said with the sweetest smile.

Ashburn turned to her, looking surprised that she called him Ash instead of Ashburn. Bayrose blushed, suddenly feeling like a trespasser.

"Hello, Bayrose." He returned the courtesy, but his expression remained blank.

A man like Ashburn didn't waste time in small talk. Social polish meant nothing to him. But Bayrose wasn't discouraged. "My sister is doing better," she said. Using "my sister" instead of Lucienne would reduce the gap between them and get Ashburn to treat her like the Siren's family.

"No, she's getting worse," Ashburn said bluntly, eyes flashing dark gray.

"You care about her," Bayrose said. "We all do."

Ashburn's gaze on her intensified as if he could see through her soul. Bayrose shivered, regretting her initial idea of making him warm up to her. Now she only wanted to flee from him. No wonder everyone in Sphinxes tried to stay as far away from him as possible. The fathomless Ashburn was completely out of her league.

"Yes, I care about her very much," he said. "Anyone who intends to harm her will meet with destruction."

Was that a threat? Her cheeks flamed hot, but her armpits felt cold sweat as a realization struck her. Ashburn knew about her plan for vengeance. He'd collected her past memories before she'd taken in the Shadow.

He can't know now, Bayrose heard the voice of Shadow inside her. *He's powerful, but not all-powerful.*

And he hadn't told anyone yet, which meant he didn't want to grieve Lucienne. He didn't want to break the Siren's heart and quicken her demise.

"People can change," Bayrose said in a regretful, submissive voice.

"I hope so," he said. "I'm watching."

That was why he hadn't said anything yet. He was hoping she could really be Lucienne's sister. He was giving her a second chance for Lucienne's sake. Bayrose could take advantage of that. She couldn't hide her past, but she could hide her feelings and future plan. The Shadow had made her a great deceiver.

Mother knew all about the Shadow too. Why did the Shadow become impotent in Mom's presence? Whenever Bayrose consulted it about her mother, it fell silent.

"Thank you for looking out for my sister," Bayrose said. "I've always wanted a sister, and I couldn't ask for a better one than Lucia." The Shadow concealed her bitterness. How could that nutcase deserve men like Ashburn and Prince Vladimir?

Ashburn straightened his back, suddenly vibrating with tension. He was about to rise to pounce. Bayrose cringed. Had she said anything wrong? No, he wasn't focusing on her.

Vladimir had moved and sat across from Lucienne on the floor.

"Who are you?" Lucienne asked him.

It dawned on Bayrose that her sister had become a little girl. That was why the loony hadn't reacted to anyone other than Aida. Usually she clung to Ashburn and repelled Vladimir in her mad state, which made Vladimir all the more eager to restore her sanity.

"I'm Vlad," Vladimir said. "We played together before."

"I don't remember you, Vlad." Lucienne tilted her head. "I have no playmates. Anyone who is too close to me will be used as a weapon against me."

"I'll never be a weapon against you," Vladimir said.

Ashburn snorted.

Lucienne swept her gaze toward Ashburn. Holding his breath, he held her stare in such a hope, as if willing her to recognize him. A spark rose in Lucienne's eyes, then vanished like a dime sinking into murky water. She turned back to Vladimir and whispered, loud enough for everyone to hear, "Who are that boy and girl?"

"They're nobody," Vladimir said. "Don't mind them."

Bayrose felt Vladimir had just scratched her face.

Ashburn narrowed his eyes, but didn't retort. He focused on Lucienne as if studying a scientific case. Bayrose realized he was looking for a crack to break through. Although he'd told Lucienne he couldn't heal her, he'd never really given up.

Let the farm boy find nothing, Bayrose whispered to the Shadow.

"They stare at me and my train," Lucienne demanded. "Are they thieves?"

"They might be," Vladimir said. "But you have *me*. I won't allow anyone to steal a thing from you."

Lucienne beamed at him, and Vladimir looked heartbroken at her smile.

"You can be my first friend, Vlad," Lucienne declared.

"An honor," Vladimir said.

"I like anything to do with honor. Will you protect me then?"

"Always and forever," Vladimir answered.

"Will you swear?" Lucienne asked intensely.

"I'll protect you until my last breath," Vladimir said.

"Like Kian?" Lucienne asked.

"Better than Kian," Vladimir said.

Lucienne laughed. "You can't compete with Kian. He's bigger than you. People are scared of him."

"Not me," said Vladimir. "Some people are scared of me too."

Lucienne laughed harder. "You hope! I guess I can trust you. But I'm not supposed to have toys. Grandfather won't be pleased." A sad, lonely look entered her eyes. "He doesn't want me to be a normal girl. That's why I don't have a friend my age."

"You have now," Vladimir said. "And we're more than friends."

Ashburn growled a warning.

"That will be our secret." Lucienne darted a glance at Ashburn and Bayrose. "Do you see the way they look at me? They must be spies."

"I can kick them out," Vladimir offered.

"That's enough, Blazek!" Ashburn called.

"Blazek?" Lucienne blinked. "You said you were Vlad! And the spy boy knows you. Are you working together to get me?" She looked like she wanted to slap the liar in front of her.

Bayrose willed Lucienne to hit Vladimir, only to realize that act simply wouldn't turn off the Czech prince. Lucienne had put a knife to his chest, and he still went back to her. How fair was it that he could forgive her sister forever, but not her?

"Not in a million years would I work with that farm boy," Vladimir said.

Lucienne looked back and forth between Ashburn and Vladimir. "I guess you're right. He just gave you the evil look. He doesn't like you much."

"The feeling is mutual," Vladimir said.

Lucienne's gaze roamed over Ashburn again. Bayrose cursed her sister for not showing the slightest interest in her. Raised as a princess, Bayrose was used to being the center of the universe. Until she was in her sister's presence. Even in her insane state, Lucienne wasn't sharing the limelight. Damn the Siren to hell!

"The farm boy is clean and nice to look at," Lucienne said.

"You know me, Lucia," Ashburn said with an encouraging smile. "Try to remember. You—"

"Lucia," Vladimir called, his knuckles tracing her face. Lucienne turned away from studying Ashburn, distracted by Vladimir's touch. Then she leaned forward toward him, wanting more, and Vladimir conjured the most charming, lopsided smile.

Bayrose wanted to pick up the toy train and hammer it on her sister's head. But she was also puzzled. Lucienne was usually unkind to the prince in her mad state. What had changed? Did Vladimir's healing help his chances with the mad Siren?

Ashburn leapt to his feet, clenching his fists, but then probably thought better and slumped back down in his chair. The leather made noises under his force.

"I made the train run for you, Lucia," Vladimir said.

Creak. Crack. The electronic train raced around the circular track.

Lucienne applauded. Bayrose was now so sick of the nutcase's giggling that she wanted to leave this place at once, but she glued herself to the couch.

"I always wondered what you were like when you were a little girl," Vladimir murmured.

"Little girl?" A strange light flickered in Lucienne's eyes, as if the sane Lucienne underneath fought to surface. Then the light in her eyes grew brighter, driving away the red rings around her irises.

"Vlad," Lucienne called, her voice no longer the little girl's. There was true recognition in her eyes. "You're here." Her hand reached for him.

"I'm always here, láska," Vladimir said, holding her hand in his. "You know I'll never leave you." There was gratitude in his eyes, and his tenderness was the endless sea in sunlight.

What wouldn't Bayrose kill to have Vladimir look at her like that!

"And you came back, my love," Vladimir said in a choked voice. He raised her hand to his lips and kissed it.

"Vlad," Lucienne said desperately. "I can't hold onto myself." She stretched her other hand toward Vladimir. "Don't let me go please."

So needy. So clingy, Bayrose cursed her sister under her breath. *You're the Siren. Act like one!*

Vladimir moved to sit beside Lucienne. He held her, his forehead pressed against hers. She twisted away, eyes darting around. She was looking for Ashburn, but didn't need to look far. He was at her other side in an instant. Bayrose hadn't noticed him move.

"Lucia," Ashburn said. "I'm here."

Lucienne narrowed her eyes on Vladimir. "Did you bring me back?" she asked. "I told you not to do that! You now have enough of my poison in your body." She turned to Ashburn. "Ash, you promised you'd look after him. You're the strongest of the three of us."

"Only if I can take your poison instead," Ashburn said.

"Ash!" Lucienne cried. "Don't say that! Would I wish that for you?"

"Shush, Lucia," Vladimir said. "The farm boy stopped me from healing you. You came back all by yourself."

Lucienne exhaled, more relaxed now, but also exhausted. "I'm in limbo, wandering in the dark alone. The dark is endless."

"You're not alone," Ashburn said. "You'll never be alone. You have to remind yourself of that. We're with you. Always will be."

Bayrose rose to her feet. This melodrama was making her nausous, but she didn't want to be left out of the trio's clique. As she neared her sister, a ring of redness started forming in Lucienne's eyes again.

Lucienne breathed hard. "It's returning!"

The next second, Lucienne surveyed the room like a predator.

Her sister slipped again. *She lapses easily when I'm close*, Bayrose realized. The Shadow was potent. *Marvelous!*

Lucienne shook off Vladimir's grasp. "Prince Vladimir, what a surprise!"

"No, Lucia," Vladimir said. "Come back—"

"Don't 'No Lucia' me," Lucienne said, wagging a finger at him. "I know you're the one who poisoned me."

The brokenness in the prince's eyes couldn't touch the cold-stone heart of the mad Siren, but it pierced Bayrose. The Shadow in her brought out the worst in her sister.

Ashburn folded his arms over his chest, evidently enjoying Lucienne torture his rival.

"Yes ... I caused you all this pain," Vladimir said, his face white as death.

"Then it's only fitting that I avenge myself," Lucienne said.

"Then avenge yourself," Vladimir said.

Bayrose chewed her inner cheek. *He's self-destructive.* But she couldn't risk deliberately influencing Lucienne while Ashburn was around. The last thing she wanted was the Fury boy to suspect the power the Shadow had over the love of his life.

"You didn't have the heart to harm me." Lucienne looked thoughtful for a second. "But you messed me up badly. Lucia the fair and merciful won't seek revenge but a punishment." A cruel smile made her soft, full lips harder. "We can think of an adequate chastisement, can't we, Ash?"

"We definitely can," Ashburn said. "Let's banish him—"

"Ashburn Fury!" Vladimir warned menacingly.

"—to the moon?" Lucienne asked.

Ashburn gave Vladimir a despising look before turning to Lucienne. "Not yet," he said. "Kicking him to the moon is too good to him. He'll have fun throwing rocks. Let's keep him around for a little longer until his usefulness runs out. We'll then think of a proper punishment he deserves."

Bayrose couldn't stand on the sideline anymore. "You two are cruel."

"This is the talk of the adults, little girl," Lucienne snapped.

"Lucia," Bayrose said. "I'm not a little girl. I'm your sister. Remember?" Breathing in, she sent a touch of the Shadow toward Lucienne. What wouldn't a girl do for the man she loved?

Instantly, a confused look moved across Lucienne's face, then the wild edge in her whisky-colored eyes ebbed.

Her heart about to shoot out of her throat, Bayrose darted a glance at Ashburn. He looked back at her, his expression unreadable. Bayrose immediately withdrew the Shadow's reach. Then she almost jumped to the roof as Lucienne suddenly leapt to her feet and stared down at the floor, a finger pointing at her toy in accusation.

"This is like a madhouse," Lucienne said. "Who is running the train in my bedroom? Did Aida allow this? Aida!"

Ashburn and Vladimir traded a glance, then quickly darted away from each other, looking angry and embarrassed that they could find common ground.

It was obvious that there was a gap in Lucienne's memories. One minute, she fixated on punishing Vladimir; then next she was worried about something completely different. The Siren was an express train going over a cliff. No one, including Mom, could stop that train.

Once Lucienne was gone, Bayrose, the rightful heir, would graciously give Sphinxes time to grieve over their uncrowned queen. Lucienne's demise would benefit millions. The Siren race—the plague on Earth—would be no more. There would be no more ancient feud. No more war. No more bloodshed. And Bayrose would step into the light.

For the greater good, Bayrose must push the express train to go faster. "Aida went to see our mother," she said. "You remember Mom, don't you?"

"Mom?" Lucienne asked, her eyebrows furrowed. "I have a mother. She—what's her name? I can't think straight." Then she jerked her head back, as if being pulled by an unseen force. "I—" She darted her eyes frenetically. "Stop fighting me! Let go." She dropped to the floor on one knee.

Vladimir and Ashburn each fought to pull her into his arms. Lucienne jolted backwards and fell, her back against Ashburn's chest, her legs thrashing. "Why are you so stubborn?" she yelled. "We can have fun together. I'm your better twin!"

"She's fighting herself," Ashburn said, drawing a sharp breath.

"How do you know?" Vladimir said, suspicion and pain whirling in his darkened hazel eyes. "She's hurting, so quit pretending to be an expert! Get out of my way and let me help her." He shoved Ashburn away and leaned toward Lucienne. She backhanded him across his left eye.

Ashburn lurched forward and held her from behind. "Shush, Lucia. It's us. We'll never harm you. Never intentionally."

Vladimir knelt on one knee and pressed his forehead against Lucienne. A stream of mist emitted from him and seeped into her forehead. She stopped struggling, drawn by Ashburn's hand gently stroking the side of her cheek down to her neck, then back to her cheek. She went soft in Ashburn's arms and whimpered.

It took a full minute for the red rings in her eyes to recede.

Vladimir broke the connection and coughed into his hand.

Blood was sprinkled on his fingers, his face colorless.

"Vlad!" Bayrose called out, alarmed. She moved toward him and laid a hand on his burning-hot arm in concern. He shook her off, even in his weakened state.

Lucienne gasped wide-eyed as if breaking the surface of the churning sea. Her eyes, now clear brown, looked into Vladimir's glassy ones. "I've forbidden you to do this," she said. "Why did you keep challenging me and hurting yourself?"

Vladimir tried to give her an assuring grin, but he only winced in pain. The guards moved in and helped him onto a sofa. Duncan wiped blood off his friend's hand with a napkin. When he tried to clean it from Vladimir's mouth, Lucienne stopped him. "Let me do it, please."

With a mist of tears in her eyes, Lucienne used her silk handkerchief to gently dab away a drip of blood from the corner of the prince's mouth. "One day you'll die from this," she said in devastation. "I've become the bane of your existence."

"No more than I am yours," he managed to whisper. Then his eyes went wild. Her madness was passing into him. "I see dead space. Dead stars. If you're gone, láska, I'll be stuck in the empty—" And then he passed out.

"I thought if there was any man who would never break," Lucienne said, her eyes glued to Vladimir, "it'd be him. Yet I broke him. Ash, you should leave me before it's too late. I don't want to break you too."

"Too late for that now," Ashburn said, then turned to the guards and asked them to take Vladimir back to his room.

"Let him rest on my bed," Lucienne said. "I'll tend to him."

"His connection to you hasn't broken yet," Ashburn said. "Physical proximity to you will continue to drain him."

Lucienne's face paled more. "I'm a leech."

Bayrose couldn't agree more.

Lucienne watched her guards carry out Vladimir, her hands curling to half fists at her sides. Then she looked down at her red gown. With a curse, she tore at it.

It's not your gown—it's you! Bayrose hoped, for everyone's sake, that vampire would just end her own life, and the sooner the better.

"Don't ever say that, Lucia," Ashburn said, grasping her shaking hands in his. "You're the light in our dark hearts, and we must go through any dark passage to find that light."

"I'm not the light." Lucienne shook her head. "I'm the darkness."

Bayrose stared at the empty sofa where Vladimir had rested a moment ago. "I'll check on Prince Vladimir."

"Come back and tell me as soon as his condition improves, please," Lucienne pleaded.

"Sure," Bayrose said. *Like hell I will.* She hastened out of the room to chase the prince.

In Vladimir's room in Lucienne's white mansion, Bayrose studied the prince. His chest barely rose with each breath. She'd wiped a trace of blood from his hairline. He wouldn't have let her touch him if he'd been conscious.

She pulled the chair closer to his bed.

His face was still ashen. For the past week, he'd been taking in her sister's poison and madness again and again. No matter how tough he was, he was still flesh and blood. How could Lucienne keep sucking out his life force and claim that she loved him? *That bitch!*

Bayrose darted a glance toward the closed door. The guards had left her alone with the prince, trusting her with him. Duncan had checked on Vladimir a few hours ago, as had Aida, Dr. Wren, and a nurse.

Lucienne had come by every half hour, but Bayrose hadn't let her in, spelling out for her that her presence might cause the Czech prince more harm than good. That vampire sister of hers had then left with a tormented look.

Bayrose knew Lucienne wished to tend to Vladimir instead of letting her. *Not going to happen.* Her sister had been avoiding challenging her feelings for Vladimir. The Siren might be good at sword fighting but was incompetent at dealing with emotions. At least she wouldn't come back for another twenty-five minutes to bother Bayrose and Vlad.

Bayrose bent forward and brushed her lips over Vladimir's. She'd always wondered how it would feel to have him kiss her, but she'd never pictured this—she kissing an unconscious prince.

His lips were cracked, dry, and fever hot.

He hadn't been this lifeless when they'd first met. He'd carried an air of wildness and held a fierce hatred for the two-faced Siren. He'd looked golden, even as he'd appeared half-damaged. Now he was a wrecked train that had suffered too many crashes.

As the Siren ran out of time, her vise-like grip on Prince Vladimir only tightened. Lucienne was poison to him, literally. Now only Bayrose could salvage him. She needed to make him see that. In order for that to happen, she needed to talk to him. Today was the first chance she had. She only hoped it wouldn't be too late for the two of them.

Bayrose traced the faint shadow under his long, thick lashes. "I'm good for you, Vlad. Know that I'm made for you," she whispered. "One love, one life time, and that's you." When she grazed her fingertips across his cheek, she slanted her mouth over his again. He didn't resist, as if he'd been waiting for a kiss for too long. She deepened her kiss, and slowly he responded, first soft, then desperately. Bayrose closed her eyes, lost in their hungry want for each other. The tip of her tongue urged him to open up, and he did.

Their tongues entwined. Bayrose felt his unfulfilled desire was as deep, dark, and insatiable as hers. Vladimir groaned with pleasure, needing more, but then suddenly he stiffened.

Before she knew it, he'd thrown her off him. Bayrose hit the floor. Fortunately, her buttocks landed first, but it still hurt. She sat up, dazed, and stared into the muzzle of an Armatix pistol.

Vladimir leaned up and stared at her with his gun. "I hoped it was her," he said coldly. "You're not her. I'd recognize her taste." A second later, he tucked the gun back under his pillow.

Bayrose knew Vladimir considered hitting a woman a cardinal sin, so pointing a gun at a girl was also a shameful thing to do. His manner didn't comfort her, and his harsh words stung her.

"Then why didn't she come to kiss you?" she asked, picking herself up from the floor.

A dark, dangerous look flashed in the Czech prince's eyes.

Suddenly she wondered if Lucienne had ever kissed Vladimir. The insane, slutty Siren resented the prince. The sane Siren appeared prudish and discreet. But obviously Lucienne and Vladimir had kissed before. Vladimir had just said, "I'd recognize her taste." Then why did the subject of kissing bring such a bitter, agonizing look from the prince?

"Why did she send me instead?" Bayrose plowed on.

He swallowed, the hurt evident on his face. "She sent you?"

"To keep you company and entertained," Bayrose said. "She's with Ashburn." And immediately she saw insane jealousy burning darkly in his hazel eyes. Of course it didn't sit well with him that he sucked out part of the Siren's poison so she could have fun with his rival. His pain diluted the acid roiling in Bayrose, just as his jealousy increased it.

The angry fire in his eyes turned to cold stone. "Leave," he said.

"I came because I wanted to," she said. "You need a friend who really cares about you, who will never use you and then discard you."

"You're no friend to me," he spat. "You used me to deliver the poison. I was a fool to trust you. Now wipe that innocent look off your face and get the hell out."

His words were full of venom, but to her surprise, the jagged pain in her chest only dulled. At least he was talking to her. He was telling her that they had a trust issue and that he was still hurting from her betrayal.

"Be fair. You used me first to get a hand on Nexus Tear. You didn't know Lucienne's father was going to add poison to it, and neither did I. How could you hate me for other people's sins?"

"I hate myself more for poisoning the only girl I love."

Could Vladimir hear the sizzling when he pressed a hot iron over her heart as he professed his love for her rival in front of her?

"You didn't poison my sister, neither did I," she said. "I hope one day you can find the truth in your heart and know that I'm innocent. If I had a hand in that scheme, I wouldn't have come to Sphinxes. I wish more than anything that my sister gets well soon. I pray to God every day to let me take her place and poison me instead. Do not keep hating me, please. I can't bear it. It's the Sealers founder and his cronies we should hate."

Pure hatred lit like black flame in Vladimir's eyes. "I swear on my soul I'll seal him and all of his minions in cheap coffins," he said through his perfect, clenched white teeth. "I'll bury them alive."

At least he didn't include me on the list of those he wants to kill, Bayrose thought. *That is quite an improvement.* "I'll assist you, Vlad. We have a common enemy. I'm so glad I escaped with Kian. If I hadn't succeeded, I'd never have met my only sister, and I'd never have seen you again."

"I don't need your assistance," he said.

It was strange that even though Vladimir resented her, she found it much easier to talk to him than Ashburn. She was always lost for words in Ashburn's presence. Then again, she wasn't alone. She noticed that no one, except Lucienne, knew how to engage Ashburn in conversation.

Ashburn was at ease with Lucienne. When she was her insane self, the chemistry between them rocketed so high that the Czech prince would risk his life to break them apart.

"You need me, Vlad," Bayrose said. "I'll prove myself to you. I'll earn your trust back."

He looked straight at her. "Don't think for a second that I'll trust you again. I'll never forgive you, just as I'll never forgive myself for my girl's suffering. I haven't torn you apart because you're Lucia's sister. Hurting you would hurt her. But make no mistake—if a mere thought of harming her pops out of your little skull, I'll kill you with my bare hands."

"Point taken," Bayrose said. She'd take his wrath. When it faded, she'd regain his grace, and then his affection. And when Lucienne checked out, Bayrose would be the one to comfort the prince in his grief. She'd worm her way back into his heart. She'd do whatever it took to get him back, and humiliation was part of the package. She was only being practical. Her future happiness was more important than her pride.

"Then why are you still here?" he asked.

"I need you to promise me to preserve yourself. If you keep taking in the poison, you'll burn out. You'll be like her. You can die, and I can't allow that."

His eyes sharpened to dark blades. "Allow? Who the hell do you think you are? Whatever is between Lucienne and me is none of your business. It's none of anyone's business."

He looked at her as if she were a rattlesnake. It was such a sharp contrast to the way he gazed at Lucienne—all tender, loving, and fierce. In that instant, Bayrose's heart hardened. "Have you not cared even a little about me?"

"I do not care about you. I don't even care if you were innocent or not. All I know is we both had a part in poisoning her. Lucia keeps you here, so I have to live with that. But I want to have nothing to do with you. The truth is: I can't stand the sight of you."

"I once knew you. You're many things, Prince Vladimir, but I didn't realize you could be so spiteful, unforgiving, and heartless."

"Get used to it," he said callously.

She'd heard of his notorious reputation with girls. Her ally Mirrikh and other friends had warned her. She'd been confident she would be the exception, but it turned out only Lucienne was immune to his cruelty—if only because she was even more malicious than him. The two villains deserved each other.

"Now get out of my room," the Czech said.

And Bayrose snapped. She no longer cared if it was his own venom talking or the venom he took from the Siren. "I hate you too!" she said, forcing back tears.

He wiped his lips with the back of his hand to clean off her scent.

Bayrose fled to the door and almost tripped over the toppled chair.

She'd lost everything, including herself, because of the Siren.

Hate was a bottomless well, and the Shadow hovered above it.

Lucienne and Vladimir had doomed Sphinxes. Soon, a war the likes of which the world had never seen would rain its wrath on the Siren and her people.

Bayrose's pain evaporated. Her heart had never felt so inhumanly cold.

Chapter Twenty-Seven
SLEEPLESS NIGHT

The cacophony of billions of living and dead strangers' memories echoed relentlessly in Ashburn's mind, but they couldn't dull his awareness of Lucienne's presence. She was near. It was another sleepless night for her.

Ashburn left his bed and exited the mansion.

Lucienne wandered in the dark forest. The rim of her white gown, almost shining in the moonlight, glided over the leaf-paved ground. The wind hugged her thin gown to her body, revealing her shapely figure.

Ashburn drew a long breath and trekked toward the girl of his dreams.

Two of her guards immediately whipped around toward him, guns drawn.

"It's Ash," Lucienne said without turning.

Adam lowered his gun as he saw it was indeed Ashburn.

Lucienne now looked at Ashburn over her shoulder. Ashburn's pulse spiked. His heart forever beat for her. His soul sang to her. He only hoped the sane Lucienne could hear it.

"Ash," she greeted.

He gave her a smile and joined her. He rarely smiled these days. "Can't sleep?" he asked with concern.

She shook her head, then asked, "What kept you up?"

"I sensed you," he said, "without tracing your guards' memories."

Adam and the other guard looked uncomfortable. They gave Lucienne and Ashburn a wide berth, wishing the distance would weaken Ashburn's mental intrusion. Ashburn ignored their futile resistance. He didn't mind them. He didn't mind anyone, except Lucienne.

He'd changed and continued to change. TimeDust bestowed him great power, but it also took away part of his humanity. The bond he had with his parents and Violet was now as thin as a piece of paper. He gazed at the only person he still cared about and wanted very much to wrap his arms around her. The Lure swam around them, dwelling on his skin. But Ashburn wouldn't touch her without her permission. He willed her to give him a hint of invitation.

A twitch of muscles on her beautiful, stubborn jaw told him otherwise. Ashburn swallowed as pain slammed into him as well.

The mad Lucienne would never fight their attraction, with or without the Lure. The uninhibited Lucienne indulged it and welcomed it. She wore her feelings for him in the open. She was wildly enchanting and more stunning than the sane, regal Siren. Ashburn suddenly realized that part of him preferred the insane Lucienne, and that thought shamed him.

"I sensed you as well," Lucienne said, holding his guilty gaze. She must have mistaken it for the punishing pain he was enduring. For a fleeting second, he swore he saw her ruefulness as she appeared puzzled by why she had to fight the Lure and their connection.

"Ash, I want—"

"What do you want?" he asked urgently. He knew what she wanted. He felt the same desperate need too. He wanted her.

Was this Lucienne going to give in at midnight, when her will weakened, when her need heightened?

"I—" She looked up at him, stepped closer, and laid her hand on his arm.

Ashburn regretted wearing a jacket. He should have put on a thin T-shirt so his skin could feel her touch. Silently, he watched desire and reason battle in her whiskey brown eyes. A second later, she withdrew her hand and stepped back. Her reason and loyalty won again. Blazek, the forever nuisance, was still between them. And

Ashburn couldn't get rid of the Czech before his worth expired.

"I need to go away for a little while," he finally said.

An alarmed look widened her eyes. Her need for him became palpable.

"Lucia, I'll be back," he immediately added.

"It takes longer and longer for you to come back each time."

"I can't sense the passing of time inside the Rabbit Hole."

"I understand you need a break. You need the silence in your head, but—"

"I need to find an answer."

Lucienne tilted her head. "But you had the answer."

"I've seen Jekaterina's memories," he said. "I've been watching her lab work. She has the partial code." But he didn't trust her selective memories. He'd never known anyone who could manipulate their own memories like she did.

And some of her memories made him wince. He'd seen her tremendous labor pain giving birth to Lucienne. The baby survived, but who would have thought it'd grow up to be the most gorgeous girl in the world? The squirming baby was quite ugly.

Jekaterina's partial code could fix Seraphen's broken memories, and Ashburn would have the final answer to the cure.

"Jekaterina told me the code," Lucienne said.

"You know what it's about?"

"Ash, I don't trust her."

"Can you trust me?"

Her gaze on him softened, then saddened. "With my life."

The love for her churned inside him. He couldn't help but step toward her and brush away a strand of hair blown by the wind from her face. Her eyes glinted with longing, but it was gone the next second. Again, she repressed it.

"I must know if it's the only solution," he said.

"If it is?" Lucienne asked.

"For our sake," he said, "I hope it isn't."

"It doesn't matter," she said. "I don't want you to do it."

He swallowed hard. She was never as selfish as she claimed to be. Then he forgot that he was waiting for her invitation to touch her and pulled her into a tight embrace. She didn't protest, but stood very still. A second later, Ashburn tore himself away from her softness and warmth and summoned his ride.

In the air on Spike, Ashburn couldn't tell if the sharp pain was from the Lure or from his own heart. And he couldn't bear to look back at her standing far beneath him amid the dark maple trees under the moon.

Chapter Twenty-Eight

A PIE

Bayrose had never imagined this could happen to her—she'd fallen into the ranks of those girls subjected to the Czech prince's cruel treatment.

She was the princess and the secret new leader of the Sealers, and she'd humbled herself before him. "I just want us to be like before."

He'd said impatiently, "Before was a mistake."

He was right. He and all those he cared for would soon pay for that mistake. When Sphinxes fell, all would know that Bayrose wasn't just any girl to be dismissed easily.

The moment she'd snapped, she'd no longer wanted to follow through on her plan to infiltrate the Siren's circle and take over Sphinxes at Lucienne's death. She wanted her enemies to see her glory before they went down. She wanted to see their dumbfounded looks when she proudly revealed her true identity. She hadn't asked for this war, but both Lucienne and Vladimir had forced her hands. One killed her father, stole her mother, and took her great love; the other killed her hope and her ability to ever love again.

Together they'd turned her into an invisible shade.

The Shadow affected her every minute of the day. She couldn't remember how long ago she'd actually laughed. But the Shadow granted her a strength she hadn't possessed as the former Bayrose. With its superpower, she was no longer petrified of leading the Sealers into war.

The Shadow agreed. "You're taking back the birthright that was cheated out of you and your ancestors."

Bayrose knew the story: at the start of the human race, twin boys had fought to be the heir to the first Siren. The younger one had tricked and threatened his older brother into giving up his birthright.

Lucienne Lam was the last descendent of the treacherous younger twin. Bayrose was the other side of the coin.

"You're the *true* Siren," the Shadow confirmed. "You'll right the wrong of the secret history of the world."

"I was the only one who ever took in the Shadow," Bayrose said.

"You're brave."

"And naïve," she said. "But as long as Lucienne Lam lives, I'm doomed to be in her shadow. I must end the Sirens' line."

"And become the one and only Siren yourself."

It was one thing for Bayrose to want to take out her sister, but when she saw how fervently the Shadow wanted to murder Lucienne, she felt a chill slice up her spine. "Will I be free of you once I kill her?" she asked.

"You know the cost."

Yes, the cost. She'd never get rid of it. She'd become a slave to the Shadow in her.

"You must act before Jekaterina interferes," it said.

Yes, Mother knew that Bayrose had taken in the Shadow. Did she know about her daughter's plan for vengeance? Would Mom betray her to her sister? The hollow panic that arose in Bayrose soon eased. With Shadow shielding her, no one could read her true intention. Yet, the look her mother had given her was more than unsettling. There had been no sunlight in Mom's look.

But Bayrose had other advantages over her powerful mother besides the Shadow. Kian and the generals considered Bayrose innocent. Lucienne accepted her. Their security no longer put her under their radar as they did Jekaterina. Furthermore, Sphinxes wouldn't expect the Sealers to rise again so quickly to strike back, and the Sealers' founder, Bayrose Thorn, was right in the enemy's heart to direct the blow.

The Sealers had no need of their own army. They were the

shadow government behind many nations, and those nations, including the United States, were anxious about Sphinxes' growing power. The Brotherhood would keep pumping fear into those nations' veins.

Their combined nations' forces would hit Sphinxes at its weakest point—its uncrowned Siren queen was half-mad and fatally poisoned, leaving her nation-to-be unstable and vulnerable.

The prince and all those who had underestimated Bayrose would see how great and terrifying she was, and the Siren would be forever diminished in Bayrose's shadow. History would reverse and right itself.

That night, Bayrose baked a yogurt and apricot pie from one of her mother's recipes. When she brought it to Lucienne, her half-sister was in the middle of a bath, singing a bawdy song.

Vladimir was in the sitting room, shaking his head at the song and waiting for his insane girlfriend to come out. He barely gave Bayrose a glance when she brushed past him and stepped into Lucienne's bedroom.

When she was sure to be out of anyone's direct sight, Bayrose picked up Lucienne's phone on the vanity table. She hit the password that the mad Lucienne had revealed to her. Within two minutes, Bayrose sent Mirrikh Schwartz the maps of Sphinxes' military bases, classified labs, and the location of the Siren's white mansion.

Then she texted Mirrikh the access code to Devourer.

Bayrose put the phone back and wiped the sweat from her palms on her pants.

The last thing the Sphinxes' team would check was their Siren's private phone line. And before they had the chance to look, Bayrose's army would be here.

She was cutting the pie when her sister threw open the bathroom door and danced out in a scarlet mini skirt.

"A pie!" Lucienne cheered.

Probably your last one, Sister, thought Bayrose. *Enjoy it while you can.*

Chapter Twenty-Nine
THE TALK

Lucienne gazed into the telescope at the vast heavens, at God's fingerprints in the universe.

In contrast, her existence and insanity were less than insignificant. She'd come to accept that. Yet the ancients believed that every person's destiny was strung to the celestial clock that reflected through the star patterns and planets in motion.

Maybe even dust had a place in the universe as it was also a part of God's creation and the material God used often. And who were we to measure the value of all things by their size?

She heard heavy boots scrambling up the stairs toward the rooftop and turned away from the sky. Kian appeared at the doorway, where he dismissed her guards.

"Hey, kid." His voice sounded bright for the first time since the Polynesian war.

Kian McQuillen was never a stargazer or a dreamer, but he tied his dream to hers. Standing tall in front of her, he was clean-shaven with renewed energy. The weary, ragged Kian, once on the verge of broken, had disappeared overnight.

"Did you come from Jekaterina?" Lucienne could guess.

Kian seated himself on a chair before the white wooden table and gestured for Lucienne to sit across from him.

"Is it going to be a long talk?" she asked.

He quirked an eyebrow. "You have some place to go?"

"I have a life, you know." She slid onto a soft chair. She wasn't ready for the talk, but since he'd demanded it—

Kian's expression was serious, bright. "Your mother figured out the cure."

The cure, of course. Lucienne had known about it since she'd paid a visit to the Eye of Time. Ashburn was the cure— only after he linked to the Eye of Time and became its slave could he heal her. She wasn't surprised that Jekaterina had reached Kian first. Her mother knew best who to use to execute her perfect plan, knowing that Kian and his men would do anything to keep Lucienne alive.

"I sent a team to Nirvana to retrieve Ashburn," Kian said.

"If he doesn't want to be summoned, he won't come back."

"It's not up to him."

She'd expected this, but still her back stiffened. Her people would hunt down Ashburn and force him to save her. They'd put him under the mercy of the Eye of Time. Ash had lightning, but he was only one man. And damn it to hell would she allow Ash and her people to turn against one another while she lived. "I don't want you or anyone to go after him," she said, her voice harsher than she intended. "Ashburn is off-limits."

"When it comes to you, nothing is off-limits."

"You'll go against my will?"

"If I have to," Kian said. "We're out of options. Ashburn should do what we ask of him. It's his duty as well."

"It's not his duty! And you don't know what you ask of him."

"It doesn't matter."

"It matters to him and to me! It isn't my right to take something so precious from him, nor is it your right."

"I don't particularly care whose right it is. He can't be more important than the whole of Sphinxes. He's one boy."

"How ironic. You forgot I'm one girl."

"You're our queen! The Siren I used to know wouldn't have blinked to do what she must do to reach greatness. You've become soft. You've let your feelings drive you instead of reining them in. Lucienne Lam, it's time to be who you are again!"

"I *am* who I am. I am not black-hearted. The Lucienne Lam you knew would never put you above her either, Kian McQuillen."

"You lost your perspective, Siren. You're always above us. You were born with a great destiny. We'll bleed our last drop of blood for you."

"Then tell me what my destiny is! Is it all scripted on the scrolls? The tradition on the stone once said there should never be a female Siren, yet here I am. You of all people fought against tradition to get me here. Now all of a sudden you believe in things written on some scrolls?"

"I'll tell you what your destiny is. Your destiny is not to die! Tell me, what are we going to do without you?"

"You'll keep going. I've wanted to talk to you about the day that I'm no longer here. You—"

"Stop!" Kian punched the wood between them. The legs snapped and the table toppled down.

Thaddeus, Duncan, and another guard rushed onto the rooftop, their weapons drawn. They darted their nervous glances at the table, Kian, and Lucienne, back and forth.

Kian waved them off, still in his fury.

Duncan and the guard retreated, but Thaddeus stayed. "I want to make sure my cousin will be fine."

Kian turned to him with a murderous look. Everyone couldn't wait to run away fast enough when McQuillen was pissed. Thaddeus flinched, but stood his ground. "I'm serving my cousin Siren."

"Go, Thaddeus. The last person on earth who will ever hurt me is Kian."

Thaddeus reluctantly left the rooftop. Lucienne knew he was waiting just on the other side of the door.

Kian had panicked when she'd revealed that she wanted him to go on without her. He'd constantly feared for her life since she was a baby, but he'd never panicked like this. Deep inside, he knew, though he refused to accept, that they were both facing their undefeatable enemy—death. She'd never seen fear wreck him so mercilessly. Lucienne inhaled. That fear would drive him to do anything to preserve her, which meant she could no longer protect Ash from Kian. Her chief would sacrifice anyone, including himself, to save her. He'd proved that over and over.

She placed a hand on Kian's, which still shook from raw fury and fear. He calmed a little at her warm, firm touch.

"What you said is unacceptable," he said, looking straight at her. His fury may have ebbed, but not the determination of destroying the whole world to keep her alive.

"I haven't given up, Kian," she said.

"You haven't asked what the cure is," he said.

The only way to dissuade him was to counter Jekaterina. "I have a hunch," she said. "Jekaterina excels at spinning lies and sugarcoating them as truth. You can't trust her."

"I do not trust her, but if her solution can save you, I'll go with it."

"The code and the cure are the ruse. She wants to push Ash and I together for her own agenda."

"I don't see how she can benefit from that."

"There is a menacing, 'grand' design manipulated by a force greater than you and me. This force has been pushing Ash and me to join together—physically. I believe Jekaterina is working with the force. She decoded part of the prophecy on the third scroll. She knew about the poison, but waited until I took it before coming to Sphinxes to enact her next plan. She's using the promise of a cure to manipulate you to help her turn the tide in her direction. The woman, the greatest manipulator the world has ever seen, is hell bent on setting things in motion at the expense of Ash and me. Jekaterina has thousands of faces and names. Do not trust her. Do not let her play you like a pawn in her unfathomable scheme."

Kian cautiously peeked into Lucienne's eyes, evidently trying to detect if the red rings were forming. Lucienne sighed inwardly, helplessly, knowing how she'd sounded. Even if Kian was sure she had utter clarity at the moment, he'd still think she was paranoid.

How could she discredit her cunning mother while her unstable mental condition had condemned her? Lucienne stopped saying more, realizing from that moment on, that whatever she said would backfire.

Her mother could easily turn her people against her, all in the name of saving her. As long as the poison was in her, no one, not even Ash or Vladimir, would count on her judgment. Not even when she held the coldest, utter intelligence.

"I just want to have a talk with Ashburn. That's all," Kian said.

He was being coy, and Kian had never been devious with her before. Which meant he already had a solid plan in place that couldn't be swayed. He'd let Ashburn volunteer to sacrifice himself first, and if Ash turned it down, Kian would pounce and deliver a fatal strike.

She must stay a step ahead of her chief; a step ahead of all of them.

Chapter Thirty

RIVER OF FIRE

Lucienne put the platinum chain around her neck, the Eye of Time inside the gold locket at the end of the chain.

The ancient power was no longer safe in her most guarded treasure house.

Her chief would set it on Ashburn to save her. Very likely, Jekaterina could get her claws on it. Her Forbidden Glory had sensed the power in her mother, and the Eye of Time had made an effort to stay out of Jekaterina's way.

It'd taken Lucienne to be the victim of this "grand design" to see beneath a train of sequences—her attraction to Ash, the Sealers' vegence, her mother's resurfacing, the prophecies, and the final, though partial, revelation of the code.

She was sure more of the chain reaction was on its way, but what was the endgame?

She'd rebuked Ashburn for his cosmic conspiracy—when the Eye of Time completed TimeDust in him, he'd come for her and force her to be with him. They'd then carry out the horrific purpose implanted in him and forged by the force behind the Eye of Time: to bring the human race to extinction.

What if Ashburn was right? But how could she tell truth from fiction when she was half mad? When she couldn't hold onto one consistent thought for long? Her insanity had leaked into her sane consciousness. The poison was in her every pore. She hoped she was only paranoid. She also had this nagging feeling that her enemy had come to the heart of Sphinxes. Was it her mother? Her sister? They were former Sealers elders, and they'd gotten too close to her. Or was it herself who was becoming Sphinxes' worst enemy?

The world had shifted. She couldn't decide which side was up and which was down. But she knew her duty as Siren. She would serve and protect those she loved. She would defend her people from any harm, including any harm from herself. Mostly from herself.

So she must kill her dream of a magnificent future to preserve theirs.

Lucienne closed her hand over the gold locket. The weight of the Eye of Time was now a burden and grief rather than comfort.

"Wrong turn, Melton," Ziyi Wen barked at a member of her team in the SX1 lab. "Don't make me yell at you again."

Under the lab's artificial sunlight, young, energetic scientists and technicians were monitoring broadband electromagnetic receivers, adjusting quantum devices, or just staring at the computer screens, their thoughts too deep for anyone else to track.

"But you just yelled, Miss Wen," Melton grunted, typing in a series of commands on the keyboard.

"Just follow the pathway I showed you earlier," Ziyi said impatiently, then widened her eyes at the sight of Lucienne strolling toward her.

Lucienne wore a white blouse and pants, which brought a grin to Ziyi's face.

"Lucia!" She flew from her chair in her pink qipao and stilettos, the gold chain bouncing up and down her slim ankle.

Lucienne hugged her friend with a doting smile. "Let's talk alone."

"When and where?" Ziyi asked.

As soon as they stepped into the satellite lab, Ziyi drove out everyone, and the soundproof glass door glided shut behind them.

"It'll be a covert mission." Lucienne leaned against the edge of a desk.

Ziyi threw a stick of gum into her mouth. "The more dangerous, the merrier."

"First," Lucienne let out a breath, "we'll have to break a few laws."

"But you're the law here."

"I wish. They watch my every move. I'm a prisoner in my own land."

"I hear you, girl, but I'll trade places with you any minute without blinking an eye."

"You want my place? I'm like a mad cow two-thirds of the time now."

"You'll get well! Jekaterina has found the code. And Ash—"

"The code is a weapon against Ash. I'm going to counter it and guarantee his safety and everyone else's. I need you to back me up and even go against Chief McQuillen. Do I still have your six?"

"Forever."

"Then go with me on a short trip. It might involve kidnapping and hijacking. Are you up for it?"

Ziyi rubbed her hands together. "Anytime." Then she appeared anxious. "I love to run on the wild side once in a while, but I'm not a warrior. I just date them. You think I can do what you do?"

"Better."

"You aren't kidding?"

"Look into my eyes."

"Clear. No red rings."

"Then let's do it."

"Now?"

"Yeah."

Ziyi narrowed her eyes to look menacing. "Looking forward to it."

"Send in a request to have Valkyrie take you to pick up a personal package for me. I'll confirm it when the base calls. Don't leave without me. We're making the trip together."

"But Kian will never let you on that jet. The guards would rather take a bullet from you than let you march out of Sphinxes."

"Leave that to me. But will you take this risk for me? For Ash? I might lapse in the middle of it. I know I'm asking too much, but I need you, and only you can help me."

"I'm with you," said Ziyi, "even when you're your evil twin. If we die, we die together. I don't have a warrior's skills, but I have a warrior's heart. I suggest we both carry an instant death pill. If shit happens, we won't die slowly and painfully."

"This won't be a death trip. I'd never ask my best friend to go down that path."

"Okay then! Since I'm more relaxed now, let me backpedal a little. You said this *covert* mission has something to do with Ash. Are we going to sneak out to see him? Is that it?"

"I'm not that clinging," Lucienne said with a sigh. "And Vlad is here. What would he think of that? I hurt him. I hurt both of them more than I thought I could. But what I'm about to do is to protect Ash, you, and everyone. Kian went to Nirvana to hunt down Ash an hour ago. This is the only time window for me to get off Sphinxes."

Ziyi's eyes went wild. "What is chief planning to do to Ash?"

"Misguided by Jekaterina, he thought he could save me by sacrificing Ash."

"But—" Ziyi hesitated. "Is it true—if Ash goes down, then you'll live?"

One glance at her friend, and Lucienne knew Ziyi would go along with Kian's arrangement if the girl was convinced that Ash's ultimate sacrifice could save Lucienne.

"No," Lucienne lied. "It'll only clear the path for Jekaterina to take what she came here for— the Eye of Time."

Ziyi hissed, "I thought she came to find the cure for you. What kind of a lousy mother is she?"

"One of a kind."

"I'll punch her in the eye!" Ziyi balled her fists. "But first let's make sure she'll get nothing."

As Lucienne and Ziyi emerged from the satellite lab, Melton stepped up eagerly. "Miss Wen, your pathway turned out to be brilliant!"

"Tell me something I don't know," said Ziyi with a dismissive wave.

Lucienne, however, eyed Melton with interest. He was almost her height and as slender as her. "Come with us, Melton," she ordered, jogging toward the lab's exit.

Ziyi shifted her perplexed gaze from Lucienne to the geek, then back to Lucienne.

"I didn't break security protocol, Miss Lam." Melton hastened after Lucienne and Ziyi. "I, at best, participated in a few games for a million bucks. No one could trace me—"

"Ziyi won't fire you," Lucienne said. "We need to discuss the pathway, and you'll be accompanying your boss to pick up a package."

"Okay," Melton said, looking relieved. "What package?"

Melton stepped inside the White Mansion, looking giddy and awed until he received threatening glares from the guards for following Ziyi and Lucienne all the way into her vast bathroom.

The guards were evidently puzzled why their Siren summoned a male geek into her bathroom. "The pathway Ziyi and Melton found might help me solve an ancient code," Lucienne told them. Everyone knew how obsessed she was with ancient technology, symbols, and codes.

"But why do you have to discuss it in the bathroom, cousin?" Thaddeus asked. "Isn't the sun room brighter and more comfortable, or the library quieter?"

"Why not in the lady's lounge?" Lucienne asked back. "Lately, I find it's the ideal place to think clearly."

"I'll be with Lucia," Ziyi said, "and Melton isn't going to do anything. He's a sheep."

"I'm not a sheep," Melton said, his face reddening from embarrassment. "I challenged someone last month!"

Ziyi ignored him and barked at the guards, "Why should your boss even explain to you what she's doing? Do not overstep your boundaries!" She slammed the bathroom door in their faces.

"You're good, Ziyi," Lucienne whispered.

"Where are Aida and Bayrose?" Ziyi whispered back. "If the guards send them in, they'll break up our plan."

"What plan?" Melton joined the whisper. "And why are we whispering?"

"I sent them both on an errand that should take a few hours," Lucienne said, then turned to Melton. "You go to sleep," and hit his Meridian point.

"Awesome. You gotta teach me that trick." Ziyi stared at Melton's slumbering form on the cushion on the bathroom floor. "What are we going to do with him when he wakes up?"

"Say we're sorry and give him a raise, and he'll probably get over this."

"Mmm," Ziyi pondered. "Let me think about it. I don't want anyone to overspend your money."

"Don't think. Help me strip him."

"Then we really need to give him a raise."

They quickly undressed Melton, and Lucienne put on his T-shirt, cargo pants, and hooded jacket. "It's nice of him to bring a jacket."

"Yeah," Ziyi said. "However, if you want to impersonate Melton, a hooded jacket might cover your big boobs, but your face is still Lucia's."

"Go out and flirt with the guards, then come back in half an hour. I need you to distract them."

"What about discretion? You have a man in your bathroom. Even your guards gossip among themselves."

"My guards know that even the mad me wouldn't stoop so low to make out with your assistant. Just go make tea and chat with them. A handful of them are already smitten with you."

Ziyi smirked knowingly.

Lucienne closed the door behind Ziyi, pulled out a disguise kit from a hidden closet, and started to transform her looks. She learned this art from a master of disguise when she was in Desert Cymbidium, just as she learned the ancient Meridian—the lost martial arts so few on earth still grasped—from Master Nameless.

Half an hour later, she was almost done when Ziyi rapped five long beats on the door. Lucienne opened it a crack, and Ziyi squeezed in and shut it.

"Blazek is here!" the girl said, and she threw her hand over her mouth, staring at the new Lucienne.

"How?" Lucienne said. "I gave him a strong sedative tea last night to make him sleep through the day." Then she frowned in realization. Vladimir could absorb her ancient poison after the ritual in Tibet. A sedative might not have much effect on him.

"You!" Ziyi looked back and forth between Lucienne and the unconscious Melton on the cushion. "Lucia, you look like his twin."

"I have to if I want to sneak out with you," Lucienne said. "But we have a new problem."

"Blazek." Ziyi nodded. "When is he not a problem? But even he can't tell that you aren't Melton."

"He can tell," Lucienne said in frustration. "He and Ash."

"Ash might know, but Blazek has no superpower."

"He's attuned to my scent."

"Wicked," Ziyi said.

"You need to get him out of here before we move."

"That devil is devious. If I try, he'll know we're up to something." Ziyi darted her eyes left and right. "Think. Think. Think." Then she grabbed toothpaste from the cabinet and squeezed it all over Melton's T-shirt Lucienne was wearing.

"What are you doing?" Lucienne protested.

"To cover your natural scent," Ziyi said, tossing the empty toothpaste tube away and zipping up Lucienne's jacket. She then found an expensive perfume, sprayed it on her neck, armpits, and wrists with the full bottle, and grinned. "Now the smell will confuse Blazek."

"You'll do the mean talk if he asks something," Lucienne said. "He's gotten used to that side of you."

"I'll guarantee he gets more of it today."

"Just don't bite him too hard."

Lucienne, as Melton, followed Ziyi out of the bathroom. Ziyi shut the door behind them.

Vladimir leaned against a sofa, his muscular arms folded across his broad chest, his eyes fixed on the inner room, obviously waiting for Lucienne to emerge. He straightened up, ready to pounce, as soon as he saw a "guy" coming out of the bathroom.

Lucienne stationed herself on the other side of Ziyi, away from Vladimir, and jogged toward the door as steadily, casually as she could manage.

"Hey, dude!" Vladimir called. "Stop."

Lucienne wanted to flee out the door, but she knew Vladimir would give a chase and grab the collar of her jacket to find out why her feet were on fire. So she stopped, shoulders sloughed, and turned to Vladimir with a confused nerdy look of "Were you talking to me?"

Vladimir narrowed his suspicious eyes, his jaw tightening in jealousy. "What the heck are you doing in my girlfriend's bathroom?" He then frowned in displeasure, sniffing the air.

The smell of toothpaste and absurdly strong perfume had succeeded in covering up Lucienne's scent. But Vladimir was Vladimir. He'd figure it out if she and Ziyi lingered for his interrogation.

"Stop harassing my assistant!" Ziyi hissed. "Lucia called me and Melton to verify the code to the cure Jekaterina cracked. She doesn't trust Jekaterina. And thanks to you, we're all in this mess!"

Lucienne winced. She'd advised her friend to show Vladimir her bad side in order to disarm him, but not like this. However, she couldn't object under the circumstances.

Vladimir's face paled, then he swallowed and looked at Ziyi hopefully, totally ignoring "Melton" now. "There'll be a cure soon?"

"Do I look like the one who owes you an explanation?" Ziyi barked. She then turned to shout at Lucienne, "What are you waiting for, Melton? Wait at the rooftop! If the jet arrives, tell the pilot to wait for me."

Lucienne reached the door, about to slip out.

Vladimir moved. "I need to talk to Lucia."

He was going to knock on the bathroom door, which couldn't be securely locked. Lucienne felt her heart jump to her throat. If he thwarted her plan today, she might not get another chance. Kian would return with Ash any time now, if Ash obliged him.

"Stop, Blazek!" Ziyi shrieked at Vladimir. "Lucia needs a quiet time to figure out the final link of the code in her bath. I'm going to pick up a tool for her so we'll all finally know the answer. You don't just go interrupting her bath."

Vladimir looked at Ziyi with reservation and displeasure.

"Thaddeus," Ziyi called, "make sure *no one* disturbs your cousin, especially Blazek, before I come back. Blazek is the one who got her into this bad shape in the first place. This code is very important to the cure. If you're loyal and able to protect your cousin Siren, as it says in your résumé, you—"

"I don't have a résumé. Never needed one!" Thaddeus said tersely. "And I don't care you're my cousin's best friend. You'll never again show me disrespect and doubt my skills and loyalty, Miss Wen!" But he stepped up and blocked Vladimir from going toward the bathroom.

The guards outside the door gave "Melton" an annoyed look of "Are you in or out, dude?" before turning back to the drama in the room.

Hearing the mechanical humming outside, Lucienne knew Valkyrie had arrived. She gave the guards an apologetic glance and ducked out the door.

~

The girls boarded Valkyrie.

The pilot flirted with Ziyi and completely ignored Lucienne/Melton.

When the jet put in some distance from Sphinxes, Ziyi and Lucienne entered the cockpit cabin. "Ethan, let my assistant Melton fly Valkyrie," Ziyi said, "and feel free to sit back in the passenger cabin and enjoy a drink."

The pilot had a brief laugh until Ziyi pulled out a gun, aiming at him with a shaking hand. "Now, Ethan! I'm not joking! And I don't have time to waste."

"Don't be ridiculous, Ziyi," Ethan said. "You—"

Lucienne's hand struck out like a cobra, hitting the Meridian point at the joint of the pilot's jaw and neck. He sagged in his chair, unconscious at once. Lucienne and Ziyi dragged him from his seat. Lucienne let her friend keep hauling the man toward the back of the jet as she took over as pilot. "You stay with him in the back, Ziyi."

"The man's damn heavy," answered Ziyi. "And I'm wearing stilettos."

"Take off your stilettos then," Lucienne said as she entered a series of commands on the dashboard.

The jet no longer headed to California as the pilot had reported to the control tower.

Ashburn had once flown Lucienne over an endless sea of rainforest on Spike. She'd tried to seduce him, spurred by her insanity and maddening lust. Ash had resisted. He'd tried to distract her with the spectacular view. He'd told her that the uncharted jungle was the most dangerous place that housed deadly species and that a volcano would erupt within two months from one of the mountains.

The volcano was right on time. Through the lens of the satellite Dragonfly, Lucienne had seen the river of fire flowing from the top of the brown mountain.

Valkyrie flew right toward the volcano site.

Lucienne pulled out the platinum chain around her neck. The locket that encased the Eye of Time grew heavy in her hand. She pushed the pin, and the charm slowly opened. The Eye, in its silver metallic color, stared back at her amid the Twilight Water.

Since ancient time, all Sirens had been driven mad to find it, but all of them had failed except Lucienne. She now had it in her palm, but she was about to get rid of it. By doing so, she was betraying the whole Siren race and denying her own destiny.

But there were things more valuable than family obligations and personal ambitions. Lucienne rebuked her former thoughts. And only when she learned to let go of the idea that she held onto all her life would she be truly free.

No, she was being incredibly selfish thinking of her own freedom. Her duty was bigger than her. Kian, Vladimir, and her people had gone through countless hardships to get there. Many of her warriors had perished for her and her cause. Once she cast away the Eye of Time, she'd never get it back. Everything she'd accomplished would be lost. All her people's efforts wasted. Their deaths would count for nothing.

Was the Eye influencing her, or was she fighting herself?

You see the truth yourself, Siren, the Eye answered urgently.

Valkyrie approached the coordinates.

The volcano spewed fire even in its break. Lucienne had timed it well.

The aircraft's sensor blinked, warning of the hazard of getting any closer to the hot air. Lucienne let Valkyrie hover at the safe edge, staring down at the boiling lava far beneath.

If you feed me to the fire, you unmake yourself. Do not throw away your birthright, Siren. You were born, as the greatest one, to rule with Ashburn Fury.

It was right. How could she even conceive of exterminating the Eye of Time, her lifetime's pursuit? This was more than madness. It was the most hideous crime!

Valkyrie made a sharp U-turn, returning home.

The Eye of Time let out a sigh of relief, but cold dread sank into Lucienne, in contrast to the molten lava outside the jet. She was heading back to hand the Eye of Time to Jekaterina. Instead of undoing herself, she was going to erase Ashburn and rip out the last humanity in him.

Conflict warred in her, like magnetic poles pushing against each other. Lucienne suppressed a shriek. Then a shock wave of violet light shot out of her burning eyes, hitting the Eye of Time.

Forbidden Glory had acted upon her extreme emotions, but its power didn't damage the ancient entity, but made a connection.

A vision hit Lucienne like a hailstorm.

On the deck of a futuristic spaceship shaped like an eye atop two other interlinked eyes, she and Ashburn held hands and watched the world burn beneath them. Time passed by like the wind. Wherever the wind went, all living things turned to ash.

The wind of time reached Kian first, then Ziyi, Aida, Vladimir, and all the loyal warriors in Sphinxes. They were reduced to swirling dust in the air.

Lucienne, an immortal like Ashburn, was untouched by the sight.

"New earth," Ashburn said. He wasn't the Ash she'd once known and remembered.

He'd become one with the Eye of Time, and she one mind with him. The power to erase the world came from the completed TimeDust in him, with the aid of her Forbidden Glory.

The ancient poison was no longer in her. It would never claim her again. Never.

Ashburn glowed beyond glory. Her glow wasn't as intense as his, but she knew she was beautiful beyond words, a hundred times more beautiful than any mortal female could ever be. She saw admiration in Ash's silver eyes, just as she adored him.

"Eterne is ours," she said.

He nodded. "For eternity."

Jekaterina led a race of beings resembling the image on the ice-pillar of the Rabbit Hole out to the deck, where they watched the destruction alongside Lucienne and Ashburn.

"Earth is ours," Jekaterina said.

The race knelt before Jekaterina in worship.

"You've waited patiently," Jekaterina said, "but I've brought you home as promised."

"Your Imperial Majesty," her race said in chorus, "you've sacrificed much for your people. You've endured time."

"And behold my beautiful, powerful daughter," Empress Jekaterina said. "She sacrificed her people so we can have this day—"

Lucienne gasped. She was back in Valkyrie, her labored breathing filling her ears. Her blood ran hot and wild at the vision, yet she'd never felt so cold.

If she returned to Sphinxes with the Eye of Time, she'd be saved, but at the expense of her people.

Was her glimpse of the alternative future a possible reality or an illusion? How could she decide when the poison of Blood Tear had altered her mind? She turned her gaze to the Eye of Time amid the Twilight Water. Its color turned blood red, just as when it'd hunted Ashburn and hooked into his mind.

It was suddenly crystal clear to Lucienne that it needed her and Ash. It needed them to do its dirty work. It had powers beyond measure, but only humanity could end humanity. Somehow *that* was the rule out there in the corner of the universe—and only she and Ash had the right genetic code, as the Eye of Time had revealed.

The ancient entity showed her its version of the future, believing she'd desire to live forever with the perfect man and choose to let her people and the world burn. It believed that sheer selfishness was at the core of human nature.

Lucienne turned Valkyrie around toward the volcano.

You will die, Siren, the Eye of Time said. *You will not be cured without me. If you choose to do this, you will never see Eterne. You will never taste the intimacy and fruit of love.*

"So be it," said Lucienne.

The prophecy said you were either the greatest of the Siren race or the worst.

Lucienne slammed shut the locket as the Eye of Time whimpered.

Valkyrie's intercom buzzed.

Sphinxes' control tower must have noticed Valkyrie's change of course and demanded an explanation. Lucienne ignored that too.

General Fairchild's threatening voice came through the jet's radio. Valkyrie's computer indicated three approaching jet fighters.

"General Fairchild." Lucienne opened the communication channel as she removed her disguise. "There's no need to pursue me. I'll be returning."

"Lucia? Siren?" General Fairchild sounded stunned. "How did you get in Valkyrie? Aren't you in the middle of the bath in your mansion?"

General Fairchild did have ears among those who were close to her.

Lucienne heard the general ordering the jets to stand down and escort the Siren back.

Valkyrie hovered at the perimeter where it could get no closer to the volcano.

A triangular side door opened. Lucienne stood before it, holding a hybrid weapon of a compound crossbow and sniper rifle. Looking into the scope, she nocked the arrow, the chain that held the Eye of Time tied to its shaft.

She had no right to sacrifice one person for her people or sacrifice the whole of Sphinxes for Ashburn. But she had the right to sacrifice herself for them.

Lucienne released the arrow that was covered by RCC material with resistance to high temperature. The arrow pierced the air and shot toward the hottest fire on earth.

The Eye of Time plummeted into the glare of the volcano's molten core and vanished in the churning ocean of lava.

As the side door slid shut, a deep shade of blood tear rolled down from Lucienne's eyes.

Chapter Thirty-One
ONE NATION

When Valkyrie touched down, General Fairchild, Admiral Enberg, Director Pyon, and other high-ranking officers were waiting at the air force base.

"You see the line?" Ziyi asked. "This is bad. They'll do more than yell at me."

"I'll take care of the generals," Lucienne said and pressed a Meridian point on the space between the pilot's shoulder blades.

Ethan woke up with a gasp, staring at Lucienne with a shocked, confused expression. Then he spied Ziyi also towering over him. "She—she hijacked the Siren's—your jet!" He pointed a finger at Ziyi. "She threatened me with a big loaded gun, and her assistant hit me without mercy and knocked me out."

"It's a G43, 9mm pistol. Not a big loaded gun," Ziyi said. "Now stop complaining. We have a bigger issue."

The cabin door opened.

Lucienne, who had changed into a white suit from the jet's onboard wardrobe, stepped out of Valkyrie. "Gentlemen." She nodded at the military crowd in a cool manner, as if nothing had happened. "I've returned. I'm going back to my house now."

"I'll accompany the Siren to her house," Ziyi said timidly behind Lucienne. "Uh, who's going to give us a ride?"

"We need to talk, Siren," General Fairchild said grimly. "Chief is very upset. He's on his way back from Nirvana."

"Then the talk can wait until he comes back," Lucienne said. It was better to be shouted at once than twice.

"Please, Siren," Admiral Enberg said, "we've been waiting to have this meeting with you for a long time."

That was why they'd ambushed her. They were taking advantage of her hijacking her own jet to make their points. Lucienne sighed, "Fine. Let's get it over with." She let the officers escort her to the castle's underground conference room.

She hadn't been to any of their meetings in a while. Her generals were running Sphinxes, along with Kian.

The room smelled of espresso, Cuban cigars, and cologne, just as she remembered. An officer brought her a mug of black coffee. She nodded a thank you and sat at the head of the table.

"Siren," Pyon started, "according to the doctors, coffee—"

Lucienne grabbed the mug tightly. "I need it today."

She took a swig, thoughts whirling in her mind. She'd wanted to converse with her officers about her leaving the Sphinxes' leadership. Kian's strong objection had stopped her. Now was probably the best time to talk to them when Kian wasn't around. She needed them to brace for the day, which would come soon, when she could no longer be with them.

She put down her mug, waiting for her generals to make the first move.

"Siren," General Fairchild began, "do you understand the severe consequences of leaving Sphinxes today?" His dark-skinned face looked grim.

"I returned, didn't I?" Lucienne said.

"That isn't the point," General Fairchild said.

"Then what's the point?" asked Lucienne.

"You left without authorization," General Fairchild said, removing a fat Cohiba Esplendido from his cigar box.

Admiral Enberg and Director Pyon kept their mouths clammed up and their expression stony. The other officers watched silently, but Lucienne could tell they held their breaths. They must have talked among themselves before this meeting. They must have chosen Fairchild as their mouthpiece. If they won this battle against her, they could lock her up in the tower and forever make her a figurehead before her last breath eventually went out.

A queen, my butt.

"You think I need *your* authorization to leave my house, General Fairchild?" asked Lucienne in a soft, lethal voice.

"Chief McQuillen set the security protocol to protect you," Fairchild said. "We all must follow the rules."

"Then let McQuillen deal with me," Lucienne said, eyes sparking dark fire and fixing on Fairchild. "And please don't smoke in my presence."

Fairchild looked taken aback. Lucienne had never taken that tone with him. He shut off his lighter and put the cigar back in the box. "I apologize, Siren."

Admiral Enberg cleared his throat. "Siren," he said, "your leaving Sphinxes today caused panic. You have responsibilities. Your people look up to you. If anything happened to you, Sphinxes would fall apart."

"I should not be the reason that Sphinxes falls apart," Lucienne said. "I've wanted to talk to you about it. You want a new nation born of ideals. A nation without the baggage other nations carry. I wanted to give you something better. I wanted to give you Eterne— what the ancients named the realm of the gods. Some of you know that I acquired a power that's beyond this world; a power that could lead us to a quantum plane. But then I was poisoned. Most of the time I've been wandering in the land of the insane." She surveyed the officers' faces, meeting their eyes. "And today I've accepted the fact that there's no cure for me."

"Siren!" Director Pyon called urgently.

Lucienne raised a hand to stop him. "I can no longer lead. I can't be your queen, but I can ask you not to fail me even though I've failed you."

"You never failed us, Siren," the officers said almost in sync, some of them in tears. "We failed to protect you from our enemies."

"You're our Siren queen forever," Admiral Enberg said.

Lucienne shook her head in regal sadness. "You'll have to move forward without me. You must not let Sphinxes fall apart. This land is home to you. From this day forward, I remove my burden and place it on you. I lay my trust in you, in all of you. I believe you'll not abuse my trust."

The officers looked grief-stricken and stunned.

"We won't give up on you, my Siren," Pyon said. "There's a cure. You must hang in there for your people. There's hope!"

There was no hope. Not anymore. When she'd tossed the Eye of Time into the boiling lava, she'd let the last hope of saving herself die. She doubted if the melting fire could demolish the ancient entity, but with it buried deep in the core of the volcano, no one could dig it out.

And no one knew the real reason she'd gone to the volcano coordinates. They must have thought that she'd gone mental again. Ashburn wouldn't know about it either. He couldn't reach her memories, and she'd made sure no one witnessed her last act inside Valkyrie.

A loud knock sounded on the door. Thaddeus stormed in. "Siren," he said between labored breaths from running, "our cousins have arrived. They brought news. War is coming to Sphinxes. We have less than three days."

"My spies will confirm the intel tonight," said Pyon. "I didn't expect war to come to our door this soon."

"Where are our cousins?" Lucienne asked Thaddeus.

"Waiting at the meeting hall," Thaddeus said.

"Bring them here," Lucienne ordered.

Within minutes, Lucienne's seven cousins, who had all sworn allegiance to her, filed into the conference room. They kissed Lucienne's Siren ring as she greeted them.

As soon as Claude Lam, Sphinxes' ambassador, delivered the news of a looming war, a slow, deadly silence settled across the room before it boiled into heated debates and shouts.

Pyon's intelligence had warned Lucienne that many nations had formed alliances under the leadership of the Sealers. Sphinxes crippled the shadow government in the Polynesian war, but didn't destroy its real power. As long as the Sealers' founder—a powerful, formidable ghost inside the machine—was alive, war would always find Lucienne and her people.

The enemy had now regrouped.

"They won't stop until they level Sphinxes," said Lucienne's cousin, Patrick, who was in charge of the Lams weapons industry.

"The news of your sickness has leaked and spread to every corner, Cousin Siren." Claude eyed Lucienne. "Our enemies choose to strike when we're most vulnerable. They mean to take us out before we become an elite country."

"Will America go against us too?" Lucienne asked in a soft, icy voice.

"The United States sees the benefit of having Sphinxes as its ally," Claude said.

"We've been sharing intelligence with America," Pyon said. "They sought a military base in Sphinxes, but Chief McQuillen gave them a firm no."

"The Sealers already have control of the United Nations," another cousin said. "Sphinxes isn't a country yet, so the UN will turn a blind eye on an attack."

"Some of our former allies have secretly shaken hands with the Brotherhood," Patrick added.

"Friends aren't forever; neither are enemies," said Claude. "It all depends on mutual benefits and circumstances. We can sway back some of our allies, like Australia, Canada, India and China."

"If they can't make up their minds when we need them, then we won't waste time on winning them back," said Admiral Enberg.

"Let our enemies come," General Fairchild said. "We have the best military hardware. We've tested our success in Polynesia and South Russia."

"There is a difference," Pyon said, rubbing his temples. "We haven't fought the war in our own land. This time they're coming here to throw bombs, missiles, and only god-know-what else at us."

"One unformed nation against many," Lucienne said. "We can't fight all of them. I don't want Sphinxes to lose any more men than necessary. We should evacuate to preserve our forces and resources." She would never have considered a retreat if she had the hope to survive. She would have chosen to fight until her last breath. But her fight was over, even before this impending war. She couldn't speak for her people or encourage them to fight when she couldn't. When she accepted her approaching doom, all she wanted was to preserve her men.

"If we run, our enemies will hunt us," said Admiral Enberg. "The day we answered your call, we vowed to give our lives to you, to Sphinxes. This land has become our home."

"And no one will drive us from our home!" many officers declared.

"What about our soldiers and civilians?" Lucienne asked. "I want to give them a choice."

"They chose to follow you when you were crowned Siren at the age of eight." Kian's voice boomed from the outer room. He'd come back. He stalked into the conference room like a force of nature. His aides hastened after him.

Ashburn wasn't among them.

She'd told Kian that Ashburn wouldn't answer to anyone except her. Ghost House and the Rabbit Hole were a closed, alien world without Lucienne accompanying them. So it was no surprise that Kian failed to escort Ashburn back.

"We'll follow you anywhere you go, Cousin Siren," the Lam cousins proclaimed one by one. "When we found out about the war, we came right away. Your family stands with you."

Her family had truly become family, and it kept expanding. Waves of warmth washed over Lucienne. Her chief was right. Even if she gave the men leave, they would stay.

She'd set out to fulfill her family obligations and personal ambitions. In the process, she'd bonded with her men. She'd gone from chasing her own dreams to sharing a new world with them.

She'd wanted to remake history with her people, for her people, but her blessing had turned into a curse. The curse that should be hers alone now fell on her people and brought a new war upon their heads.

She was poisoned. She was the mad Siren beyond reason. Yet, her people refused to abandon her. They chose to defend her, to shed their blood and that of her enemies for her.

"We won't just fight for you, cousin," Thaddeus said softly. "We fight for our new home, our future, our right to exist as a free and independent nation."

"Well said, Thaddeus," Pyon agreed.

Lucienne swallowed. Yes, her people had made a life for themselves on this new land. Sphinxes was as much their home as it was hers. They had every right to hold onto this land. "Then we fight," she said. She would fight with them. She would do everything in her power to protect them and shed her last drop of blood for them and for Sphinxes.

That night, Lucienne in her white gown stood on the rooftop of the castle addressing her people. Her warriors, scientists, and civilians gathered on the ground. The air force, military bases, and navy fleet were watching her hologram live feed.

"People of Sphinxes," Lucienne called, gazing down at the crowd that filled the castle and far beyond. "Within three days, our enemy, made of the combined armies of all nations, will come to drive us from our homeland," her voice reached the far end of this burgeoning nation, "because we represent new ideas, new hopes, new strength, and a new future. You came from different races and from every corner of the earth. You have now built this new world together, and our enemy hates it. I won't lie to you. Their force is powerful. So I'm giving everyone a choice: stay and fight or leave for safety today. Should you stay, many of you will lose your lives defending this land you now call home—"

"We'll defend our homeland!" The soldiers' furious shouts rose from the ground. "We'll defend Sphinxes and our queen till the last of us stands! We'll kill any enemy!"

Lucienne raised a hand and the soldiers' fierce cries gradually subsided.

"We're the beginning, not the end," she continued. "We'll build the strongest nation in the world, for us and for our children, and our children's children. On the land where you stand, there will be playgrounds and schools for them. No enemy can take that away from us! We'll fight. We'll prevail. We'll show the world our strength and willpower. They'll think twice before ever coming to Sphinxes again." She paused, tears moistening her lashes. "I'm proud that I have you—the best of the best, and the strongest of the strong. We are one nation and one people!"

Tens of thousands of warriors roared, "One nation! One people! One and true Siren Queen!"

Kian, her officers, and her cousins shouted with all the warriors, proud tears burning in their eyes. Ziyi wept, searching for napkins. Lucienne met her Czech prince's gaze for a moment and saw an ocean of love, profound pride, and fierce protectiveness. There was no ache or torment in his hazel eyes for the first time since she'd been poisoned in the Temple of Lemuria.

The light that had once upon a time shone on Eterne reignited in her heart. One day, one among her people would find a way to bring the realm and a new future to Earth and to the human race. The hope was lost to her, but not to her people.

Under the crescent moon, the Sphinxes flag—half red and half white, with the Siren's symbol, a full circle containing an all-seeing eye in the center—rose to the tip of the pole atop the castle's tallest tower.

A horn blew, and the trumpets joined in. A new nation's pride vibrated in the air.

Every man and woman in Sphinxes stood tall and saluted the flag.

The nation of Sphinxes was born.

Part Three

Chapter Thirty-Two
THE CODE

The code Jekaterina had given Ashburn was a symbol of infinity. Three infinities—heads biting tails—locked in triangular positions.

The code appeared so simple, but when Ashburn tried to extract its meanings, his database flashed thousands of them.

No matter. With this code he could fix Seraphen's broken memories.

The door to the Ghost House opened upon Spike's approach. Ashburn rode straight through the ice-like pillar into the Rabbit Hole. The barrier was impossible for others to break, but to him, it was immaterial. This whole place was his playground, imprinted with his genetic code.

Ashburn flung himself off Spike and squatted before Seraphen's head.

Seraphen's golden eyes stared up at him. "How long have I been here, Ashburn?"

"Does it matter to you?" Ashburn asked, then felt like an asshole for saying that. The remaining humanity in him stretched thinner every day. His empathy was close to the dead.

Seraphen studied him. "It matters not. Time stopped having meaning ages ago. As the generations pass me by, I feel only the slightest echo of time. You'll feel the same after the passing of this generation, if they survive."

"They'll survive," Ashburn said.

"So you still care. I see. You still have some humanity left. If you merge with the Eye of Time, you'll have none."

"I need answers from you, Seraphen." The last thing Ashburn

wanted to discuss was how he hung onto his fast-fading humanity.

"You keep coming back for the same answer. You need not look to me, but yourself. If you want an excuse to save her at the expense of mankind, you aren't going to get it from me."

Seraphen spoke the brutal truth.

Ashburn had thought he was ready to spend Lucienne's last moments with her, but he could no longer stand it. He couldn't watch her fade away. Every moment it killed him more than it did her. And how could he go on once she was gone?

Jekaterina had taught him to embed the code into his TimeDust so he could link to Seraphen's mind inside the Rabbit Hole. Without the vast noise of human consciousness crushing him, he heard only Seraphen's thoughts. Through their link, Ashburn sent the symbol of three locked infinities to Seraphen's head.

Seraphen looked baffled before fear showed in his golden eyes. "Impossible."

"You recognize it," Ashburn asked. "What is it?"

"Bad news." Seraphen drew a breath, a habit he had, even though he no longer needed air. "Where did you get this?"

"From Jekaterina."

"Jekaterina?"

"Lucienne's mother." Ashburn sent Seraphen Jekaterina's image. "The Eye of Time said that Jekaterina has a thousand faces."

"A thousand faces? It can't be her, can it? No, she couldn't survive on this planet when time formed on earth. Her race left, so did she."

"Who is she?"

"The Queen of the Exiles, a goddess who once lived among humankind. She had a human daughter Niamh, who tricked me."

Ashburn knew the tale of Niamh—the mythical princess of the Land of Promise. She was the mother of the first Siren. Niamh was also Lucienne Lam's middle name, given by her Siren's mark in the ritual. The subject of Niamh always riled up Seraphen, and he'd been hell bent on ending her bloodline. Lucienne was Niamh's last descendent.

"Jekaterina can't be the queen," Seraphen murmured to himself, distraught. "She can't be Niamh either. Niamh was half mortal. But if she turned into an immortal because of her mother's blood … and the Exiles are coming. Niamh … the hybrid …."

"What's the bad news, Seraphen?"

The head went into a tirade of gibberish.

"Seraphen!"

Seraphen wasn't responding.

Ashburn flashed the code of three infinities in front of Seraphen, and his former protector jerked back to the present. "Destroy the code!" Seraphen yelped. "Never use the key. It's the first beacon for the Exiles to come through the portal—"

"It has been embedded in TimeDust," Ashburn said. "Now I'll have to fix your damaged memories. I must know what else I can do to save Lucienne."

"Your obsession with her has doomed your race."

"I think not," Ashburn said and burned the code into the depth of Seraphen's consciousness.

A tiny, black spot emerged inside the maze of Seraphen's mind, then exploded into bright light. The light spread like tree branches until all the "trees" were shining.

And Ashburn had the final answer—only by melding with the Eye of the Time could he purge the poison in Lucienne. There was absolutely no other way and no other cure in heavens or on earth.

So either he walked toward his own nightmare of losing himself or toward the other—losing Lucienne Lam.

Chapter Thirty-Three

DEVOURER

The Sealers' fighters came like locusts. Lucienne's warrior fighters met their enemy halfway, stopping them from reaching the soil of Sphinxes.

In the Defense Room, Lucienne stood with Kian, Prince Vladimir, and her high-ranking officers. A satellite hologram displayed the ferocious air battles.

Missiles, rockets, and lasers shot across the sky in all directions. In their wake came red fire and black smoke. Fighters broke into shards of metal, plummeting into the churning sea. It was hard to tell which remains were the enemy's and which Sphinxes' fighters.

The ground forces were like arrows notched on bowstrings, ready to spring into action.

The castle trembled now and then from the explosions miles away.

"The Sealers outnumber us seven to one," General Fairchild said grimly.

Lucienne breathed deeply. It was one nation against many.

"We'll hold," Admiral Enberg said. "Our warships have joined the fight."

Kian gave Enberg a nod. "Give them hell, Admiral."

Admiral Enberg spoke into a link, "Champions, go!"

Champions I, II, and III broke the water at the edge of the Sphinxes Seas and shot toward the enemy in the air. They were the first warplanes equipped with a force field that could absorb impact from more than one hundred missiles. Champions were Lam's Industry's new darling, and now the world's most advanced fighters were unleashed.

The killing fighters pierced the enemies' ranks like blades cutting grass. The rest of the Sphinxes fighters regrouped and flanked the Champions with renewed vigor.

A line of enemy fighters plunged toward the ground in a cluster of fire balls.

"Now who's the bitch?" General Fairchild snorted.

"You *are*," a voice came through the Defense Room's intercom.

The room turned deathly silent except for the noises of the battle in the background from the hologram.

"I'm Mirrikh Schwartz," the voice continued. "I've come for you all, especially you, little Siren."

Mirrikh Schwartz, the ogre who had persecuted Kian. Old and new hatred roared in Lucienne's blood. Before she found him, he'd come to her. *Good.* Then a dread fell upon her.

Many nations' intelligence agencies had tried to infringe her network, but Sphinxes kept those bugs out. How could the Sealers have access to Sphinxes' most fortified communication channel? The enemy had heard all of their commands. A traitor must be among them, but Lucienne couldn't think of who it might be with the battle raging on.

Before she and the generals called Ziyi, the girl pitched in through the comm link. "Lucia, Generals," Ziyi's voice was laced with terror, "our system has been compromised."

"Uncompromise it," Kian shouted.

"We depend on you and your team, Ziyi," Lucienne said. "You can do it."

"I know, but something's very wrong." Ziyi's voice filled with panic. "I've never seen anything like this—"

The enemy fighters started to retreat, except one jet.

Its distinctive black plates featured giant red letters that spelled Predator. The Sealers' menacing symbol—an arrow piercing the Siren's all-seeing eye—stood carved on its snake-like head.

Lucienne felt her hair rising on her neck as a chill like no other surged up her spine. Her Forbidden Glory had sensed something terrible in the air, something so dark no words could define it.

Champion I immediately fired at Predator, its laser beams hitting its head and engine. But instead of blasting Predator to pieces, the green laser beams dissolved as if they were toy beams. The black jet pulsed, and a gray mass of mixed smoke and fog crept out of its head.

Now all three Champions fired upon the black jet, but their missiles melted to drops of liquid.

"What the hell is that thing?" General Fairchild demanded, wiping sweat from his brow.

Airbase and the fleets launched a hailstorm of missiles and rockets toward Predator, but all the weapons dissolved.

"Fall back!" Lucienne cried into the command com.

"Disengage!" Kian, Fairchild, and Enberg's shouts overlapped her.

The smoke from Predator moved at lightning speed. It tossed Champion I up. The fighter flapped like paper in a storm. In the blink of an eye, it disintegrated, leaving a small flame in its wake. The flame plummeted toward the ground.

"No!" Lucienne screamed.

Her cousin Thaddeus was inside Champion I. He'd been fidgeting miserably as her guard and nurse all these months. A born warrior, he'd craved the thrill of battle, so she'd indulged him and let him fight on the frontline. Now, he was dead. One of her tight family members was gone. Grief blinded her vision. *Grieve later. Put it inside a box for now.* She forced herself to breathe in and out. Tears still streamed down her face.

The storm of smoke wrapped the other two Champions, and the two fighters turned to tiny flames instantly. The smoke and fog kept expanding until it blotted out the sun and half the sky.

Sphinxes sank into darkness. Three small flames that were former Champions swayed and fell from the darkened sky.

"Isn't the candlelight beautiful?" Mirrikh's holographic image appeared in Sphinxes' Defense Room, right beside Lucienne. Kian and Vladimir both lunged and pulled her away from it.

Mirrikh's image smirked. "This is just the beginning, I promise." He gestured, and a section of the smoke moved like a spear with supernatural speed, piercing hundreds of Sphinxes' fighters. Hundreds of flames dropped from the sky like flickering candles.

The rest of the Sphinxes' warplanes and battleships all fired at Predator. The blanket sky became a web of fire from missiles and laser beams, but the lasers dissolved and the missiles melted inside the net of smoke and fog.

"The world has never seen such a spectacular sight!" Mirrikh was choked with tears, then chortled with pride. "Devourer can destroy the whole world's population in mere seconds if I'm in the mood!"

His hologram flickered off.

Ziyi's voice came through. "Lucia, I blocked his access. The channel is secure for the moment. My team is working on fortifying our network."

"Keep at it," Lucienne said in an even voice.

"We can't fight this thing." General Fairchild turned to Kian and Lucienne, his face drained of color. "Nothing can touch it."

Lucienne knew what the general meant. Soon the smoke and fog were going to descend upon Sphinxes. Her people would all become flames and burn for a few seconds, and then nothing would be left of them.

"Take the Siren under," Kian ordered.

He wanted her to escape with the civilians and scientists through the underground tunnel. He thought he could still save her. "No." Lucienne raised a hand to stop her guards as they moved toward her. "I won't flee while my men fight. I'll live and die with you all." Over Kian's furious look, she said softly, "Besides, there isn't time. You know that."

"Ziyi," she called, "hail the Sealers elder."

A faint chime bleeped. Mirrikh's image appeared on the screen in the Defense Room.

"Mirrikh Schwartz," Lucienne asked, her voice emotionless, "are you the true founder of the Sealers—the Ghost in the Machine?"

"I will be," Mirrikh said, "after this war."

An illumination passed by, and Lucienne drew a breath. "You launched this war against my country to rid yourself of someone higher than you in your Brotherhood's rank, but haven't you come to the wrong place?"

Mirrikh gave a low chuckle. "I've never hit a wrong target in my life."

"So you believe your superior is in my land, and you're eager to remove him or maybe her," Lucienne said. "Tell me who the Ghost in the Machine is among my people, and I'll give you your founder as a peace offering. You can go home happy."

"Razer-sharp." Mirrikh roared with laughter. "They say with you there is never a dull moment. We're much alike. It's a shame we're at war, otherwise we might become friends."

"You call the shots," Lucienne said. "You and I have the power to create different reality. Let today be the start of a new relationship."

"Siren, Siren," Mirrikh shook his head, an amused smirk on his face, "you're indeed a seductress."

"I do not try to seduce you," said Lucienne, "but I am eager to open a dialogue so our people can have peace."

"Did you request a peace talk when you blew up my father and his fleet in Polynesia? Oh, no. You completely forgot. But I don't come to avenge him. As a leader of high vision, I'm not that petty. However, the world is too small a place for two superpowers. If you had what I have, you'd have struck me long ago. So today I must bring the powerful Siren to her knees and establish my sole leadership in the world."

"You've brought me down," said Lucienne. "You've displayed

Devourer's power. There's no need to shed the blood of the innocent. Nations won't regard you as a benign superpower if you commit a massacre today. Mirrikh Schwartz, show the world you have mercy, and the nations will follow you willingly."

"A valid point," Mirrikh said. "Mirrikh Schwartz is also merciful. I like that. My benevolence will depend on your next performance. I'll spare Sphinxes if you kneel before me. My operatives will videotape this grand historical event for the whole world to see."

"You and the world will see my humble side," said Lucienne.

The elder laughed again in delight. "You aren't as horrible as they say, little Siren. You put your people before you. After your unconditional surrender, your people will be mine. They'll live to serve me since they all owe me their lives."

It would be a horrible fate for her people to be under the whip of a psychopath. He would have to slaughter most of her warriors to enslave the rest of Sphinxes' residents.

Cold rage filled her veins, but Lucienne kept her blank mask in place. "I'll yield to you on the rooftop of my castle. It's spacious enough for your filming." She'd need the open space to unlatch her power and not hurt her people.

"I appreciate you being mature and considerate, Siren," Mirrikh said. "But be warned: if you fail to show up in three minutes, I'll unleash Devourer on your island." He wiggled his pampered pinkie at Lucienne. "And all of you will become my big collection of little flames."

Lucienne ordered Ziyi to turn off the communication to the Sealer elder, and his image vanished along with his sneer.

"I won't let you sacrifice yourself." Kian gritted his teeth. "We'll fight the prick!"

"Even if you surrender to save us, he'll still level Sphinxes," Pyon said. "I saw the kill in his eyes, and I haven't read people wrong."

"We'd rather turn to flames than serve that snake!" the officers declared, fury burning in every one of them. "We'd rather die free than live in chains!"

"If we go down," Vladimir roared, "we take down as many mutts as we can!"

"We'll fight, but my way." Lucienne scanned the fierce faces of her officers. "Can you trust me?"

"With our every breath," they said, pressing their fists against their hearts.

"I'll never let my people be slaves," said Lucienne.

Chapter Thirty-Four
DOUBLE BETRAYAL

Bayrose stood with a few soldiers on the platform while the rest of the civilians waited anxiously in the underground train. At the first signal when the combined nations' armies breached Sphinxes, they'd leave through the tunnel, crossed the ocean, and reach the safe shore beyond.

Bayrose didn't plan on leaving with them. She was only to lay low, away from the raging war outside, biding her time. As soon as the island fell, she'd move up to the ground to join her army and take command.

Aida, Ziyi, and many civilians refused to leave without Lucienne. Even Mom stood with her firstborn. Well, they would all perish. Bayrose couldn't get to her mother. Mom knew about the Shadow in her. She would know that it was Bayrose who had summoned this war and brought Devourer upon this land. If Mom's loyalty wasn't with the Sealers anymore, then sadly there was nothing Bayrose could do for her.

Prince Vladimir would fall too. Bayrose wrung her hands. She hated him for his heartless nature, but did she really want him to die? No, she shouldn't think of him right now. She was the true Siren and Sealer. A great leader must learn to accept a personal sacrifice.

She jolted as the image of Mirrikh Schwartz flickered on screen on the station's wall.

"Mirrikh Schwartz, are you the true founder of the Sealers—the Ghost in the Machine?" Bayrose heard her half-sister ask.

"I will be," Mirrikh said, "after this war."

"You launched this war against my country to rid yourself of someone higher than you in your Brotherhood's rank," Lucienne asked, "but haven't you come to the wrong place?"

Mirrikh chuckled. "I've never hit a wrong target in my life."

Blood pounded Bayrose's eardrums. Was Mirrikh going to throw her to the Sphinxes' wolves? She looked around to see if anyone had come for her. The soldiers glued their eyes to the screen. No one paid attention to her reaction.

Then the screen went black. Lucienne's tech team must have stopped the broadcast.

Sphinxes would soon discover her true identity. Bayrose chewed her lip and tasted blood. She would deny any accusation. *Who should you listen to*, she would demanded, *me or the psychopath?*

But then a terrible realization hit her. It didn't matter if the Siren knew she was the Sealers founder and a traitor. Mirrikh, her most devoted ally, wanted her dead.

He'd demonstrated the terrifying power of Devourer, but wouldn't stop there. He wouldn't be satisfied that the Sealers had stepped from the shadow into the spotlight. He *wanted* to become the founder of the Sealers. He wanted to be the most powerful man on earth. That was why he'd come and showed the world his face.

She'd given him the access code to Devourer. She was gullible, stupid to hand him the most lethal weapon in the world. He'd figured out she was the founder. After he removed her, he would control the Sealers. He wouldn't just hit the marked spots that she'd permitted him to strike. He would demolish all of Sphinxes with her in it.

Mirrikh was a true psychopath. Nothing excited him more than shedding the blood of innocent people. Bayrose could see that clearly now, but it was too late.

Cold sweat soaked her armpits.

Her childhood friend might even keep her as an insignificant flame in a glass container as a souvenir. Bayrose balled her cold, sweaty palms. She'd sacrificed so much. She'd come to the heart of the enemy's land for the righteous cause, for the Sealers Brotherhood, and this was how Mirrikh and her army would repay her? Her rage was pitch black, yet useless.

Can you shield me from Devourer? Bayrose asked the Shadow in her.

I can shield your mind, the Shadow said, *not your mortality.*

The ancient feud between the Sealers and the Sirens no longer mattered when facing extinction together. Enemies or friends, their ashes would be mixed—no, there wouldn't be any ash left when the smoke from Devourer reached the ground.

Bayrose rushed toward the elevator.

"Miss Thorn," a lieutenant assigned to escort the civilians to safety called, "where are you going? We're leaving."

"I'm going to save the day," she said as she dashed into the elevator.

If Mirrikh refused to remember his childhood love for her and spare her after he saw her face, she'd reveal to her army that she was the true founder of the Sealers and take over command.

She clutched the founder's ruby ring in her pocket.

Chapter Thirty-Five

PHOENIX IN ASHES

Lucienne stood on the rooftop of Sphinxes' castle, more regal than any mortal queen.

She looked over her island. Her people had built a modern kingdom amid the lush forest and white beach, but it was now devoid of color under the smoke of Devourer. Hundreds of little flames and shards of jets littered Sphinxes' once turquoise ocean.

Her enemy invaded her realm to harm her people, yet her troops stayed their ground, guarding the land they realized would soon be lost. The Sphinxes' flag with the Siren's symbol flapped in the wind under the black sky.

She was alone at first for a second, then Kian, Vladimir, and her officers joined her. Her cousins were with her as well to face the direst day. Thaddeus wasn't among them. Her beloved cousin was dead.

Predator, the Sealers' symbol piecing the Sirens' on its snake-like head, hovered above them. Under its red hull, Lucienne saw her holographic image projected by the elder's operatives. The world was watching the downfall of the Siren and the terrible fate of Sphinxes through the live feed.

Lucienne ignored her own stony image and the fury on her warriors' faces. She fixed her attention on Predator.

Forbidden Glory stirred in her, sensing the greatest threat its host had ever encountered. With her power on high alert, X-ray vision came to her like a blaze. Lucienne saw an orb expanding and contracting like a dark heart inside Predator. Devourer!

The ancient weapon kept emitting the dirty gray mass, and Lucienne suddenly knew—as if the knowledge had long been stored in her genetic memory—that Devourer was made to swallow souls. When it turned Sphinxes' fighters into flames, it was digesting the brave souls of her warriors. Having had a taste, it was thirsty for all the souls in Sphinxes, particularly hers.

She also realized that it couldn't be turned off once its safety switch was lifted. After it finished with her and her people, it would turn on another land, then another, until it consumed all the souls on earth. That stupid, arrogant Sealers elder didn't truly understand what he'd unleashed.

She must summon Forbidden Glory's full power. The only way she could fight this beast was to let her power take her over completely. The consequences would be unimaginable. She'd be utterly consumed and never regain her sanity. Worse yet, she could become the phantom—the shell of Forbidden Glory—if she survived.

And then, like Devourer, her Glory might harm her people when she couldn't reign over it. It had displayed that treacherous trait again and again when she'd been in the grasp of her madness.

She exhaled. One last tough decision she had to make.

Just then, Jekaterina slipped by her side. Strangely, her mother's presence had a calm effect on her at this frenzied hour. Jekaterina placed her cool hand on Lucienne's shoulder. Lucienne shivered. It was the first time her mother had touched her.

"Lucienne, summon your Glory now," Jekaterina said. "He'll come."

How did Jekaterina know she was going to call upon her Forbidden Glory? Did her mother also know the consequences of her giving in to defeat Devourer? As she sent Jekaterina a tired, skeptical glance, she saw Bayrose dashing toward them, frantically waving a ruby ring toward the black jet in the sky, and shouting, "Stop!"

Jekaterina moved, inhumanly fast, slamming into her younger daughter with a cuss from an ancient language. Following that was a word "*useless.*" After that, Bayrose was out of sight, currently forgotten.

"Lucia," Vladimir whispered beside her, sensing the sudden shift in her. He was attuned to her after becoming her healer and sharing her poison. The Czech prince now carried part of her curse, but he'd rather be trapped with her in an inferno than be away from her home free.

Could she finally set him free after this?

One gaze into his hazel eyes and she knew wherever she stood he'd stand by her. It had been that way ever since he'd fallen for her. What she wouldn't give to have a chance with him and tell him how much she cherished him, and that she wanted him to live happily after she was gone.

Kian also realized what Lucienne must do. "Lucia—" He swallowed and couldn't speak more.

"You've protected me," she said with a brave smile. "Now it's my turn to protect you all."

"The farewell is touching." Mirrikh's holographic image descended before her. And then many holograms appeared behind his in a half-ring. Viewers—foreign leaders, military personnel, journalists, and regular people with children among them packed the hologram screens. Mirrikh Schwartz had picked a sample of the world's population as his hologram's live audience to witness the Siren's surrender. "But the world that's watching this unprecedented historic event is running out of patience. Time to kneel, little Siren."

The world's representatives held their breath, eyes sparkling with anticipation. At that moment, they were all bloodthirsty predators.

Vladimir spat at Mirrikh's face in the hologram and flipped a bird to the worldwide audience.

"Who said I'd kneel?" Lucienne purred. "I don't kneel. Nor do my people. Sphinxes will *never* surrender." From the astounded expressions on the representatives' faces, she knew the world had felt her mesmerizingly seductive power. She was truly the Siren.

The Siren seduced before striking.

"But you promised you would!" Mirrikh asked incredulously, "You lied in front of the whole world?" With the ancient power shielding him, he was immune to her influence.

"Surprise," said Lucienne.

"You'll die a horrific death, Lucienne Lam!" Mirrikh screamed. "No! You won't die that easily. You'll watch while I dust and flame Sphinxes. I know your weakness, Siren! You care too much. Watching the terrible deaths of your people, the deaths of those you love, is the worst kind of punishment for you. Now behold my wrath!"

Devourer pulsed, and Predator vibrated violently. The thick, gray mass that blocked out the sun shifted, plunging toward Sphinxes, toward Lucienne and her warriors, its black mouth wide open, its jagged teeth lengthened, eager to devour all the souls in Sphinxes.

It'd been starved for too long.

The faces in the holograms were masks of horror.

Lucienne threw her hands into the air, sending out Forbidden Glory.

Waves of light burst from Lucienne like a volcano erupting. Metal, water, fire, earth, and the poisoned aether all came into play. They weaved together and formed a vast membrane, covering Sphinxes like a flowing rainbow net. The gray mass hit the edge of the rainbow and bounced back.

"You will not harm my people!" Lucienne shouted.

Fury blazed through her, light and fire shooting from her eyes toward Predator. The angel's wings in fire crashed into the gray mass. The two forces tore at each other. Fire drove parts of the mass away from the land of Sphinxes, but the gray thing ate the roaring fire.

As seconds went by, the gray mass increased, diminishing the fire.

Devourer was too powerful and obscene, and Lucienne was fighting it with the poisoned Forbidden Glory. As she pushed her power toward its limit, the burning in her ignited, almost as painful as when she'd first suffered from Blood Tear's poison in the Polynesian cliff.

While she felt depleted and on fire, Devourer renewed its energy from its supply of newly consumed souls. Her knees buckled, but

Lucienne fought to hold on. She wouldn't allow it to devour more of her people. It had taken her cousin Thaddeus' soul and thousands of others. Grief and hatred fueled the Forbidden Glory, but the pain and burn made her double over. As she shoved the gray mass back, she vaguely noticed her mother stopping Kian, Vladimir, and her warriors from reaching her.

"Do not touch her!" Jekaterina shouted a warning, power exuding from her. "Do not disturb the Siren!"

Blood beaded on Lucienne's hairline.

Devourer's gray mass breached the front line, its dirty, violent tongue licking Lucienne. It had the first taste of her soul as its blackness crushed into her. It now knew her darkest fear and desire. Lucienne had never felt so disgusted, violated, and terrified, but she couldn't afford to retch. Trickles of blood streamed down the sides of her face. The evil essence could lick her, but she wouldn't let it touch her people again.

Lucienne diverted part of her energy—the water and metal elements—to strengthen the membrane that was shielding her people. The earth element rose to lend her strength as she kept hurling fluxes of fire at Devourer. Inch by inch, she forced back the tip of the gray mass that had defiled her.

Take all of me and burn that thing into oblivion! she commanded her power. As it drew from the depth of her draining well, Lucienne felt the burst of blood vessels in her veins and behind her eyes. *You must not consume me before I vanquish my enemy!*

Another wave of gray matter struck back. Lucienne staggered under its brutal, brunt force.

"Daughter, defense only!" Jekaterina called. "You can't overcome it alone with your poisoned Glory. Hold your line until he comes. He'll come!"

Lucienne couldn't hold on any longer, though she knew she must. She just couldn't hold on … even with all she had. The well had completely drained.

Then the dirty mass breached her membrane.

A stream of blood poured from Kian's nose. He was the first to be affected—Devourer was playing with her now. It knew she had reached the end of her resources, and it knew what Kian McQuillen meant to her.

Then Vladimir spewed blood.

Then more of her warriors, including her generals and officers, crouched down, their eyes bulging in agony. She heard her people scream.

With a blood-curdling shriek, Lucienne conjured one last ounce of energy from somewhere. Aether, even poisoned, enhanced the shield and amended the fracture torn open by the gray mass. Forbidden Glory's metal wrestled the thing away from the membrane and Lucienne's people.

As soon as Kian and the warriors could stand, they formed a tight circle around her.

A flash of brilliant light pierced the dark sky.

Black lightning hurled toward Predator. The Sealers' command jet flapped in the air but did not drop from the sky. Devourer sustained it.

Spike hummed with light as Ashburn landed beside Lucienne. Without missing a beat, his palm joined one of hers; his other hand pressed against her back. Black lightning gushed into her, filling the empty well inside her.

Air shimmered all around Lucienne and Ashburn.

Forbidden Glory's fire rekindled. Then a carnal pleasure from Ash's touch surged through Lucienne waves after waves. All she longed for at the moment was to wrap her legs around his waist. To hell with the battle! She wanted to leave with Ash and abandon her people to their horrific deaths.

No, no, not now! Lucienne cursed. The Lure had never been so potent, fueled by the combined powers of Forbidden Glory and TimeDust and the reunion between the pair after their long separation.

Ashburn rasped, then half closed his glowing silver eyes. The Lure always had a stronger impact on him, either in pleasure or punishment. Lucienne twisted her torso to face him, to silently warn him that they were still on the battlefield, her people's lives at stake.

He read her, but could do nothing about the Lure without breaking his connection to her. A mix of longing, fear, lust, and fury distorted his face. The Lure had put them in the worst possible situation.

Devourer caught on to their predicament. It charged them with all its might, determined to suck in their souls once and for all. Lucienne and Ashburn shared a look of horror. It was impossible to fight the Lure and Devourer at the same time.

Jekaterina stepped forward and laid her white, porcelain hand on their joined hands. The Lure rippled once, twice, and then, like a static that crackled, it was gone. Lucienne hadn't time to think how Jekaterina knew about the Lure or had the power to subdue it. Drawing from Ashburn's undivided strength, Lucienne let a renewed river of fire erupt from her.

A rampant flame whirled up like a tornado, joining Ashburn's black lighting. Together, they pierced through the living gray mass. Lightning flashed, and a firestorm raged. They relentlessly struck the being's dark heart. Following the assault, the other four fundamental forces all smashed into the orb of Devourer.

Thunder rolled across the sky as fire and metal descended. It was an earthquake in the sky. Ziyi screamed, as did Bayrose and many others. They threw their hands over their ears and cried in agony. Sphinxes' warriors gritted their teeth, but held their ground and watched their queen's back.

Rattling violently, Predator fled, but Ashburn's black lightning caught it, pinning it in the air like a giant iron hand. Forbidden Glory moved in without hesitation, its metal cutting through the hull of the black jet.

"It can't be!" screamed Mirrikh's image in the hologram. "No one can beat Devourer! It's the most advanced, ancient technology—"

Predator disintegrated. Mirrikh's image flickered off and never returned. No one even heard his last whimpering. As the black jet and the Sealers' symbol on its snake head shattered into pieces, the dark orb was exposed, hanging in the air.

Black lightning and red fire circled the orb, then closed in, savaging it again and again. The orb vomited the darkest mass, in a last attempt to swallow the lightning fire. But the lightning sliced the mass, and the fire roared and vacuumed it with absolute brutality.

Devourer screamed as if the whole world was in a collective labor pain.

The world's representatives echoed its scream in the holograms, the shockwave from the Devourer reaching them across vast oceans and distant mountains. People fell to their knees, screeching as blood burst from their eyes, noses, and ears. The pain across the globe was unbearable.

The Siren's warriors couldn't stand it either. They screamed with the whole of Sphinxes and the world.

Jekaterina appeared untouched. Her brown eyes turned steel gray—cold and tired.

The inhuman shriek from Devourer lasted for nearly half a minute—the longest thirty seconds in human history.

Then silence. Blessed silence.

The orb of the black heart shrank to a drop of grey liquid.

The smoke and fog receded from the sky, like an old, dirty blanket being rolled away. The sun broke through. The warriors had to cover their eyes to adjust to the sudden brilliant light. The ocean returned to its sparkling blue. The forest swayed like a rhythmic poem as if it hadn't faced near extinction. The sea birds twirled, making circular shadows on endless white sand and waves.

Only the shards of broken jets littering Sphinxes' land and sea reminded Lucienne and her people of the battle they'd just fought.

Splash! A muddy liquid that was once Devourer dropped in front of Lucienne's feet.

Lucienne stepped on it and twisted her torso to face Ashburn. "We won," she whispered, her breath labored. The tears came as blood, tainted her eyelashes. Before he could wipe them off, she returned her gaze to the sky.

"Lucia," Ashburn said, "show mercy."

"No," she said, a killing light still in her eyes, and flung her hands into the air again, palms toward the sky. "You came, you saw, but you'll never conquer," she announced. "And you won't return."

At the same time, Kian ordered a full-frontal attack with a battle cry.

Sphinxes' air force, naval, and ground troops caught up with the fleeing Sealers' and their allies, blasting the invaders from the sky, sinking them to the deep ocean, and cutting them down on the ground.

Lucienne's fire, mixing with the earth element, went before her army. Wind fueled the fire, and materialized metal speared the remaining enemy's fighters before fire finally incinerated them.

The Siren's fury was terrifying to watch, but the world watched it.

Lucienne erased the whole army of the multiple nations in mere seconds.

She was Sphinxes' most deadly weapon.

With a snap of her fingers, Lucienne cut off the live feed, and the holograms vanished. The world had seen enough. The next moments belonged to her and her people.

"The nations of the world will think a thousand times over before they come to Sphinxes again!" General Fairchild waved his hands in the air and shouted, "Sphinxes stands stronger than ever!"

"Well done, Siren," Director Pyon said in tears amid the warriors' roaring cheers.

"My fight is over," Lucienne said, completely spent. But the nations wouldn't know she'd exhausted all five fundamental forces of her Forbidden Glory. "From now on the fight is yours."

"I'll always fight for you," Ashburn said gently.

"I'll forever defend you, my Queen," Vladimir said fiercely.

"Long live our Siren Queen!" her warriors shouted, awe and pride etched on their faces.

Sphinxes, as a united new nation, had risen.

Kian looked bitterly proud and devastated. He knew what the battle had cost her. She held his gaze, trying not to show the pain burning in her every fiber. She needed to make him promise to press on and protect Sphinxes without her, but a red tide had arrived. She hadn't an ounce of strength left to dodge it or fight it.

Lucienne collapsed.

Before the floor met her face, Vladimir and Ashburn had both caught her. Lucienne struggled to hold on to the thread of her last consciousness.

"I'll save you, Lucia," Ashburn swore in glinting tears, "no matter the cost."

You can't. The Eye of Time is gone. You won't need to go down that horrible path.

In the end, Ashburn Fury still chose her above all. He would sacrifice the world and himself to save her, just as Kian wanted. As Sphinxes would pursue. But neither her protector nor her people knew the consequences of keeping her alive.

She'd stopped the wicked wheel from spinning in order to keep them and the world safe.

No one will ever need to sacrifice for me again.

Her consciousness lingered outside her body a second longer. Ashburn held her in his arms while Vladimir pressed his forehead against hers to heal her. Their efforts were futile. Her gaze swept over Kian, Ziyi, Jekaterina, Bayrose, her cousins, and her warriors, all of whom surrounded her in a protective ring as she, alone, kept falling into an alien world of nauseating red and absolute cold.

Blood tears tainted her lashes, face, and messy hair, but she also saw a trace of a winning smile freeze on her lips.

Her people were safe.

She'd protected them, though not all of them.

She was the fabled phoenix that burned to ashes and would one day return.

THE STORY CONTINUES …

THE FINAL INSTALLMENT

The Immortals

(Laments of Angels & Dark Chemistry, #4)

Sigh up to the author's mailing list http://eepurl.com/YxOcn to hear about her new release, discounts, giveaways and fun stuff!

ABOUT *LAMENTS OF ANGELS & DARK CHEMISTRY* SERIES

At the heart of *The Laments of Angels & Dark Chemistry* series is the very survival of humankind.

I left clues on the mysteries of human origin, evolution, and ancient civilizations and wars throughout the first three books, and you'll have answers in the fourth and final installment.

Long ago, Earth was filled with wars between more advanced species and wars we fought among ourselves and against them. Our ancestors called the superior race "the fallen angels," who insisted they were the first Earth natives.

As humankind increased in numbers and became a new kind of predator, our conflict with the angels could no longer be settled. Human spirits could not accept the role of "inferior race." Our ancestors chose to die free than live on their knees, and so they devised a weapon and drove the angels into the space. The cost was deadly--numerous brave men and women perished, and by turning back time, destroyed all technology and every advanced civilization.

Now millions of years have passed.

Humans stand hesitantly at the threshold of a quantum evolution, but the race we exiled has found a way to wage a new war against us. They've upgraded their magical powers and technology beyond our perception. They're coming to take back Earth.

Unfortunately, the weapon our ancestors deployed has been lost to us. We don't know anything about ancient warfare or our secret history. We don't have the slightest idea that we're facing extinction.

Our only hope rests with Lucienne Lam, the last and most powerful of the Sirens, who leads her Sphinxes nation in the fight against the returning angels. She will stand with the last of us to save our planet.

In the end, only one race can have Earth. Will it be us or them?

Sneak Preview

INTRODUCING A SIZZLING NEW SERIES:
THE EMPRESS OF MYSTH

Forbidden. Sworn Enemy. Wicked Seduction.

Savage angels have turned Earth into their hunting ground. To save all earthborns, the fey princess Rose cedes to the marriage demands of the King of Angels, knowing she won't survive the wedding night. When she comes to Atlantis to find a secret weapon to banish angels from our planet, she awakens the darkest lust in the king's lethal brother.

The most formidable angel comes across the universe and finds her. He will stop at nothing to possess her, even if he must fall.

The High Prince offers Rose an indecent proposal: sleep with him once and he'll keep her safe. Rose will turn his urge against him and destroy the angels' house. While unbridled lust burns the prince, it also torments her.

This sizzling mythological romance series centers on war and lust between an immortal race and fallen angels, before humans walked the Earth.

THE EMPRESS OF MYSTH 1: ANGEL'S LUST

PRINCESS ROSE

The golden skyscraper, where the palace of the angel king nested, stretched high into the sky. Its cold metal gleamed.

Atop the tower, the spring's sunlight backlit a figure, shielding his face in the shadow. His wings, massive and glossy, arched high before being tucked away.

A male angel, exuding immense menace even from afar, was spying on me.

The trespassers had come through the portal in the sky, and they had conquered most of the planet in two weeks and slaughtered a whole tribe of my people.

All Earth residents had been caught unprepared.

My name is Rose Jekaterina Faylinn, Princess of Mysth, the heir to Emperor Oberon. We're the oldest race on Earth, the firstborn. Other subspecies call us fey, fairies, and the fairest, among many other names.

We're the immortal Mysthians.

Each Mysthian has an inborn magic that links to earth elements. Our powers are for growing, healing, and nurturing, but useless in war. None of us possess destructive, dark magic.

So my emperor father agreed to the angel king's terms and sold me to King Agro to buy peace for himself and his kingdom.

And I arrived at Atlantis with my hand-picked team of nine.

The angels seemed surprised that I hadn't brought an army. I was being realistic.

Without the final weapon I came to seek in Atlantis, my warriors would all be slain, no matter how many troops I had with me.

Bringing only a few warriors would send a different message to the king. I must let the angels believe I'd come to hand Mysth over to them. In the mean time, I would work on turning myself into a lethal weapon against them.

I wanted my enemies to assume my team and I posed no threats, and thus the king would place fewer guards.

I needed the leverage and freedom to roam in Atlantis.

My gaze left the angel spy atop the tower while I entertained the thought of tearing out his golden feathers and letting the wind pick up the trash.

I refocused on the task of putting one foot in front of the other and marching in a proud, calm manner as my instinct screamed for me to run from the slaughterhouse of the angels' city.

Dark doubts kept whirling in my mind: I'd been tailored to be the Empress of Mysth all my life. I'd secretly trained with the best weapon-masters since I'd been a child, but could I really crush the mighty angels?

I bit my lip. I'd been pushed back to the corner. If I failed, the Mysthians would be wiped off of the Earth, and Mysth, the twilight realm, would be an empty echo and a wasteland.

I stepped on to the golden bridge that led to the king's palace. There was no turning back now. Armored angel warriors lined each side of the wide bridge, raising their long swords from their sides— the blades that had bled my people.

Rage burned in me, yet I put a cold mask in place.

The angels' wings stretched high, a terrifying sight.

Their king, who indeed had a sadistic sense of humor, had selected only those of his soldiers who had massive, black wings to greet me, or more accurately, to intimidate me.

I wouldn't give my enemies the satisfaction. I did not give those wings a second glance, and I treated the soldiers as non-existent. Angels were known to understand only arrogance and power.

I looked straight ahead, letting my peripheral sight pick up the rest of the details.

The long swords the angels held high suddenly came down over my head when I reached the first row of the soldiers. Were they going to behead me right here? My heart jerked violently in my rib cage, and fear rammed into me like a cold ice-pack.

My face drained of blood.

Fortunately, I'd prepared. I'd brushed the powder of rouge on my cheeks in case my face paled in a situation like this, or worse.

Roaring, my royal guards lunged forward with their swords. Lexa, my disguised lady-in-waiting, pushed me backwards. Souline, my true lady-in-waiting, threw her hands at the angels with a string of curses, but there was no offensive magic coming out of her. She was a healer.

I shrugged free of Lexa and raised a hand to stop my guards, then I kept walking.

My people hesitated for a second, and Hector, the captain of my guards, gestured for them to fall back. He stayed closer to me.

My companions held back their wrath and moved forward as if accompanying me to my funeral.

The angels' swords didn't descend but crossed with the ones from the opposite side, forming an arch of blades over my head as my team and I marched under it.

All this was meant to terrorize me, yet disguised as the angel king's stately greeting to a foreign princess.

I was more worried that the angels could hear my thundering heartbeat.

Relief washed over me as the deafening sound of waterfalls under the bridge returned. I'd blocked all environmental noises when I'd fixed my attention on the angels.

As my heartbeat resumed to normal, I wearily regarded the angels' city in front of me.

It was a great work of engineering—wild nature seamlessly immersed into the polished, modern high buildings. Atlantis seemed to float in the air, much to the taste of the sky beings.

That was why they'd taken this city from the Dragonian when they'd first landed on Earth.

The Dragonian had been our rival before the arrival of the angels. The race of engineers had been busy inventing weapons to break into our magical realm, the land of dreams. Ironically, they'd focused on the wrong target; and look where it had gotten them. The majority of the Dragonian were now the angels' labor force, and the remnants had gone into hiding, gathering around their rebel leader, North, while vigilant angels constantly hunted them down.

I sighed. We weren't doing any better. My emperor father had had to whore his only heir to preserve Mysth.

Only I had a different plan than being a whore.

I'd vowed on my mother, the late empress regnant, who had died at my birth, that I, Rose Jekaterina Faylinn, would destroy the angels.

My wedding to King Agro was set for two months' time, on my twentieth birthday. I had to find the angel's power source, their ultimate weapon, before then.

"Princess," Hector warned beside me.

I nodded slightly. The captain must have had the same doubt as I. Could we—the ten of us—succeed in Atlantis?

We had to.

We were the last line of defense against the angels.

My eyes turned harder.

Earth belonged to us, and no one would take my inheritance from me. I raised my chin higher, then I realized that Hector was alerting me to an angel approaching from the air at high speed.

The spy had left his post at the top of the tower. His wings stretched, glinting in the sun and vibrating with power.

In a blur, he was on us.

The king's soldiers on the bridge withdrew their swords to pay him respect. So this angel wasn't just a spy, he was high-ranking, but he couldn't be the king. King Agro was said to have one black wing and one red, a lesser line from the angel royal house, born by one of the concubines to the Lord of All Angels.

In a blink I knew who this angel was: King Agro's half-brother, the formidable High Prince of Angels.

The prince pivoted around me and my ladies-in-waiting above us, sniffing at us in turn like a dog sniffing the scent of his playthings.

A barbarian! But what more could I expect from an angel?

I maintained my cold composure.

Then he fixed his attention on me.

I couldn't ignore him at such a close range, so I stared up and met his confused, icy gaze. Despite my loathing toward his race, my heart lurched at his glacial, lethal beauty.

His hard, muscled long body was clad in black leather. His golden wings extended full, blocking the sunlight. High cheekbones settled proudly on his sun-kissed yet arctic marble face. His eyes that had been piercing ice grey an instant ago now were a bright silver. He looked at me like a big, nasty cat that had just spotted a squirming mouse.

Only I wouldn't be a mouse.

I did not fear this big predator, or any of his kind.

My heart brimmed with hatred. The High Prince of Angels was a battle-breed. He had probably led the legion to bleed my people and root out the whole village, just to show off their merciless power.

I would return such a favor. I'd bleed them, soon and profusely. This angel and his brother king would be among the first to suffer my wrath.

My glare didn't leave his eyes as I glided on the long bridge toward Atlantis's gate.

The angel's firm, sensual lips twitched at the corner, as if he was amused that I showed no intention of backing down from his bullying. For sure there might not be too many who wanted to stand up to him when he emitted such pure menace.

If I had had the slightest offensive magic the prophecy promised, I would have blasted him with waves and waves of it and see who would be more amused.

My guards and lady-in-waiting tensed like bowstrings behind me, but I didn't break my gait, and telepathically I commanded them to stay put.

The high prince grinned, evidently sensing my royal warriors' fury, but he didn't glance at them again.

You'll pay for your arrogance, angel.

He fixed his attention on me completely, the silver glint in his eyes turning darker. He looked hungry now, like I was his last dessert on Earth.

I expected myself to experience nausea and prayed my breakfast would stay in my stomach, but the repulsion didn't come. Instead, a sensual delight fluttered in my stomach, as if a coming-of-age girl had just met her first crush.

I blinked, appalled by my physical reaction. How could I feel an instant attraction toward an angel, my sworn enemy that I had vowed to destroy at the first opportunity?

His good looks shouldn't have touched me.

Mysthians outshone any race in beauty, and even the angels weren't above us.

I glared at the High Prince of Angels. I'd spit at his face if I weren't a princess.

Then he soared into the air and left me alone.

Just as I'd thought I could finish the parade toward the king's palace relatively serenely, he howled. The bridge and the mountains behind us echoed, and the air rippled with formidable power.

I shivered and was furious at once.

Uncivilized creature!

My guards pressed their hands tightly on the hilts of their swords. My lady-in-waiting quivered, becoming even more fearful for me.

The angels on the bridge shifted uncomfortably. Everyone could feel the high prince's power—ancient, potent, and violent.

The barbarian soared higher and flew back to the golden tower.

A second later, he dove through the ceiling of the tower and disappeared from sight.

His roar stuck in my mind. If this one was wild like that, then what kind of beast was the king, his brother? What kind of monster was I going to face?

Anxiety boiled in me. Fortunately, the sound of the waterfalls covered my deafening heartbeat.

When I stood in front of the angel king, I couldn't afford to show any dread. I couldn't afford to sweat, go pale, or have such a racing heartbeat.

Earth Mother, I lowered my head slightly and said a silent prayer, *if you indeed favor your child, then protect me. Do not let me fall. Do not let me fail.*

I crossed the bridge with my companions and halted before Atlantis' cold, massive gate. Portraits of little fat children with wings crawled on its metal.

They were the Dragonian's work as well. Wasn't it enough for them to invite the angels to take their capital city?

"We're here," Hector said softly, in an effort to lend me his warrior's strength. "Are you ready to enter, Your Highness?"

Was I ready?

Could I ever be?

The gate that couldn't keep the monsters inside swung open before me.

Like what you read?
THE EMPRESS OF MYSTH 1: ANGEL'S LUST
Available on Amazon!

ALSO BY AUTHOR

Available on Amazon!

THE EMPRESS OF MYSTH SERIAL

THE EMPRESS OF MYSTH 1: ANGEL'S LUST
THE EMPRESS OF MYSTH 2: ANGEL'S OBSESSION

THE EMPRESS OF MYSTH 3: ANGEL'S INDECENT
PROPOSAL
THE EMPRESS OF MYSTH 4: ANGEL'S GLORY
THE EMPRESS OF MYSTH 5: ANGEL'S FURY
THE EMPRESS OF MYSTH 6: ANGEL'S MATE
THE EMPRESS OF MYSTH 7: ANGEL'S WAR

THE EMPRESS OF MYSTH 8: ANGEL'S HOME

LOVE'S PREY: A SWEET ROMANCE

ABOUT THE AUTHOR

Meg Xuemei X is an award-winning author. She loves dark chocolate and gazing at the stars. She lives in Southern California with her husband, a panther, and a fox.

She is always happy to hear from readers and welcome new friends on Facebook.
Facebook: http://www.facebook.com/MegXuemeiX
Email: megxuemei AT gmail.com
She'll be giddy if you sign up to her mailing list at http://eepurl.com/YxOcn to hear about her new release, discounts, giveaways and fun stuff!

www.ingramcontent.com/pod-product-compliance
Lightning Source LLC
Chambersburg PA
CBHW070012110426
42741CB00034B/1196